CHRONIC ILLNESS and THE QUALITY OF LIFE

CHRONIC ILLNESS
AND THE QUALITY OF LIFE

ANSELM L. STRAUSS, Ph.D.

Professor of Sociology,
Department of Social and Behavioral Science,
University of California, San Francisco

and **JULIET CORBIN, D.N.S.**

Research Associate,
Department of Social and Behavioral Science,
University of California, San Francisco

SHIZUKO FAGERHAUGH, D.N.S.

Associate Research Sociologist,
Department of Social and Behavioral Science,
University of California, San Francisco

BARNEY G. GLASER, Ph.D.

Formerly Professor of Sociology and Currently Visiting Lecturer,
Department of Social and Behavioral Science,
University of California, San Francisco

DAVID MAINES, Ph.D.

Research Fellow, University of Illinois, Chicago

BARBARA SUCZEK, Ph.D.

Assistant Research Sociologist,
Department of Social and Behavioral Science,
University of California, San Francisco

CAROLYN L. WIENER, Ph.D.

Assistant Research Sociologist,
Department of Social and Behavioral Science,
University of California, San Francisco

SECOND EDITION

The C. V. Mosby Company

ST. LOUIS   TORONTO   1984

A TRADITION OF PUBLISHING EXCELLENCE

Editor: Alison Miller
Assistant editor: Susan Epstein
Manuscript editor: Judy Jamison
Cover design: Suzanne Oberholtzer
Production: Judy England, Barbara Merritt

Second edition

The C.V. Mosby Company
11830 Westline Industrial Drive, St. Louis, Missouri 63146

Library of Congress Cataloging in Publication Data

Main entry under title:

Chronic illness and the quality of life.

   Rev. ed. of: Chronic illness and the quality of
life / Anselm L. Strauss. 1975
   Bibliography: p.
   Includes index.
   1. Chronic diseases—Social aspects.   2. Chronic
diseases—Psychological aspects.   3. Chronically ill—
Care and treatment.   4. Quality of life. I. Strauss,
Anselm L.   II. Strauss, Anselm L. Chronic illness and
the quality of life.   [DNLM: 1. Chronic disease
RA644.5.C47   1984   362.1'0422   83-22061
ISBN 0-8016-4825-4

TS/VH/VH 9 8 7 6 5 4 3 2   03/C/350

For
IRENE, HELEN,
HILARY, PAUL, AND RUTH,
whose courage ennobled us all

PREFACE

Chronic illness or long-term illness as it is sometimes called, is here to stay. It will not vanish, despite the amazing advances in medical knowledge and technology. In fact, no matter how useful, helpful, or desirable, many advances (organ transplantation, for example) tend to bring in their wake certain new problems. Or they may simply, for specific persons, put off until another day the appearance of some relatively inevitable chronic condition. Not all conditions are fatal or even terribly discomforting, but many are and, as we shall shortly see, may "hit" fairly early in life and affect sizable portions of our population.

Many readers of this book—most of them health personnel, skilled at giving some specialized kind of care to the ill—will themselves be sufferers of one or more chronic conditions. These may plague them daily or occasionally prevent their working, until the condition eases up or is treated. If lucky enough not to have a chronic illness, then they are very likely to have a parent, spouse, child, or close friend who suffers from chronic illness. Indeed that is most probable, given the great number of chronically ill people.

Stop a minute, then, and ask: How much do health personnel take into account their knowledge of chronic illness when caring for the ill persons who come to health facilities? How well do they translate their own experiential knowledge into their actual working with ill persons? Presumably the answer is that sometimes they act wisely on that experiential knowledge. Often, however, they do not. One reason for their failure is that the health facilities often, and perhaps even usually, do not especially reward them for employing that special wisdom. Beyond that, we ought to ask ourselves (the authors included) how much we really know about the problems of living to which certain chronic illnesses give rise. Our personal knowledge tends to be somewhat restricted, and that derived from our work tends to pertain to the experiences of ill persons while at the hospital, the clinic, or other health facility, rather than being rich in details about what life is like "back home," given their particular disease symptoms and their regimens.

In this second edition, we have added materials to show some of the experiences of chronically ill patients when they are hospitalized; however, the main focus, as in the original edition, is on the ill person and his or her family at *home*. The focus is on how they all manage to live their lives as normally as possible in the face of the sick person's disease. So the emphasis is very much on the social and psychological aspects (not the medical) of *living with chronic illness*. In the terminology of a now widespread phrase: How is the *quality of life* affected by having a chronic illness?

The specific differences between the first and second editions are as follows. All but one case illustration, of the several used originally, have been eliminated, because it is the framework of the original book that seems most useful to readers. In their place we have, first of all, expanded substantially the introduction and both the chapters on managing the trajectory and the family's experiences with managing and living with illness at home. Then we have written additional chapters on patients' experiences—and work—while hospitalized, because although the experiences at the hospital are secondary to what happens at home, rehospitalization is nevertheless frequent enough for many of the chronically ill to be very important. The hospital and the home stand at two ends of the same continuum, and one needs to understand the experiences associated with both. Moreover, the prevalence of chronically ill patients in today's hospital makes it quite a different place than when genuine "acute care" was its mission. Again, these added chapters are based on our recent research. Finally, we have added new material on health policy issues with regard to the chronically ill, notably on the issue of rising health costs and some of the trends leading to heightened awareness of the implications of chronic illness prevalence. All of the original edition, except for the case illustrations, then, has been kept intact.

Our approach to understanding the chronically ill and their care has always involved the idea that work—hard work—is part of what they and their families must do to stay alive, afloat, and "functioning" as physiological and social beings. In this edition, the implications of *work* as essential, unavoidable, and central are emphasized in more detail. This emphasis will be especially visible in the new chapters.

Part 1 introduces the issue of chronic illness—its prevalence and some of its larger implications for health organization and patient care. This section of the book closes with a framework for thinking about the daily and persistent problems faced by the chronically ill and their families.

Part 2 is devoted to a discussion of some of those problems, including the management of crises, the handling of regimens, the controlling of symptoms, the handling of social isolation, the management of time, the management of the trajectory, and the attempt to live normally and maintain normal social relations.

The title, "The Family in the Picture," suggests the substance of the last chapter in Part 2.

In Part 3 we turn to the hospital, the place where chronically ill people go during acute phases of their illnesses, emphasizing particularly the work (often unnoted or disregarded) done by the patients and their kin—work often essential and certainly contributory to getting effective treatment there. We discuss also in separate chapters two kinds of work in hospitals that have been profoundly affected by the combination of medical technology and prevalent chronic illness: comfort work and clinical safety work.

Among the new material we have addressed the question of how health personnel might obtain the kinds of biographical information needed from chronically ill patients to give better care. We also discuss chronic illness in terms of larger health policy issues. We first note trends pertinent to heightened awareness of chronic illness and comment on the theme of rising health costs in the national debate over health policy, relating it to the prevalence of chronic illness. Then we write about health policy in terms of ensuring that the chronically ill get better health care.

The senior author of this book is a professor of sociology and, for many years, a faculty member at the School of Nursing, University of California, San Francisco. He has been fortunate in being allowed ready access to many health facilities. He and his associates—who are coauthors of the second edition of this book—have been able to observe and interview a great many staff members. During one research project on terminal care in hospitals, we finally realized that most of the patients, terminal or not, were chronically ill—from cardiac diseases, cancer, asthma, and the like. As a result, eventually we and our students began to interview patients at their homes to see what life looked like from their viewpoint. The first edition of this book and several research papers were the result of those studies. Later we did studies of chronic illness in the hospital and at home, and some of those materials have been included in this edition.

Understandably, we owe a very great deal to our students, research associates, and colleagues. We have drawn on the interviews and field observations of Jeanne Quint Benoliel, Marcella Z. Davis, Laura Reif, Theresa Louie, and George Chu. At the end of each field note quotation used, the researcher's name is given, except where it is our own. We are indebted to all of them, as well as to Barney Glaser's seminar on sociological analysis of qualitative data, and to Kathy Calkins Charmaz, Elihu Gerson, and Erma Zuckerman for stimulating conversations over the years about the social and psychological aspects of living with chronic disease. Deserving of our gratitude also are several German colleagues who worked with us in San Francisco while doing their own related research: Wolfram Fischer, Christa Hoffman-Riem, and Fritz Schuetze. We also learned a great deal from the student nurses with whom we worked, from Anselm Strauss's course on chronic disease, taught annually since 1971, from our colleague at the School of Nursing, Jeanne Hallberg, and from a former colleague there, Mildred MacIntyre. We must thank Helen Nahm, formerly Dean of the School of Nursing (but, more importantly, a wise woman), for commenting on a draft manuscript of the first edition. Our thanks also to the Russell Sage Foundation for generous funding of some of the research that lay behind that edition of the book. Furthermore, we are deeply indebted for long-term funding of our research to the Division of Nursing, Public Health Services.

Perhaps most of all, we need and wish to thank the patients, their kin, and the health personnel who have taught all of us by freely, so amazingly freely, giving us the information we needed. And without Fran, neither this book nor, quite literally, the first-named author . . .

Anselm L. Strauss
Juliet Corbin
Shizuko Fagerhaugh
Barney G. Glaser
David Maines
Barbara Suczek
Carolyn L. Wiener

CONTENTS

xi

INTRODUCTION
AND FRAMEWORK

INTRODUCTION

In essence chronic illness is THE challenge of this era to hospital and public health officials, and to the medical, nursing, and other professions concerned with sickness and disability. . . . [It is] America's No. 1 health problem.[6]

Those words were spoken in 1956 by L. Mayo, chairman of the famous Commission on Chronic Illness, in a keynote address to a conference on chronic illness, just on the eve of the commission's influential four-volume report. The commission's definition of chronic diseases is still serviceable:

All impairments or deviations from normal which have one or more of the following characteristics: are permanent, leave residual disability, are caused by non-reversible pathological alteration, require special training of the patient for rehabilitation, may be expected to require a long period of supervision, observation, or care.[6]

The commission's views were astute but focused too narrowly on the task at hand. In fact, humankind was about to enter a new era in its long civilizational history. Although hardly as dramatic as the arrival of the atomic bomb, or as well noted as the current population explosion, there is unquestionably something startlingly new about the biological condition of a considerable, and increasing, portion of the Earth's population—namely, the prevalence of the *chronic* rather than acute illnesses. Yet neither the general public nor the health professionals, as we shall see, recognize anything like the full implications of this for training, care, insurance—indeed for the health institutions themselves. We are only beginning to pass into a period when chronic illness per se (rather than specific or categor-

1

ical chronic diseases) will be referred to, thought about, acted on as a general reality. This seems to be no less true in England, Sweden, and other medically advanced nations than in the United States.

Until the late 1930s, in industrialized countries, as in the third world countries today, the prevailing and often terrible afflictions were due to bacteria and parasites: the so-called acute diseases. The dramatic medical and public health battles of the last centuries, and the great medical discoveries, were directed against and were about precisely those kinds of illness. Although the incidence of such diseases began to drop decades before the introduction of the sulfonamides and the antibiotics, the picture before their introduction during and just after World War II is captured by these sentences: "The thing to worry about [then] most was catching something. Infectious diseases were all around."[10] The words are by Lewis Thomas of the Sloan Kettering Foundation, and they refer to his medical school days just before the war. He remarks that the main disease then to worry about was tuberculosis, which anyone could catch at any time in his or her life; yet little could be done about that illness. He went on, "For all the others, the streptococcal infections, epidemic meningitis, staphylococcal septicemias, whooping cough, polio and all the rest, there was absolutely nothing to be done beyond providing good nursing care and hoping for the best." A dramatic change took place when the antibiotics and various improved immunological measures turned out to be so effective against many of the infectious and parasitic diseases. Those diseases still reign in the less fortunate countries, but in the highly industrialized ones (especially the United States, the Soviet Union, Japan, and western Europe), what people suffer from mostly are the chronic illnesses. They include the cancers, arthritis, and a great host of others that are currently "incurable." Men and women have always suffered from these, of course, but they never were the prevalent illnesses. These now constitute the equivalent of plagues and scourges of yesteryear. They are what bring people to the doctor's office, the clinic, and into the hospital: they are what people in developed nations usually die from.

Genuinely accurate figures about the incidence of chronic illness in the U.S. population are not to be had, but a rough idea can be obtained from the following. A survey carried out during the period July 1965 to June 1967 by the U.S. Public Health Service substantiates the prevalence of long-term illness as *the* major health problem.[2] During the 2-year period of the survey, approximately 50% of the civilian population, excluding residents in institutions, "had one chronic condition or more." Of those 94.9 million Americans, about 22 million "experienced some degree of activity limitation and 6.3 million . . . had some form of mobility limitation as a result of chronic conditions."

The magnitude of the activity and mobility problems[1] is further suggested by the following and more precise figures. About 4 million persons, or 2% of the total U.S. population, were unable to carry on major activities (work, housekeeping, school or preschool activities, participation in recreational, civic, or church activities). Another 12 million were limited in major activity. Concerning mobility, or the ability to move about freely, about 1.4 million Americans were confined to their houses except in emergencies; 1.8 million needed the help of others or some special aid (cane, crutches, wheelchair) to move about; still another 3 million persons had some trouble in "getting around freely." As for the number of chronic conditions per person, the average was 2.2—that is, *multiple* chronic illnesses are very common.

Just what kinds of conditions are chronic? The authors of the survey give these figures:

Heart conditions	16.4%
Arthritis and rheumatism	14.8%
Impairments of back or spine	8.2%
Mental and nervous conditions	7.8%
Impairments of lower extremities and hips	6.1%
Visual impairments	5.6%
Hypertension without heart involvement	5.4%

People of different ages are likely to suffer from different chronic conditions. For example, the two chief conditions affecting mobility limitation are, by age group:

Under 17 years	Paralysis, complete or partial	28.2%
	Impairments of lower extremities and hips	15.3%
17 to 44 years	Paralysis, complete or partial	13.6%
	Impairments of lower extremities and hips	13.6%
45 to 64 years	Arthritis and rheumatism	25.1%
	Heart conditions	13.0%
65 years and over	Arthritis and rheumatism	29.3%
	Heart conditions	15.4%

It is true that elderly people are much more likely to have chronic conditions (and more of them), but it is not at all true that chronic disease is merely a geriatric problem. The survey's figures show the following:

Persons having no chronic conditions:

Under 17 years	77.2%
17 to 44 years	45.9%
45 to 64 years	28.9%
65 years and over	14.4%

**Persons with one chronic condition or more,
some or total limitation in a major activity:**

Under 17 years	0.9%
17 to 44 years	4.7%
45 to 64 years	14.2%
65 years and over	39.5%

In 1981, a National Health Interview Survey published by the National Center for Health Statistics[7] yielded the following data:

Persons with limitation in a major activity:

Under 17 years	2.0%
17 to 44 years	5.4%
45 to 64 years	19.1%
65 years and over	39.2%
All ages	10.9%

Thus even very young children can be afflicted, whereas youthful to middle-aged persons are considerably impaired.

Figures from a 1977 Health Interview Survey by the National Center for Health Statistics show clearly that the burden of chronic illness falls more heavily on low-income American families[2]:

Percentage of persons limited in activity because of chronic conditions, by age and family income: United States, 1977

Age group	Percentage limited in activity		
	Family income <$6000	Family income ≥$6000	Difference between income categories (%)
All ages	26.6	10.4	156
Under 17 years	4.5	3.2	41
17-44 years	14.2	7.1	100
45-64 years	46.8	19.1	145
65 years and over	50.3	37.8	33

Prevalence of the 10 leading causes of limitation of activity due to chronic conditions, by main cause of limitation and income: United States, 1977

Main cause of activity limitation	Number of persons limited in activity per 1000	
	All incomes	Income <$6000
Heart disease	17.6	36.9
Arthritis and rheumatism	16.3	38.8
Impairments of the back or spine	9.4	14.7
Impairments of the lower extremities or hips	7.2	14.6
Other musculoskeletal disorders	6.8	7.3
Hypertensive disease	5.2	12.4
Asthma	4.8	7.5
Diabetes	3.3	7.2
Senility	3.3	9.4
Emphysema	3.3	7.3

The magnitude of many of the figures in the foregoing tables is certainly startling, reflecting as it does the prevalence and extent of today's chronic illnesses. Thus it is rather strange that health personnel—from physicians "on down"—still tend to refer to hospitals as places where acute illness is treated, whereas people with chronic illness are housed mainly at special facilities, such as nursing homes, and of course are treated as ambulatory at the physicians' offices, clinics, and community health centers.

It is perhaps the disease-oriented training and interests of the health professionals that lead them to refer to hospitalized patients as acutely ill. After all, the shoulder-to-shoulder battle against fatal or at least crippling disease is a deservedly recognizable part of modern medicine. Yet even cursory scrutiny shows that most patients visiting the hospital for specialized treatments are not there because of acute diseases but because they currently suffer from an acute phase of one or another chronic disease: cancer, cardiac, kidney, respiratory, and the like.

This is no particular news, for hospital staffs actually do realize that many, if not most, of their patients have diseases for which a genuine cure does not exist. What can only be accomplished is, in common parlance, mainly "checking the progress of the disease," "getting them back on their feet," "slowing up the inevitable," and so on. If pressed, most personnel would agree that they were not engaged in "cure" in the old-fashioned sense of curing pneumonia or measles.

Nevertheless, they tend to reserve the contrasting term "care" for those patients whom one can only make more comfortable, who definitely seem so "chronic," their condition so "hopeless," so bad that "nothing much can be done," that they belong somewhere other than in a highly specialized work place such as a hospital. That is why one researcher could report that hospitalized stroke patients seemed, from the staff's viewpoint, to be out of place.[4] Or, in the somewhat plaintive words of Dr. Steinberg, the Director of Mount Sinai Hospital in New York, some years ago:

> I am a director of a general hospital for the treatment of the acute, not chronic diseases. In such an atmosphere, chronic disease is an accusation. . . . On the one hand . . . there is a movement to begin to widen the hospital's usefulness [to chronic patients]. On the other hand, we are frustrated because of the difficulty of carrying out our primary mission—the treatment of acute disease.[6]

These contrasts of acute/chronic and cure/care reflect something of a paradox so characteristic of contemporary health care. On the one hand, health personnel can believe, and assert with conviction, that chronic disease is the number one problem. On the other hand, they can continue to think about conquering chronic disease (and handling the number one problem) in terms not much different than when the prevalent diseases were genuinely communicative or parasitic.

Of course, it is perfectly true that some chronic diseases eventually will be conquered and even prevented, but perhaps not all and certainly most of them not very soon.

However, the astonishing progress of medical technology allows us to hope for conquered disease and increased longevity. Understandably, those people who aid in progress toward that magnificent goal are given special rewards and honors. Those who merely help to care for, to give comfort to, the incurably ill tend to get far less money and prestige for their efforts, whatever may be the psychological rewards accruing to the work. Additionally, in countries where specialization is far advanced and where specialists usually have great prestige or even great glamour, the organization of medical care and health care tends to be along categorical lines (heart, cancer, stroke, and so on), rather than focused on chronic disease in general.

Why should the focus not be in categorical terms? After all, specialists in neurological disease, for example, will best understand and battle such disease, not specialists in skin disease or some other bodily part or system far removed from the brain functions! Furthermore, even in terms of public support (in the United States) for attacks on given diseases, money can best be raised and research effectively concentrated if the public interest is sharply focused. In the words of Mary Switzer, a former director of the Office of Vocational Rehabilitation, it is all very well to talk of rehabilitation in general, but to be practical one must

> recognize that we would not be as far along the road as we are now if we did not have the emotional investment that has gone into the development of "special interest" programs. . . . It is . . . important that special groups strike out and dramatize specific problems like polio, cancer and mental illness.[6]

Many people would argue persuasively that agencies organized across the board, rather than along somewhat limited disease lines (cardiac, respiratory), would simply be and are ineffective.

Against such considerations, it is possible to make two arguments. First, to treat medically the problems of any chronically ill patient, one has to supplement the strictly medical knowledge with psychological and social knowledge—about the patient's family and other intimates, as well as about the patient himself. That knowledge will include not only how he or she and they handle the disease and the associated medical regimens but how the disease, regimens, and symptoms affect his or her and their lives—and so possibly, or even probably, the ultimate progress of the disease. Presumably, however, different chronic diseases will have different impacts on their victims' lives. Thus, although not strictly medical, this is still a categorical approach to all persons. However, the current categorical approach is mainly, often totally, medical; hence it tends to hamper thinking about *chronic disease* in more than a piecemeal—one at a time or one group at a time—fashion. This point can be illustrated graphically by the following case report, as summarized by a somewhat astonished pediatrician[5]:

> Rickey is a three-and-one-half-year-old boy residing in Baltimore City. His mother was afflicted with German measles in the first trimester of her pregnancy. Rickey was born with the full-blown picture of the rubella syndrome.

He had congenital cataracts and congenital heart disease. He developed a bleeding disorder (thrombocytopenic purpura) and hemolytic anemia. His blood disorders improved, and he began to gain weight. Heart surgery was done at age three-and-one-half months, and he was finally discharged.

Rickey showed slow motor and mental development. He was essentially blind, and it became apparent that he was also deaf. He developed an intolerance to milk and required a special soybean formula. At age twenty months, after close study, a hearing aid was prescribed and obtained. Soon after, his cataracts were removed surgically. He has been evaluated and followed by the director of admissions of the School for the Blind. He attends the Gateway Pre-school for communication disorders. . . .

The agencies, clinics, and services from which Rickey is receiving services are as follows:

Baltimore City Health Department
   Western Health District, Well Baby Clinic
   Division for the Handicapped
Maryland State Department of Health
   Division of Crippled Childrens' Services
   Division for Community Services to the Mentally Retarded
The Johns Hopkins Hospital
   Cardiac Clinic
   Hearing and Speech Center
   Child Growth and Development Study
   Wilmer Eye Clinic
   Pediatric Clinic
   Emergency Room
Greater Baltimore Medical Center
   Comprehensive Pediatric Clinic
The Children's Hospital
   Orthopedic Clinic
The Hearing and Speech Agency of Metropolitan Baltimore
   The Gateway Pre-school
The School for the Blind
   Mrs. Minturn, Director of Admissions
Day Care Services for the Mentally Retarded (tentative)
Rosewood State Hospital (tentative)

It has come to the attention of the staff of one of the involved agencies that the family of this child is being run to death and has incurred considerable expenses despite multiple resources for assistance. Virtually without a break, this mother had continuous appointments over a two-week period. . . .

This child has received regular follow-up for his various diagnostic problems. However, his family is run ragged and so near the end of its rope that they are considering institutional placement despite the inappropriateness of such placement. . . .

. . . Many of the services given this child just grew, like Topsy. Countless medical summaries and notes exist, but they are scattered in the records of several facilities.

It is neither a popular nor a constructive attitude to criticize the weaknesses of a system without enumeration of its strengths and assets.

Rickey's case illustrates the strengths in the abundance of willing hands, the adequacy of specialized skills, and the appropriate utilization of a number of resources designed to help the child in his special areas of need. However, somehow the family got lost sight of, and through this loss, all the efforts, time, expense, and personal commitment may go down the drain.

The second argument against a strictly categorical approach rests on the fact that persons who are chronically ill share many social and psychological problems. Of course, each disease or group of diseases also brings different social and psychological problems. Nevertheless, an understanding of the common, rather than only the different, problems can be of considerable aid in improving the lives of the chronically ill. These common problems are complex and need to be studied and their implications thought through for particular patients and groups of patients.

In advancing these two arguments, we do not mean to deny the usefulness of a strictly categorical approach. We are, however, asserting that a more general approach can also be very useful; it helps to shift some of the focus from rather strictly medical matters—and from the acute phases of chronicity—to the daily lives of the chronically ill and their families. Without understanding a great deal about how the chronically ill get through their days outside of health facilities (and inside them, too), health personnel will never understand what they really need to know to give effective care at the facilities—and to ensure that the patients will not return more quickly than they should.

Of course it would be foolish, and downright incorrect, to believe that physicians, nurses, social workers, physical therapists, occupational therapists, and other health personnel know nothing about the personal lives of chronically ill patients and their families. Many a patient is an open book to those who attend him or her. Of course, many a patient is a closed book, too! More to the point, however, is that the training of health personnel is rarely focused on social and psychological matters (every reader will find exception to that statement, but generally speaking, it is true). Worse yet, at the health facilities, the staff's accountability is for medical and procedural actions, not particularly for those pertaining to psychological and social matters—witness the charting and the reporting.[9] A log of nonmedical information (most of it oral in nature) does build up on particular patients, but that information mainly tends to be couched in terms that competent psychologists or sociologists (or perhaps psychiatrists) would often find more harmful than genuinely useful for effective health care.

As for an informative literature bearing on the daily social and psychological problems of the chronically ill and their families, it is fairly sparse. The vast literature about various of the diseases pertains mainly to their medical aspects and to their medical management. Much discussion about the emotional and personal concomitants of chronic disease tends to be anecdotal and experiential rather than researched or deeply studied. The information is better than nothing, but all too often it does not add up to very much.

Of course some diseases, such as asthma, seem to have psychological components and so have been studied by psychiatrists and psychologists. To understand how a given disease affects the daily experiences of the afflicted persons, however, one is likely to find better information in the increasing numbers of perceptive and eloquent autobiographies by patients, than in the standard literature about their diseases (see the bibliography).

Although the detailed medical discussions of etiology, symptomatology, treatment, and regimens often do touch on the social consequences for patients and their families, generally there is not much focus on how they might all better manage their lives, given the particular disease. Neither is there much focus on how health workers might help with the problems that come in the wake of chronic illnesses and their treatments—problems like social stigmatization of the patient, isolation, family disruption, marital discord, transformation of domestic roles, or even such more strictly medical matters as how to prevent fatal physiological crises through making necessary arrangements within the family or in the neighborhood.

Gradually more attention is being paid to the social and psychological aspects of chronic disease by psychiatrists (as in recent studies of the families of children dying of leukemia), by nurse scientists (as represented in this book), and by behavioral scientists. Nevertheless, there is still a paucity of literature on which to draw in order to obtain either an intimate feeling for the problems of the chronically ill or systematic knowledge about their problems in general.

How can we begin to think about long-term illnesses in terms that are not strictly medical? How can we learn to see with some directness and clarity the *social* and *psychological* problems faced by the chronically ill (and their immediate families) in their daily lives? Before confronting those questions directly, it will be useful to discuss more generally some salient features of the chronic illnesses and how those illnesses—as well as their impact on patients' lives—tend to be handled by contemporary health professionals and health institutions.*

---

* The following discussion is adapted from Gerson, E., and Strauss, A.: *Time for Living.*[3] Although our discussion pertains strictly to the United States, it is probable that there are no major differences between the United States and other highly industrialized countries where modern medicine and its institutions are widespread. Of course, there are striking differences in their total health systems, the political influence of the medical profession, the methods of payment for service, and the proportion of national expenditures for health. But the larger implications of the shift to the prevalence of chronic illness seem not yet to have affected profoundly the organization of care in any of these countries.

1. *Chronic illnesses are long-term by nature.* The time scales for the treatment of acute illnesses usually span days or weeks; rarely do they span months. Often, significant differences in a patient's condition can be achieved within minutes of the start of medical care. The long-term character of chronic illnesses requires a form of organization suitable for repeated interaction over months and years between patients and health workers, and for the complex social relationships that grow up between them over the course of illness.

2. *Chronic illnesses are uncertain* in a variety of ways. Often *prognosis* is uncertain, and only the evolving course of the disease provides enough information to make possible a reasonable estimate of what is going to happen—and when. Such uncertainties in prognosis can often cause considerable stress for patients and medical workers alike. The inability to make long-range plans under these conditions contributes an additional burden, especially among younger patients who have the bulk of their major life decisions before them. In addition, patients find themselves participating in the development of "frontier" medical technology as physicians use a variety of new drugs, devices, and surgical procedures in an attempt to bring the illness under better control. The very existence of major research efforts adds uncertainty to the long-term course of illness, as patients and medical workers alike look forward to the emergence of new procedures, each of whose potential can be evaluated only by direct experimentation.

In addition, many chronic illnesses are inherently episodic in nature; acute flareups are followed by apparent remissions or quiescent periods. Often the crisis themselves are not predictable, and so patients and medical workers both must prepare for occurrences at any time. The variety of uncertainties present in many chronic illnesses forces patients to reorganize and restrict their lives in a continuing attempt to prepare for the unpredictable. Thus planning, both short- and long-term, in patients' lives is often extremely difficult.

3. *Chronic diseases require proportionately great efforts at palliation.* The level of pain and discomfort, restricted activity, and quality of function experienced by chronically ill patients necessarily loom larger than for patients with acute illnesses. Because the cooperation of the patient (as well as his or her family, friends, and associates) is vital in the care of chronic illnesses, relatively more attention and effort must be paid to palliative measures. These include not only the efforts to control pain or other physical discomfort, but the anxiety and grief of the patients and their associates as well.

Since sick persons must learn to live with their symptoms (and the side effects of medical procedures), palliation becomes an important part of the overall treatment technology, as does the care of medical or quasi-medical problems ancillary to the primary diseases. Symptomatic relief often means as much in the short term to patients in such situations as does the overall progress of the treatment. Persistent pain, dizziness, nausea, or interference with normal functions (such as sleep, elimination, palatability of foods) can wreak havoc in a sick person's household, especially when the person is a child. In the extreme case such palliative efforts may involve major medical procedures in themselves, for example, neurosurgery to bring about the relief of pain.

Such efforts at palliation often run afoul of narrowly conceived notions of what is "medically necessary." With the emergence of ever-increasingly stringent controls on expenditures, palliative procedures become relatively difficult to justify; hence attending health workers find themselves in the position of attempting to balance the demands of the patient, their own opinions of appropriate treatment, and the regulatory procedures of interested agencies. Because the concept of care based on the acute illness model provides no organizational means of conducting this balancing process, both physician effectiveness and patient's quality of life often suffer substantially and directly.

4. *Chronic diseases are multiple diseases.* For a variety of reasons, long-term illnesses tend to multiply themselves, a single chronic condition often leading to multiple chronic conditions. First, many chronic diseases are systemic and degenerative in effect, so that the long-term breakdown of one organ or physiological system leads in turn to the involvement of others. Thus, for example, there is a frequent interconnection among renal failure, certain cardiovascular involvements, and diabetes—the presence of one often leading to one or both of the others. Second, the long-term disability or morbidity associated with chronic diseases implies greater susceptibility to additional diseases. Finally, the use of extremely powerful chemotherapeutic agents and radical surgical procedures as treatments for one chronic disease often implies additional iatrogenic disability.

If these tendencies provide additional medical problems for the physician and patient, they also imply a multiplication of management problems, as various treatment and management options for individual conditions are shut off by other involvements. The multiplication of symptoms often means that patients' abilities to adjust to and compensate for disease-induced limitations are sharply curtailed. Thus a series of minor partial disabilities can interlock with one another to become, effectively, a total disability. Of course, this is exacerbated by the increasing psychological stress experienced by the sick person watching his or her body literally "falling apart," despite (or occasionally because of) the heroic efforts of attending health workers. Often the stress per se becomes a factor contributing to additional medical complications, as in syndromes involving hypertension. The fear, frustration, and anger accompanying the stress often lead to additional trouble in the relationship between staff and patients, and between patients and associates. Thus the necessity for close cooperation and trust between patient and health workers is jeopardized by the course of the disease, and a vicious circle may come into play.

5. *Chronic diseases are disproportionately intrusive* on the lives of patients. The need to adjust to the demands of a regimen and the limitations on activity imposed by symptoms imply a reorganization—often radical—of the sick person's life-style, commitments, and activities. Because the disease is for the long term, the sick person cannot "drop out" of normal activities temporarily; he or she must rather make major structural changes in the manner in which life is conducted. Often these changes imply large costs to both the patient and his or her associates.

Household routines must often be rearranged to accommodate physical limitations on activity, the use of special equipment, the demands of the symptoms, or the scheduling of the regimen. This in turn reflects itself in the lives of other household members, requiring changes in how they conduct their activities. These changes, combined with the not infrequent changes in physical appearance and temperament that sick persons undergo, can be quite enough to destroy otherwise stable family relationships. If it is not, there is always, in the United States, the pauperization process to contend with. Such indirect social side effects can be both subtle and far reaching, as when the chronic illness of a child disrupts the schooling of a sibling.

People with chronic illness must also face the need to adjust their work lives in some degree to the demands of the disease. Even if the disease and its regimen are not totally disabling, there remains the possibility that the demands on time, energy, and skill made by the illness and its treatment may interfere with work to an intolerable degree, forcing the ill person to give up an otherwise satisfactory career. In addition, there are relatively few guarantees that ill persons will be able to return to a position that they left temporarily to accommodate the acute phase of their illnesses. Employers are often reluctant to hire chronically ill people because they represent potential insurance liabilities. Often they appear to be unreliable or transient as a result of the continuing threat of incapacitation by their illness. Employers also are only rarely acquainted with the specialized needs of chronically ill persons and are unwilling to make relatively minor changes in scheduling and work arrangements on a case-by-case basis because this implies additional overhead costs to them.

Sick persons also can pay a high price for diseases in the form of *social isolation* from their friends and community activities. The direct demands of symptoms and regimen may of course, make it impossible to maintain the former pace of activities, but there are other consequences as well. Chronic diseases can be stigmatizing; changes in appearance, rarely for the better, may cause both the ill person and associates enough discomfort that the person simply withdraws from social activities. The impact of stigmatization varies with the social identity of the stricken person: young women are more apt to suffer than older men. The combination of social and medical factors involved in a chronic disease complex can therefore often result in a significant withdrawal from community life, in the loss of friends, and in the abandonment of hobbies and recreational pursuits.

6. *Chronic diseases require a wide variety of ancillary services* if they are to be dealt with properly. Depending on the degree of complexity and the number of involvements, a chronically ill person may require service from an enormous number of ancillary professionals. The services of a social worker may be needed to help the sick person through the bewildering maze of regulations, forms, and agencies involved in financing his or her care; in addition, social workers often serve as specialists in referrals, providing knowledge of specialized services and agencies needed. Often some form of psychological counseling or therapy is needed to cope effectively with the disease-induced stress and its consequences. Psychiatrists may be consulted for this purpose, although elaborate psychotherapy is not always needed. The chronically ill often need educational services to inform them about their disease, its medical and social consequences, alternative strategies for management open to them, and the like. Usually these educational services come from the physician or nurses attached to the medical service, but these people are often far too busy to provide adequate detailed information. Sometimes organizations made up of persons with similar illnesses (self-help groups) are available, and these provide not only the necessary educational services, but also moral support, the advantages of group purchasing of specialized equipment and supplies, and a public voice for the needs of similar patients. For the most part, however, educational services are haphazard, intermittent, and poorly organized.

Special tutoring or educational services may be necessary for chronically ill children and occasionally for their siblings. The public schools generally are not equipped to handle the special situations of chronically ill children, and these children must therefore suffer inadequate or improper education. Alternately, their parents must make special arrangements; however, since there is little in the way of organized service in this regard (except in a very few "categorical" instances, as for the deaf or blind), usually the solution is simply to do without. Technical services such as physical therapy and training in the use of prosthetic devices or special equipment are more readily available, although occasionally there are problems here, too. Occupational counseling and retraining are available only if the sick person happens to fit the criteria of a program organized primarily around the needs of the healthy unemployed. Effective advice on occupational career management in the light of chronic illness is not usually available. Domestic counseling is widely available, but relatively few counselors are well acquainted with the specialized needs and problems of the chronically ill, and funding for these services is problematic. Legal and financial services are available only through the usual channels of the marketplace from professionals who rarely, if ever, have any significant acquaintance with the problems of the chronically ill.

Perhaps the most pressing need is for simple general counseling from a sophisticated and sympathetic third party who can suggest plausible strategies for managing a wide variety of the problems that continually arise in the course of chronic disease management. Sometimes such counseling can be achieved "under the table" by psychiatric referral, but increasing stringency of cost controls by funding agencies (public and private) are eroding the effectiveness of this tactic. Social workers, the traditional source of such counseling, tend to be committed to a perspective that defines the patient as *ipso facto* psychopathological. Further, they are often so swamped with administrative work (and the demands of private practice) that they can provide little beyond the most general sort of advice and a referral service. Public health agencies engender similar institutional requirements that block even well-intentioned public health nurses in their attempts to work with chronically ill clients.

7. *Chronic illnesses are expensive.* Even where extremely elaborate and expensive technologies are not normally used in the care of a particular illness, the need for routine monitoring, the occurrence of crisis, the use of drugs over long periods of time, and the extensive interaction with patients and associates all make caring for chronic illnesses expensive. In addition, the complex and multiple nature of many chronic illness courses, as well as the need for a variety of ancillary services, drive up substantially the direct costs of chronic illness care. Furthermore, the opportunity costs of chronic illness are very high in comparison to acute illnesses; lost work alone often requires patients to become welfare recipients, and of course the restriction of activity often attendant on chronic illness means the sacrifice of many recreational activities, even inexpensive ones. Furthermore, the long-term, repetitive, and complex character of chronic illness care naturally implies proportionately greater overhead and administrative costs for patients, health organizations, and funding agencies alike.

A most important aspect of this process is the conversion of self-sufficient American families into paupers. As a result of the extraordinary continuing expenses of some chronic illnesses, families are forced to consume their savings and may even become welfare recipients. Even with the development of Medicaid programs and the evolution of health insurance in various forms, the vicious indirect consequences of this process continue: dissolution of families, gross damage to the psychological integrity of patients, social stigmatization, and the like.

It will perhaps help to recapitulate the important features of the chronic illnesses. They are long term, uncertain, expensive, often multiple, disproportionately intrusive, and they require palliation, especially because they are "incurable." These characteristics of chronic illness are essential to keep in mind when thinking about the impact of illness on patients and families and health personnel. We will see their impact all through this book.

A FRAMEWORK

To repeat our earlier questions: How can we begin to think about long-term illnesses in terms that are not strictly medical? How can we learn to see with some directness and clarity the *social* and *psychological* problems faced by the chronically ill (and their immediate families) in their daily lives?

To begin to develop both an empathy with the ill and some effective ways of thinking systematically about their experiences, we suggest the following framework.

First of all, one must think of any given disease as potentially causing *multiple problems* of daily living for the person so unfortunate as to have the disease, Among those problems are:

1. The prevention of *medical crises* and their management once they occur
2. The control of *symptoms*
3. The carrying out of prescribed *regimens* and the management of problems attendant on carrying out the regimens
4. The prevention of, or living with, *social isolation* caused by lessened contact with others
5. The adjustment to changes in the *course of the disease,* whether it moves downward or has remissions
6. The attempts at *normalizing* both interaction with others and style of life
7. *Funding*—finding the necessary money—to pay for treatments or to survive despite partial or complete loss of employment
8. Confronting attendant *psychological, marital,* and *familial* problems

These are among the *key problems.* It takes no great imagination to see why. For instance, if a dying cancer patient and his or her family cannot adjust to his or her downward course or to the swings of good and bad days or weeks, then they are all in for psychological and domestic trouble. If a regimen necessitates radical changes in life-style (as when a person with heart trouble is forbidden to smoke, drink, or eat sweets), that medical injunction is likely to have a considerable impact on the person's social and perhaps domestic life.

To handle such key problems, patients and their families and friends must develop *basic strategies.* They must work out standard methods or techniques that will yield some measure of success with those key problems. For instance, a person with cardiac disease may have to avoid even slight inclines and so must learn to take new routes through neighborhood streets, even if this means taking "the long way around." Someone with ulcerative colitis may have to develop techniques of gracefully disappearing from social occasions for several minutes without causing any suspicion of what he or she has to do after getting to the bathroom.

Many of these strategies call for the assistance of family and friends, or even acquaintances and strangers, who act as various kinds of *agents.* Thus, in the pages to follow, we see people who act as *rescuing* agents (saving a diabetic individual from dying when she is in a coma), or as *protective* agents (accompanying an epileptic person so that if she begins to fall she can be eased to the ground), or as *assisting* agents (helping with a regimen), or as *control* agents (making the patient stay with her regimen), and so on.

The basic strategies for coping with the key problems call for certain kinds of *organizational* or *family arrangements.* People's efforts must be coordinated—with all the understandings and agreements that necessitates. Thus disabled patients have standing arrangements with neighbors and friends who do their grocery shopping for them. The parents of diabetic children need to coach neighbors in reading the signs of oncoming coma as well as to warn them against allowing the child to have sweets while at their homes. A man with a cardiac condition and his wife may reach an agreement—perhaps only after much persuasion by her—that when she senses his oncoming fatigue before he does, she will warn him; otherwise he may suddenly and embarrassingly run out of energy. Clearly, to establish and maintain such necessary arrangements may require not only much trust and considerable interactional skill but also financial, medical, and familial resources. If any of those are lacking, the arrangements may never be properly instituted or may collapse. In any case, important *consequences*—for both the patient and his or her family—flow from how he or she and they have organized their efforts so as to handle key problems.

In sum, then, the important terms in our framework for understanding the daily experiences of chronically ill persons include key problems, basic strategies, family and organizational arrangements, and the consequences of those arrangements. We reluctantly add that health personnel are, in this scheme, far from the only important features. True, they can be crucial for some persons' very survival and also may give very useful counsel or aid in managing their key problems. However, medicine as currently constituted tends to be distinctly secondary—if contributory—to the sick person's day-to-day "carrying on" in the face of disease. A major reason for this book, however, is the increasing interest of health personnel in the difficulties facing the chronically ill and their desire to be of assistance in handling those difficulties.

Let us turn now to separate discussions of the key problems listed. Those problems are not strikingly different from the ones confronted by normal people when occasionally they fall acutely ill, but readers should soon see, if they cannot yet imagine, why the problems of chronicity are perhaps qualitatively different. This is so if only because of the wearing persistence and relative permanence of these problems. Whereas normal persons, once they are over their acute illness, can soon forget it, the chronically sick cannot forget; their illnesses are either always with them or, if quiescent, potentially lurking just around the corner.

In this book we will be at pains to emphasize that it is not only the sick person who faces these problems but also, in all likelihood, the immediate family. Her or his fate is, in a real sense, also theirs. We shall signalize their mutual struggle—to manage their living despite the chronicity—by referring most often to him or her as a sick person rather than primarily as "the patient."

We should also add that the various key problems facing the sick persons and their families involve them not only in a variety of different kinds of *work*—crisis work, symptom control work, regimen work—but also in a host of other kinds of tasks that can for convenience be called comfort work, clinical safety work, the work of preparing for dying, the work of keeping marital relationships repaired, and so on.[1] The heavy requirements of this work can exhaust patient and family, tearing some families apart but tightening the family ties of others, making new and sometimes "better" persons of both the sick people and their helpers.

Before turning to the separate discussions of the key problems in the next chapters, it will be useful to consider some drastic differences between hospital and home that affect management of chronic illness at home. It will be useful also to consider what it means to have at least a partly "failed body."

There are at least six contrasts that "make all the difference" between hospital work and home work, similar as the work may be in other respects. First, in the hospital the patient is living under relatively controlled conditions, whereas at home, life's contingencies are always breaking in on the management of the illness. Some of those contingencies are so minor as to require only slight adjustments; others can be disastrous.

Second, the caring agents in the hospital are, with much variation of course, relatively knowledgeable about and experienced in their medical work, whereas at first the agents at home have much to learn about their medical work. Later, they may know much more about the unique or idiosyncratic features of the particular illness with which they are dealing.

Third, although the hospital staff may be much concerned with the care and fate of their patients, generally speaking they cannot be as concerned as the spouse or other kin. This is not only because intimate relations with patients are not characteristic of hospital work, but also because kin have only one (or only a few) sick people to care for and work with, whereas in the hospital, patients silently—sometimes even explicitly—are in competition for staff's time and energies. However, the kin's "more time" with the sick family member raises interactional and identity issues, as well as purely medical ones, not so frequently encountered in the hospital situation. (We will see some of these later.)

Fourth, even when a hospital is understaffed, at least there is a multiplicity of workers with a shared division of labor, and potentially at least some flexibility in reallocating tasks when staff members are temporarily very rushed, tired, exhausted, bored, or cannot "stand" being with a specific patient. At home there may quite literally be only the spouse who does all or most of the medical work (as well as medically related work *and* housework). There may not even be a spouse. Alternately, certain tasks can be allocated to or assumed by children or friends, but that may only be a temporary expedient. In any event those arrangements must be made, often negotiated; they must then be sustained, thus remade and renegotiated. Those arrangements often prove to be very fragile.

Fifth, there is another great difference between hospital work and home work insofar as the former is relatively short term, whereas the latter can be very long term indeed—to the point where kin, and sick person too, feel they are in a no-exit situation, whether or not they have ever heard of Jean-Paul Sartre!

Sixth, a last contrast is particularly important because, although it is generally recognized, its implications frequently seem to escape even relatively astute physicians and other health workers, since their tendency is to focus interest on the technical aspects of illness work. In contrast, while chronically ill people carry a burden of symptom and regimen management, shared to some degree with spouses at least, they also are doing life's other work (domestic, office or school, or other "work"), which in turn impacts on, is impacted by, and is all intertwined with the medical tasks themselves. All or most of life's other work becomes suspended, of course, while the patient is in the hospital; if kin, friends, or colleagues take over that work, at least it is not the hospital staff members who do. So, however complicated and intricate may be the medical work in hospitals, it is *far* less complex in the larger "human" sense than living and working with a chronic illness at home.

The contrasts just listed are all the more startling when another contrast is considered: that between resources available to patients while in the hospital and those available at home. *The* central resource for doing literally thousands of "things" is a person's body itself. An unimpaired body is equipped to rise, sit, stand, lie down, push, pull, stretch. Its hands and legs function in amazing numbers of ways, as does every part of the body—neck, head, lips, face—as well as the various systems within the body. At the hospital, really sick patients are admonished not to, or in fact need not, engage in most actions done outside the hospital at work or play. At the same time, of course, those things "medical" that need to be done, whether on or inside the patient, will be carried out by the personnel or by machinery—including machinery that substitutes for the patient's systemic functioning.

Everyone's body inevitably develops inabilities to perform certain actions as well as it did previously, whether the lessened functioning is due to age, tiredness, temporary ailment, or serious illness. The degree of diminished functioning varies along a continuum, of course, from slight to total loss of ability. Moreover, there are countless numbers of continuums, one for each action (stretching the neck to the left, stretching to the right, being able to hold an object in the right hand or in the left hand, and so on). Different illnesses affect different body functions, affect them differently as different phases of the illnesses, and with greater or smaller degrees of severity and permanence. In consequence, the body as a basic resource itself is an immensely variable phenomenon and would be even for two persons who suffered from exactly the same disease—even if they were identical twins. Essential body functions such as maintaining the heart's beat or controlling a failing heart can be managed by a pacemaker or proper drug intake, but most of the resources needed to *substitute* for an ill person's loss of body ability may not permit such easy substitution.

Furthermore, what anyone's body is required to do—other than just to stay alive—cannot possibly be separated from what is normally but rather globally referred to as his or her "life-style." Since personal, cultural, occupational, domestic, financial, and other conditions—including accidents and other potentially fateful contingencies—profoundly affect how a person lives, it follows that what a sick person's body must ordinarily do will also bear on what his or her body must face up to. A badly arthritic finger may make all the difference in a surgeon's or pianist's life (even if the latter is just an amateur). Loss of ability to lift sizable objects may finish off the paid activities of a plumber or carpenter but leave the life of a professor or lawyer relatively undisturbed. Inability to climb even modest slopes is easily managed if one lives in Chicago but not in San Francisco; however, slopes can throw a very large monkey wrench into the expressive life of the same Chicagoan who is passionately in love with mountain climbing. So, voluntary or imposed tasks as well as the body's abilities or inabilities are inextricably linked in everyone's life, but perhaps more so in the lives of the ill.

What the body as resource cannot do effectively, easily, or at all—but is, alas, required to do—leads to the necessity of obtaining an adequate *substitute resource.* Some other person's body or some piece of equipment must supply what is lacking, but under what conditions will he or she—or it—be available? For how long? And at what cost, either to the sick person or to the substitute agent? To raise such questions analytically is to do no more than every sick person must do pragmatically. Sometimes having or finding substitute body resources is not so difficult, since spouse, other kin, and friends may pitch in, fill in, proffering or even insisting on the rendering of services. However, it may be necessary for the sick to develop strategies for obtaining and certainly for maintaining effective substitutes in place of their own failed resources. The strategies may work beautifully but inevitably bring additional consequences, some of which may be negative (they cost money, they take up much time, they place temporary stress or long-term burdens on the helping persons), whereas others may be marvelously positive (as we will see when discussing spouse relationships). Paradoxically, when the consequences are negative they set conditions calling for further strategies to eliminate or mitigate their financial, physical, emotional, interactional, or other damage. In short, a failed body necessitates *arrangements*, and then inevitably sequential *rearrangements*, as contingencies arise, as conditions change.

Having covered the main items in this suggested framework for thinking about chronic illness, we are now in a position to move on to the body of this book. We begin with Part 1, "Problems of living with chronic illness."

References

1. Bright, Margaret: Demographic background for programming for chronic diseases in the U.S. In Lilienfeld, A., and Gifford, A., editors: Chronic disease and public health, Baltimore, 1966, Johns Hopkins Press, pp. 5-22.

2. Chronic conditions and limitations of activity and mobility, U.S., July 1965-June 1967, Public Health Service Publication No. 1000, Series 10-61, U.S. Department of Health, Education and Welfare, Public Health Services, Mental Health Administration, Jan. 1971, pp. 1-4, 8, 11.

3. Gerson, Elihu, and Strauss, Anselm: Time for living, Social Policy **6:**12-18, 1975.

4. Hoffman, Joan: Nothing can be done, Urban Life and Culture **3:**50-70, 1974.

5. Hopkins, Edward: The chronically ill child and the community. In Debuskey, M., editor: The chronically ill child and his family, Springfield, Ill., 1970, Charles C Thomas, Publisher, pp. 196-198.

6. Mayo, L.: Problem and challenge. In Guides to action on chronic illness, New York, 1956, National Health Council, pp. 9-13, 35, 55.

7. National Center for Health Statistics, Health Interview Survey, U.S. Department of Health and Human Services, 1977, unpublished data; and Vital and health statistics, current estimates from the National Health Interview Survey, Series 10, No. 141, Oct. 1982.

8. Strauss, Anselm, Fagerhaugh, Shizuko, Suczek, Barbara, and Wiener, Carolyn: The social organization of medical work, Chicago, 1984, University of Chicago Press.

9. Strauss, Anselm, Glaser, Barney, and Quint, Jeanne: The nonaccountability of terminal care, Hospitals **38:**73-87, 1964.

10. Thomas, Lewis: The right track, The Wilson Quarterly **4:**103-107, 1980, p. 43.

PART 1

PROBLEMS OF LIVING WITH CHRONIC ILLNESS

CHAPTER 1

PREVENTING AND MANAGING MEDICAL CRISES

Crisis. This is a striking place to begin our discussion, since it seems quite medical; yet so much that is social is involved in how crises are prevented and managed, and even in how they are triggered.

Some chronic diseases are, of course, especially characterized by potentially fatal medical crises. Cardiac conditions are rather obvious instances of that point, as is severe diabetes, which may lead to insulin comas from which the diabetic individual may not emerge alive unless rescued in time. In contrast, epileptic convulsions may not kill unless the person's breath becomes totally cut off, but the convulsions may occur so suddenly as to endanger the person by falling or by moving automobiles. To prevent these crises—when that is possible—and to minimize their potentially fatal effects when they do occur, vulnerable persons, and probably their close kin too, must organize their lives for crisis management. They must literally construct and maintain necessary organizational arrangements. After a given crisis, they may need to reconstitute or to improve those arrangements.

Relevant to crises are these questions. How probable is their recurrence? How far can they go (to or short of death)? How frequent are they? How fast do they appear? How clear are the signs of their coming to the patient or kin or bystanders or even health personnel? Can they be prevented or their effects mitigated, and by whom? How expected are their appearances? How complex are the rescue operations? What resources are available to prevent the crisis or to pull the person through it relatively undamaged or at least alive? The following discussion will touch on these questions.

READING THE SIGNS

First, let us look at the organization of effort that can be involved in properly reading signs that portend crisis. Thus diabetic people or the parents of diabetic children are taught by health personnel not only how to prevent potential crises (caused either by sugar shortage or by insulin shock) but also how to recognize the signs of oncoming crisis itself. They are also taught what to do in case of an actual crisis. In turn, diabetic individuals or their parents teach their kin, friends, and possibly their neighbors, schoolteachers, and fellow workers what to see and do when the crisis is appearing or actually occurs. Likewise, epileptic persons and sufferers from sickle cell disease, if they are so fortunate as to have signs immediately preceding their convulsions, learn to recognize the signs and so prepare themselves for the oncoming crisis. They sit down, lie down, and if in public get themselves to a place of safety.

To prevent mistakes on the part of others when in crisis, or to get proper action that will save themselves, diabetic individuals may carry instructions on their persons. If they do not, bystanders will not read the signs correctly and so will not know what to do or may do the wrong thing. As a book on ileostomy warns:

> Fluid or electrolyte imbalance is the most serious danger to the ileostomy patient. It can occur very precipitously and endanger the patient's life within a day. Its cause is excessive output through the ileostomy. . . . A simple case of flu, partial obstruction, or an accident may initiate increased . . . output. For this reason diarrhea lasting more than twelve hours must be reported to a physician. It is recommended that every ileostomy patient carry an ID card giving in addition to personal identification the name of the condition, describing briefly the method of appliance removal and skin care, and listing the name and number of surgeon or hospital to contact for information in case of an accident. Ileostomy is still a rare condition and may not even be recognized by hospital personnel.[2]

Ironically enough, if the disease is rare or relatively unknown to them, physicians may even sometimes read noncrisis signs incorrectly and so precipitate a fatal medical crisis. This can happen, for instance, when a person with sickle cell disease is brought bleeding and unconscious to a hospital and immediate effort is made to stop the bleeding—because he or she has failed to carry instructions *not* to stop the bleeding!

Like properly instructed ileostomy patients, diabetic persons may carry not only instructions but also materials with which they or others can counteract their crisis: sugar or candy or insulin. A man with epilepsy may stuff a handkerchief between his teeth just before convulsions, and a knowledgeable bystander may know enough to open his jaws, get his tongue out if necessary, and employ a handkerchief.

When signs are not read properly, are read too slowly, or are interpreted as meaning something else, then people die or come close to dying. This is what happens when comas are mistaken for fainting or alcoholic convulsions. This also is what happens when a person with cardiac disease for the first time experiences severe chest pains but passes them off as unimportant or as merely signs of a bad cold. (Thereafter, she may put her doctor's name and telephone number right under the telephone—and carry the information in a wallet, too—for emergency use.) When an unconscious patient is brought into the emergency room of the nearest hospital, physicians there understandably may treat for the wrong disease. Indeed, any crisis-prone person brought to an emergency room runs the hazard of being misdiagnosed unless he is either conscious—and so can talk to the physicians—or carries something on his person that will alert them to his disease. Otherwise, the staff is at a great disadvantage because an adequate medical history is lacking.

A slower version of the same diagnostic error is when patients with cancer are misdiagnosed; only later may the correct diagnosis be made, often too late to save the patient. Moreover, not only may a patient misread her own signs but also the associated signs of crucially assisting machinery; thus inexperienced patients who are on kidney dialysis machinery may not recognize that their machinery is not working correctly and may not realize that their bodies therefore are nearing physiological crisis. Errors also can be committed even by quite experienced persons, because they have not yet learned to recognize that biological changes in their bodies—for instance, changes caused by the life cycle—can bring about crisis, so they read the signs as noncritical.

ORGANIZING FOR CRISES

That nonmedical organization of effort is necessary for preventing or managing crises should be apparent from what we have touched on before, but the point is worth further amplification. Not only must danger signs be read correctly and appropriate actions be taken by the person himself or by other people; additional kinds of organized actions—some relatively simple, some very complex—may be necessary. Thus it is imperative that a crisis-prone diabetic man or woman *not* leave the house without candy or insulin, otherwise he or she may be unable to prevent or overcome the crisis. On weekends, care must be taken that there is insulin in the house, because then most pharmacies are closed. The mother of a diabetic child needs to make special arrangements for insulin shots and proper diet with the mother of chums if he or she is to stay overnight at their house.

> One mother has arranged to have her epileptic adult daughter live with her own friends, because someone must, the mother believes, live with her constantly. Once the daughter went out alone and had to be rescued from the traffic. The friends with whom she lives now do not allow her, during heavy traffic hours, to cross a boulevard in the neighborhood for fear of her either being hit or having an epileptic fit then and there.
> *Palmer*

Mr. James, who had a cardiac condition,

> described how the phone numbers of an ambulance, his doctor, and his wife at work could be taped to the phone. He would plan to contact them in that order if he felt an attack coming on. He reemphasized that he could tell when one was approaching. Also he would not lock the front door so that if he would be unable to let the ambulance people in, they could get to him.

The adherence to crisis-preventing regimens may require, as with cystic fibrosis or kidney dialysis patients, a high degree of daily organization in the family. With such a disease as hemophilia, the entire environment may have to be controlled minutely, so that the child does not stumble against sharp edges and begin his fatal bleeding; so too must the adults institute over the child an ever-vigilant guard.

> The young hemophiliac son of Czar Nicholas of Russia had two servants to hover constantly over him and catch him if he began to fall. Sometimes he wore padded suits, and even the trees in the area where he played were padded in the event that he might brush against them.[3]

In fact, the parents of a hemophiliac child wage continual war against both a potentially fatal environment and against the potentially fatal actions of the child himself. This kind of intense monitoring of the child's physical activity and the environs can lead not only to his excessive dependency but to great friction between a resentful child and the parents as protective agents. The parents cannot even resort to mild corporal punishment if the child is disobedient.

It is worth adding that in all the examples just noted, the potential danger of death is great, as is the relative speed with which the crisis can both occur and go through to death. This eventuality can, however, be prepared against, although not always successfully, because it is relatively expectable. Certainly the specific time of a crisis may take everyone by surprise. Nevertheless, since the event is expectable, organizing against its occurrence can be fairly effective.

BREAKDOWN OF ORGANIZATION: POTENTIAL AND ACTUAL

When the crisis is not so foreseeable, then it is more likely to prove disastrous, since usually there is less organization of effort to manage it. A crisis may be unexpected not only because of the nature of the specific disease but because of the inexperience or medical ignorance of the sick person and her family.

> One cardiac man interpreted his physician's instructions to stop working as meaning just that, but he did not discontinue his daily exercise, which consisted of heavy weight lifting and bicycle riding. He could have precipitated a fatal crisis, although he did not. Doubtless his physician would have been very upset—or at least exasperated—if he had known how his instructions were interpreted!

If the onset of a disease has begun with a visible medical crisis, bringing fear but awareness to the patient, then of course he and his family are more likely to make careful arrangements against the possibility of crisis recurrence. The more likely are they, also, to get the willing cooperation of friends and extended kin, who can easily believe in the legitimacy of his requests concerning their help to prevent another crisis. If there had been no such original crisis, however, the attending health personnel may have to impress on him and his family that such a danger really does exist.

> A cardiac patient of our acquaintance surprises his friends by answering "no" honestly when they ask him if he had been afraid of death during his myocardial infarction; concomitantly, though he takes the precaution of carrying his cardiologist's telephone number in his wallet, he really does not, "in his guts," believe himself likely to have any emergency.

Understandably, too, the further away patients are from the experience of an actual crisis, the more likely they are to relax their guard. They are "out of the woods." This can be seen right in the hospital a few days after a patient's myocardial infarction. After the patient is feeling better, she begins to move around more than the staff believes she should. They reprimand; that is, essentially they tell her to organize behavior more in accordance with her crisis-prone condition. On the other hand, one can also see the staff begin, in their turn, to relax their vigilance as they pay increasingly less attention to her in favor of more critically ill competitors. Interestingly enough, sometimes the patient believes he or she is out of danger sooner than does the staff and sometimes vice versa, so that some patients are warned repeatedly to take it easy (and sometimes threatened with the imagery of death if they do not), whereas other patients who seem overly frightened of dying are urged to move around more, not to be afraid, and generally to stop acting so unrealistically sick. When the patient gets home, the same dramas may and probably will be reenacted with his family.

Assuming there is an organization of effort for crisis management, any breakdown or disruption of it can be disastrous. Thus family strain can lead to the abandonment of or lessening of control over crisis-preventing regimens. The temporary absence of protective agents or of control agents (mothers, in the instance of diabetic children who are prone to eat too much candy) can be disastrous. A divorce or separation that leaves an assisting agent (a mother assisting her child with cystic fibrosis with absolutely necessary exercises) alone, unrelieved with her task, can gradually or quickly lead to a crisis. (One divorced couple, however, arranged matters so that the husband would relieve his wife on weekends and on some evenings.) Even an agent's illness can lead to the relaxation of regimens or the elimination of actions that might otherwise prevent crisis. Other things being equal, though, slow onsets of crises do allow for the remobilization of disrupted organization. Clear signs of crisis are likely to allow more effective remobilization than do unclear signs.

The worst situation, however, is when a sick person is abandoned by kin and friends, so that the only effort he can call on against potential crises is his own. If he cannot even count on himself, then he or his family may purchase the efforts of necessary agents, but if money runs out then the following kind of situation (reported in the *San Francisco Chronicle*, April 10, 1971) can occur:

> A man dying from a rare form of epilepsy and who needs constant attendant care to stay alive received help from the State yesterday.
>
> Medi-Cal chief Dr. Earl Brian authorized the immediate hospitalization of John Herbert Roberts, 42, who is in a convalescent home, for "current evaluation" of his needs.
>
> Roberts, who is suffering from myoclonic epilepsy, needs constant attendant care to assure that he doesn't choke to death during spasms.
>
> Dr. Julian Milestone, Roberts' doctor, said, "he could die any time, if there is no one in the room to watch him, he could die in five minutes."
>
> Medi-Cal pays $400 a month for Roberts' stay in the home but would not pay the $1000 a month needed for an attendant 15 hours a day.
>
> Roberts' relatives and friends had paid for the attendant care in the past but they said their money ran out yesterday.[4]

Six months later, however, Mr. Roberts won a state supreme court case against Medi-Cal, the judge ruling mercifully that:

> Since petitioner suffers from a unique illness, with abnormal requirements (for treatment), his claim does not quite fit within any of the pigeon holes (created by Medi-Cal regulations). Respondent could, of course, issue new regulations taking account of petitioner's plight, but he has not done so.
>
> Respondent's argument stops here . . . but the inevitable, if unspoken, conclusion is that petitioner will not receive the nursing care he needs and regrettably, will die. . . .
>
> Fortunately . . . neither the statutes nor regulations compel so horrific a result.[5]

In some disease conditions, the ill person believes she cannot count on others, no matter how alert and well disposed, to prevent her dying—because realistically they cannot. "Once again I found it difficult to fall asleep," writes a cardiac patient recovering from his first heart attack. "I would lie awake thinking for hours. Would I get over it? What more was in store for me? I had nightmares."[1] Well he might, thinking he might never wake up! Again, when people suffer from myasthenia gravis, when skeletal muscles become flaccid, there is the possibility of their choking through loss of tongue control.

> One patient who takes a drug that temporarily corrects his drastic muscular defect—and which wears off rapidly after a few hours—must wake twice during sleeping hours in order to take it. When occasionally he has overslept, he has barely been able to swallow or even breathe. Understandably he is in great fright over the possibility of choking to death.

An especially poignant instance of virtually constant guarding against medical crisis is the plight of people who suffer from very extreme emphysema. The slightest psychological upset can rob them of their vital but scarce oxygen, so they tend completely to avoid social contact and interaction with other people. Any kind of emotion, even laughing, might bring them into crisis. In short, when the patient is his own protective agent, he carries a very heavy burden.

The self-against-fate feeling, and experience, can be contrasted with the experience of individuals who can really do relatively little about potential crises (other than to follow their regimens faithfully), but who must rely almost solely on their physicians' skilled efforts to prevent or manage crises. Kidney transplant patients are a good example. Some are immensely trustful of and grateful to their surgeons; it is easy to see why.

POSTCRISIS PERIOD

Now, just a word about the postcrisis period in relation to the organization of efforts. At home, of course, such patients require plenty of family organization to prevent additional crises or to manage them if they occur. What is not so evident is that signs of improvement may be read, by kin or patient, when few exist, or that a hundred and one contingencies may arise that render faulty the organization for further crisis prevention and crisis management. Relevant variables here are how far back and rapid are the recovery, since both of these may vary for different disease conditions. Paradoxically, some crises-to-death allow for rather speedy recovery (insulin shock), whereas others that may be far less dangerous, or at least have proceeded less far, allow the person to feel and act "normal" only after some days or weeks have elapsed. Postcrisis organization is correspondingly affected, being relaxed more quickly or maintained alertly for much longer.

If, indeed, there is yet another crisis, and one or more parties to crisis arrangements believe the arrangement was faulty, then there can be considerable guilt or anger, depending on who feels at fault and who feels angrily virtuous. Control agents who failed or who were disobeyed, protective agents who were not sufficiently alert to the signs of crisis or who where outwitted by careless patients—these are the kinds of actors in the crisis drama who are likely to feel guilty or aggrieved and angry. Unfortunately, these reactions can have a negative impact on domestic relations and hence on the family's ability to manage future crises.

CEDING RESPONSIBILITY TO THE HOSPITAL

It is worth adding that when a sick person is brought to the hospital just prior to or during a period of crisis, she or he and the family are, in effect, ceding responsibility for crisis management to the hospital's personnel. The family's crisis organization gives way to professional organization. Those patients who have been fighting against potential crises (such as cancer victims nearing the ends of their lives) may cede control with a sense of relief. Carrying the burden was just too much. However, sometimes such delegation to hospital personnel can be difficult for patients and even devastating to their sense of personal worth, since they no longer appear to themselves to be competent in handling their own affairs. On a less tragic scale, this same phenomenon can be observed with patients with ulcerative colitis when they enter the hospital. They are accustomed to close monitoring of their symptoms and to the prevention of potential crises by careful adherence to regimens, and they only enter the hospital when their condition becomes critical. Then their monitoring functions are quickly taken over by the hospital staff. Typically, the staff is quite unaware that the almost total delegation of control to itself can be damaging to the patient's identity. The delegation may be necessary, but it is usually not cushioned by softening gestures.

Furthermore, when the staff thinks the repeated hospitalization of specific patients is caused by personal or familial negligence, then it tends to look with some disfavor on those patients. An extreme example, of course, is the distaste that the personnel of emergency rooms have for alcoholic "repeaters," even when brought to the site in bad condition. Much more subtle is the staff's response when faced by such a situation as the following:

> Two hemophiliac men, respectively 26 and 27 years old, are called "crocks" by the staff, because they pretty frequently come back in crisis state and have to be given one more transfusion. Nobody really knows much about them, except that they seem "queer."

Well might they seem queer, having gone through a lifetime of potentially fatal crises! More to the point, however, is that the staff feels frustrated, since it feels not as if these patients were saved through skilled or efficient techniques but only as if the patients could have saved everybody time and effort by not getting into trouble again. Pressed, the staff might well admit that hemophiliac individuals cannot do much to prevent these frequent crises, but. . . . A detached observer might be inclined to say that this routine kind of rescue work probably should be going on elsewhere than in a big medical center, presumably at some medical facility where the staff does not define its work either as curing or as the immensely specialized management of acute disease.

To the foregoing discussion of crisis prevention and crisis management, it should also be added that *during* an extended period of crisis (whether the patient is in the hospital or at home), some organization of family effort is still called for. Kin may need to make special arrangements about their time (from work, for visiting the hospital, for nursing the patient at home). They may also need to make arrangements about space (having the bed downstairs rather than upstairs, living near the hospital during the peak of the crisis). They may have to juggle the immediate and even the extended family's finances. They may have to spell each other, in an extraordinary division of family labor, when taking care of the patient at home during his crisis. Even the patient—in trying "to get better" rather than "giving up" or in acting properly rather than tempting fate by improper actions—may have to contribute to the organization of effort necessary to bringing him (and his kin) through his period of danger.

References

1. Kesten, Yehuda: Diary of a heart patient, New York, 1968, McGraw-Hill Book Co.
2. Lenneberg, E., and Rowbotham, J.: The ileostomy patient, Springfield, Ill., 1970, Charles C Thomas, Publisher.
3. Massie, Robert: Nicholas and Suzanne, New York, 1967, Dell Publishing Co., Inc.
4. San Francisco Chronicle, April 10, 1971, © Chronicle Publishing Co., 1971.
5. San Francisco Chronicle, Nov. 5, 1971. Story reprinted from a United Press International Release.

CHAPTER 2

MANAGEMENT
OF REGIMENS

A second key problem encountered by many, if not most, of the chronically ill is the management of their regimens, for unless the physician is absolutely helpless in the face of a given chronic disease, he or she will suggest or command some kind of regimen. At first blush, regimen management may not seem a problem of much magnitude: regimens are either followed by obedient, sensible patients or ignored at their peril. Indeed, physicians and other health personnel tend to regard patients (or their families) as not only foolish if they do not carry out the prescribed regimens, but downright uncooperative. They talk approvingly or disapprovingly about the adherence or lack of adherence to regimens. It is true that sometimes patients and families foolishly and even willfully break the rules, as when the mother of a child allergic to chocolate allows him "just one piece."

However, the issue is not really one of willfulness, stupidity, or even medical ignorance. The issue is primarily that patients must continue to manage their daily existences under specific sets of financial and social conditions. Their chronic illnesses and the associated regimens only complicate—and are secondary to—their daily management problems. In that regard, regimens sometimes present even more difficulties than the symptoms themselves. It is no wonder, then, that every regimen—and every item in it—is actually or potentially on trial. So are the people who recommend the regimen.

REGIMENS ARE EVALUATED

Regimens, then, are *not* just automatically accepted. They are judged on the basis of efficiency or legitimacy, or both. Also, they are judged on social rather than medical bases. Hence they will be taken up and adhered to only under certain conditions. Some of these are:

1. There is an initial or continuing trust in the physician or whoever else prescribes the regimen.
2. No rival supersedes the physician in his or her legitimating.
3. There is evidence that the regimen works to control either symptoms or the disease itself, or both.
4. No distressing, frightening side effects appear.
5. The side effects are outweighed by symptom relief or by sufficient fear of the disease itself.
6. There is a relative noninterference with important daily activities, either of the patient or of people around him or her.
7. The regimen's perceived good effects are not outweighed by a negative impact on the patient's sense of identity.

Such evaluations are not just made once and for all but are made continually if not continuously! We discuss some of these conditions for evaluation at work below.

REGIMENS HAVE CHARACTERISTICS
Learning the regimen

After an initial acceptance of the regimen—whether prescribed by a physician, chiropractor, osteopath, naturopath, or someone else—the most important chronological event is that the patient (or parent or wife, if need be) learns how to administer the regimen. Regimens, of course, can have various characteristics, but two vis-à-vis learning are very important: whether they entail eliminating something (food, activities) or adding something (drugs, activities). Some additions or eliminations are very easy to learn. Some, however, involve procedures that can be difficult, especially at first, such as giving asthma shots or monitoring body wastes.

When the regimen involves a machine, as in kidney dialysis, the learning can be quite a complex matter—and then the relevant health personnel are more likely to take the time to teach the patient or kin what they need to know. Even with such a crucial regimen, however, there can be organizational "slips," as one social scientist who was working as an experienced technician on a dialysis unit has written:

> On another occasion, I took a telephone call from a patient who had been home a week and had just finished rebuilding his first Kiil. He wanted to know how to fill it with formaldehyde to sterilize it, saying he didn't remember the precise procedure. I answered his questions and mentioned to the evening staff later that he had called. Their reactions were surprising. He had been taught the procedure . . . and his calling the center was simply the usual psychological reaction of patients who had just been sent home. The patient just wanted someone in the center to talk to and reassure him that he had not been

abandoned. I tried to point out that while the method for sterilizing Kiil is simple, actually carrying out the steps can be confusing unless one had done it several times, and that furthermore this patient had been trained during the days and that evening staff had no way of knowing what had or had not been taught. Staff was adamant, however, and replied that I "had been in dialysis long enough to know better."[1]

Learning how to carry out the regimen can, at first, be very anxiety provoking.

At the initial session of learning how to give insulin shots, the mother of a diabetic child shook so much that she dropped the needle and burst into tears. *Benoliel*

When life may hang on proper carrying out of a regimen through machinery, then anxiety may be almost unbearable during the early phases of learning to use and live with the machine.

One family, whose child had cystic fibrosis, remarked that they no longer went out at night. ("I don't even trust my sister to do the right things.") Both parents were so acutely anxious about the mist-tent pump and the possibility of its going bad that they constantly listened for any change in noise or rhythm and also constantly checked the water bottle to make certain it was not empty. *Benoliel*

Sometimes the regimens are not easy for patients or their assisting kin to learn.

Mrs. F. said sometimes she just hated to go see Dr. Y. because Johnnie wasn't coughing productively. She thought the physical therapist really wanted to wash her hands of them. It is only since Johnnie's last hospitalization, a month ago, that he learned to cough productively, and to bring up amounts of mucus. *Benoliel*

Difficulties in learning regimens may result not solely from the complexity of procedures or the accompanying anxiety, however, but also from the regimen's impact on personal identity. It is one thing for a person with cardiac disease to be told, "walk," another for one with diabetes (and his or her agents) to hear that he or she must stay *for life* on that regimen! Being on a dermatological regimen that involves smearing a large portion of one's body with disgusting-looking ointment can be quite devastating. To be hooked into the frequent use of machinery—whether it be lifesaving, like a dialysis machine, or as innocuous as a bronchial inhalator—can be profoundly disturbing, if only because one feels a slave to the machinery. Identities are challenged, too, by the requirement of "staying with" the regimen: if one cannot meet the challenge (quite like fat people who are ordered onto a dietary regimen), then one may feel characterless, a genuine failure. Control agents who cannot keep their ill children or husbands on necessary regimens can easily blame themselves, not merely their sick charges, especially when they have been somewhat lax in their efforts at control or if the illness worsens despite their efforts.

Time and regimen

Various other characteristics of a regimen may call for considerable organization of personal or family effort. Consider the matter of time. Some regimens take many minutes or even hours to carry out. This means that the requisite time must be available, otherwise the regimen will be omitted or at least altered so as to be of shorter duration. Some regimens must be done twice or three times daily; this activity may run counter to working steadily on the job or interfere with very busy weekends. Some regimens must be carried out on schedule or timed in relation to the peaking of symptoms, rather than flexibly altered to fit whatever time is available.

> People who have had colostomy operations schedule their movements in accordance to the scheduling of their irrigations, which must be done at home. Their mobility, therefore, tends to be restricted to the distance that can be covered in the time between irrigations. Their sociability away from home, indeed their social contacts, are "limited to periods between irrigations." In other words, they are of rather short duration unless occurring at home. "Patients can, therefore, be considered as living 'on a leash' which is only as long as the time interval between irrigations."[2]

Regimens may even occupy so much time (entire days on a kidney dialysis machine) that they are virtually at the center of a person's life. On the other hand, time may be a relatively minor problem even when the regimen must be carried out with frequency. Thus even when pills must be taken often, pill-popping does not take much time. Likewise, sometimes duration is easily managed: patients can listen to music, or think, or even do business work while engaging in lengthy regimen procedures. When the treatment involves going to a health facility, where waiting time is added to regimen time, then patients find it more difficult to plan their daily time exactly, although they may utilize the waiting time to read, knit, or whatever.

Discomfort, effort, energy, and visibility

The amount of discomfort regimens cause is another characteristic. The discomfort can be direct, as with the pain caused by some physiotherapy exercises. The discomfort can also involve side effects, like indigestion or dizziness or lethargy induced by drugs. When, in addition, the side effects signify danger or risk to the person or his family, he is much less inclined to continue the regimen unaltered unless it signifies less risk than does continuing with the present symptoms or letting the disease go unchecked. Thus people with chronic bronchitis will cut down on their postural drainage, skipping or shortening the sessions, at least until their symptoms become quite bothersome or alarming.

Still another characteristic of the regimen is the amount of effort or energy it takes to complete it in its prescribed form. This implies not merely time consumed but quite literally the sufficient energy and effort that must be mustered up for the task. (Emphysema patients who simply do not have enough energy to climb the stairs to their second- and third-floor apartments will leave breathing equipment untouched during the day.) If someone is ill or tired, she is that much less likely to be able or want to carry out the regimen. If, in addition, carrying out the regimen requires the assistance of another person, as with cystic fibrosis exercises, then both need to have sufficient energy to do the job. If, for example, the mother has been ill and cannot muster up sufficient energy, or if the child is tired and does not wish to put out the required effort, then the exercise is much more likely to be skipped.

Whether or not it is visible to other people and what that visibility means to the patient is a consideration to be made when planning the regimen. If the visible regimen means that a stigmatized disease can be suspected or discovered, the person is most unlikely to carry out the regimen in public. Yet, the physician's orders may require that she do it sufficiently so that it *is* public. (Patients with tuberculosis sometimes have to cope with this problem.) If the visible regimen is no more than slightly embarrassing or is fully explainable, then its visibility is much less likely to prevent its public occurrence. If its visibility is partly reduced, as when someone disappears fairly frequently to the bathroom even though everyone notices how often he must go, the regimen will probably be followed.

Efficiency

Another characteristic is also important: if the regimen is "readable" as efficient ("it works") by the patient, then that *may* convince him that he should continue with it. But continuance is problematic, not only because other properties already noted may counteract his best intentions or his good sense, but because an effective regimen may mean to him that now it is time to go off it—no matter what the physician says. This is exactly what happens when patients with tuberculosis see their symptoms disappear and figure that now they can cut out—partially or totally—their discomforting regimen of massive pill swallowing.

> That this is not an unusual act is illustrated by the story of one patient who had slight back pains, and so went to a physician who diagnosed the pain and gave him a relaxant drug, but then cut down and finally ceased taking the drug as

soon as the pains totally disappeared. He was only unusual in that he told his physician—who was startled at the open revelation.

Also relevant to the seeming efficiency of a regimen is the speed with which its efficiency is displayed to the patient. To continue with a treatment, as in cancer, that does not have rather immediate results, but, indeed, sometimes just the reverse, takes quite a bit of fear of the disease itself and trust in the physician. If pain or discomfort (physiotherapy) or the elimination of favorite foods is added to the slowness with which efficiency is demonstrated, then it takes much trust in the physician or real fear of the disease or great desire to be rid of the symptoms to carry out the regimen.

Denial and confusion

The very characteristics of the regimen, then, constitute important contributing conditions for adhering to, relaxing, or even rejecting the prescribed regimen. A few other important conditions are worth mentioning. Thus if the patient simply denies that she has the disease, she may refuse to submit to a regimen or may only minimally carry it out. (As with tuberculosis, many patients actually experience no symptoms and will not take the physician's reading of the ambiguous—to them—x-ray signs as proof of illness.) Again, a patient may wish very much to adhere to a regimen, but the instructions about it leave him confused or baffled. For instance, cardiac patients told to "rest" can be much frustrated because they do not really know of what sufficient rest consists. Being told to "find your own limits" is no great help either, although it does give tacit permission to experiment with an unavoidably flexible regimen.

Expense

A very important additional characteristic of regimens is the expense for the patient, especially where drugs or machinery are involved. Patients are more likely to cut back on drug regimens if they are expensive, especially when their efficiency is not speedily demonstrated or where they bring about discomfort.

> The parents of a child with asthma were discouraged with the lack of response to treatments in light, especially of their expensiveness. They remarked that these had been costly—and it wouldn't be so bad if there were some positive results—but there's no improvement. It had been a difficult year financially; hospitalization was $400, only half covered by insurance, and none of the doctor's bills were covered; also there were bills for medicine, inhalators, and so on.
> *Benoliel*

If, however, the disease is very dangerous, patients are more likely to give funding for the regimen considerable priority over their spending for other activities and objects.

In general, however, funding problems do affect whether and to what extent the regimen is followed. Thus emphysema patients with little money who are not supposed to climb stairs cannot easily choose to move to a more expensive first-floor apartment, giving up their rather cheap third-story rent. The result is that they do not use their breathing machines, because they would have to go upstairs to use them when once downstairs. Another consideration is that if a regimen—as with drugs—involves a considerable amount of money and yet does not seem to be rather quickly affecting either the symptoms or the disease itself, then there is apt to be at least some cutback on the amount of drug taking. The balancing here is between the cost of the regimen and its evaluated efficiency.

Isolation and comprehension

Yet another condition for nonadherence or partial adherence is that the regimen leads increasingly to social isolation, so that the patient has to decide whether the regimen's effects are worth the loss of sociability and human contact.

There is one final condition: if the patient and/or kin do not have a very accurate view of the deterioration accompanying the disease, then they are that less likely to stick with an otherwise difficult, discomforting, or time-consuming regimen. Immediate deterioration or occasionally severe crises would counteract that tendency to relax or abandon the regimen; in their absence, however, only some view (even if dead wrong) of deleterious results may prevent relaxation or abandonment of the regimen. This kind of medical ignorance sometimes results from inadequate communication between physician and patient—either because the professional does not take time to explain or is not skilled at explaining, or because the lay person may not understand the technical language of the physician. Of course, sometimes the patient does not wish to hear.

Summary

Now that we have reviewed a substantial number of regimen characteristics, we can actually list them. This is worth doing to emphasize, as if underlined in red, that the view of a patient's breaking the regimen (foolish, ignorant, obstinate) that is all too often held by health personnel is just too simplistic, too stereotyped. Just scanning the list is likely to make one wonder at how anyone (including himself) manages to stay with his or her regimen, even in modified form!

1. Is difficult or easy to learn and to carry out
2. Takes much or little time

3. Causes much or little discomfort or pain
4. Does or does not cause side effects, especially if they are actually or seemingly risky ones
5. Needs much or little effort or energy to carry out
6. Is or is not visible to others
7. If known, might or might not cause others to stigmatize the person
8. Does or does not seem efficient
9. Is or is not expensive
10. Does or does not lead to increasing social isolation

To make the issue of adherence or nonadherence even more graphic, we might consider the following diagram. It involves the ideas that a *regimen* can be (1) easy, (2) difficult, or (3) very difficult, that the patient's *life-style* can be (1) much affected, (2) somewhat affected, or (3) very little affected by the regimen, and that the *disease or the symptoms* may be (1) minimally or (2) maximally affected by the regimen (as the patient sees it). Now, imagine how likely, or unlikely, a patient is to follow a regimen faithfully when it falls into any of the various situations pictured in the diagram. Certainly the two extreme cases (A and B) are, respectively, the least likely and the most likely to be followed exactly.

Life-style

Disease or symptom	Much affected		Somewhat affected		Little affected	
	Minimal	Maximal	Minimal	Maximal	Minimal	Maximal
Easy regimen						B
Difficult regimen						
Very difficult regimen	A					

AGENTS: COOPERATING AND CONFLICTING

If a person does choose to stick by his regimen, this will require some degree of personal and often familial organization of effort. We will not develop this point very much, since it was a feature of the earlier discussion of crises. It is worth mentioning, however, that there are several kinds of agents, including two to be discussed now. One is the assisting agent, as with the parent who helps the child with his cystic fibrosis breathing exercises. The second is the control agent, who helps the tempted or recalcitrant patient stick to her regimen, using various tactics such as issuing commands or manipulating indirectly ("I always take a little away from his lunch and evening meals to allow for snacking—such as popcorn at the movies"). Additional tactics include shaming and reminding. When the agent fails to do his or her part of the cooperative job, then the regimen is not likely to be implemented, or at least not effectively. The agent can be tired, ill, uninterested, or might disbelieve in the regimen.

The control agent may also not be able to get, or at least maintain, control if the ill person "has a mind of his or her own." In such instances, sometimes not even a family member is instituting influence or restraint but someone else. Thus a friend of mine who was dying of cancer

> runs her own show, with her mother as the assisting agent but not a control agent. Today Fran took specially cooked food over to Helen. Helen was about to have hamburger, but Fran put her foot down—that's not the thing to eat after yesterday's and today's bouts of diarrhea. "Can I eat your food?" Helen asks, and Fran says "yes" and explains why. Then Helen asks her mother for a glass of wine. Fran says that makes no sense. Helen then gets angry at her mother because she'd been allowing her to drink wine! In effect, Helen has never allowed her mother to be much of a control agent. Fran was able to, because accidentally she entered the act at the right time: if she'd insisted on "no wine" earlier—or maybe later—she'd have lost the argument too. Fran did feel badly in denying Helen the wine: she's not experienced at such controlling!

Also, two people in the family can disagree about a regimen, as when the father believes it ridiculous or ineffective, but the mother believes the physician. Such domestic disagreement, and even overt conflict, will certainly affect whether and how much the regimen is followed.

Where there is cooperation in the family, there is often a division of labor.

> Mr. V. doesn't participate in the coughing procedures of his son with cystic fibrosis because he doesn't have the patience to "work with" the child, coaxing, encouraging, and waiting. But he does help with the child's special tent and bed. The mother believes that if the husband didn't share the work that way, she could not live with the burden of her sick child.
> *Benoliel*

Domestic division of labor can also be much affected by relationships within the family.

> In another family affected by cystic fibrosis, both parents help with the exercises and treatments, but the husband does more because he has more authority. The mother has difficulty getting the child to do the difficult regimen without accompanying big scenes.
> *Benoliel*

Sometimes the entire family may be "in on the act" of aiding, assisting, or controlling the patient. Thus a diabetic individual can maintain his diet if everyone in the family follows *his* diet. More implicitly, if an asthmatic mother is advised to "get rid" of her child's dog, then the child, too, is participating in her elimination regimen. But siblings may occasionally rebel: "Everything has to be done for old Louise!"

The physician and other health personnel may, of course, also act as assisting agents (physical therapists, for example) or control agents. They may persuade and dissuade when they believe it necessary. They may do this with great tact or, alas, not always so nicely—although, admittedly, impoliteness and threat sometimes bring results. The two extremes:

> The physician talked to the child about giving up eating wheat, saying this was difficult but really he thought wheat was the problem and would he give it a try. He talked about his own allergy to grapes and having to give up drinking wine. Would Jim give it a try? Jim agreed and they shook hands.
> *Benoliel*

> After a kidney transplant and refusal to follow the regimen, his kidney (in an examination at the clinic) shows signs of being rejected. He makes a big scene, when told, cursing physicians and yelling that he wasn't being helped. He refuses to be hospitalized. His main physician was out of town, but when phoned told his nurse to say: "Well, Joe, if you want to commit suicide, just stay at home and don't bother us any more. We're trying to help you, but you don't want it."
> *Suczek*

Sometimes there is considerable misunderstanding between the physician or other health personnel and the person concerning the terms of his or her regimen. Even where the instructions are simple and extremely important—as in the number of pills a transplant patient should take—the patient may not hear correctly. Besides simple mishearing, conditions for misunderstanding include the health personnel's unawareness of situations that may lead to "rule breaking": specific home conditions, domestic conditions, and cultural values (as toward specific foods that are highly esteemed or tabooed). In addition, the physician may just be thoughtless or unrealistic, as was a pediatrician who put a young child on

85 units of insulin four times daily—the last dose at midnight: the mother commented caustically: "Can you imagine waking a kid up at midnight for that!"

When the regimen requires really professional skill and is a matter of life and death, then understandably the patient is called into the hospital where the treatment given him is, in fact, just another form of regimen. Out of danger, or taught the requisite skills, he can be sent home; or if need be, as with radiation therapy for cancer, he must return at intervals to have his regimen carried out by the professionals.

Given the exigencies of life and the changing patterns of symptoms, inevitably patients and kin enter into negotiations with each other, and sometimes with health personnel, over relaxing or otherwise changing the regimen (substituting one drug for another, one activity for another). They are negotiating not merely over such matters as the elimination of discomfort and side effects, but over the much more primary issue of how the management of ordinary life can be made easier or even possible. Health personnel, of course, recognize much of this bargaining and sympathize with it if the stakes seem reasonable. What they do not always recognize is just how high the stakes may be for the patient and the family. They ignore those to the peril of their mutual relationships: at worst, the patient may go shopping for another physician and other help; at the least, she may quietly alter the regimen or substitute or supplement it with something drawn from another source (a pharmacist, a friend, an aunt).

> A Chinese-American health professional with asthmatic attacks has chest specialists who, out of professional courtesy and colleagueship, checked on him at frequent intervals. He understood his medications and all the implications. Since the attacks robbed him of sleep and energy and severe attacks were unpredictable, he was ready to try anything that might work. He consulted two herbalists, took his medications and herbs concurrently.[3]

ADHERING TO AND MODIFYING THE REGIMEN

It should now be evident that sick people do not necessarily regard all elements of a regimen as having equal priority. They may strictly follow some elements but slack off or totally reject other elements, for instance, those that give indigestion or seem not to be working. Patients may do this after bargaining with the physician, or they simply may not tell him about their modifications of the prescribed regimen. Moreover, other persons may act to dissuade them from following certain parts of the regimen, or indeed all of it, and even persuade them to try alternative regimens. About the latter, they often give testimonials drawn from their own experience or based on hearsay.

Patients also shop around for alternatives, either because a current regimen does not seem to be working well or because there ought to be a better one, or at least one that works faster, is less uncomfortable, demands less effort, or is less costly. On the other hand, if life is at stake and there is considerable trust in the physician, then the ill person is likely to consider that the entire regimen is binding. Not to carry it out is to court disaster and quite possibly death. As one person on dialysis said with finality: "It's going to be done and that's it!" And another:

> It's taken me a long while to adjust. Before, especially the day before I come in, I don't want to go. There's the boredom of lying here all day, and some pain. Then I think, "You don't go, you're going to die!" and I force myself to adjust. *Suczek*

The organization of effort necessary for carrying out some regimens not only has to be instituted and maintained, it requires the "learning through experience" of everything that must go into juggling life while carrying out the regimen. So, one has to learn what are his own, unique reactions to various aspects of his regimen—and how to handle daily living in the face of those reactions. He has to learn how much of the regimen will handle how much of his symptoms, and whether he wants more or less of those symptoms controlled—in terms of the impact of his daily living. He has to learn, too, what differences carrying out his regimen will make in relationships with kin, friends, acquaintances, fellow employees, supervisors, or employers. All the foregoing amounts to learning what difference the regimen is making—right now—in his and their style and quality of life. Thus along with learning to institute and maintain personal-familial effort that will support the implementation of a regimen goes their respective learning to organize the wider realm of maintaining as much of a normal life as seems possible in the face of needing to control the symptoms or the disease itself.

If the course of the disease and its symptoms are not sufficiently held in check by the regimen, so that they all impact drastically on her life, then the patient inevitably will begin to think about whether it is all worth the price. She will be balancing life against death. Again a quotation from a dialysis patient, this one with only a couple of months of experience behind her:

> In the beginning, it's as if that machine is a human being with a brain and it's *running* you. Then you realize it is only a machine and the brain is *yours*. Then you are suddenly faced with the fact that you're very nearly at death's door and you have to depend on that machine to stay alive—*that's* upsetting. The question at that point is why bother? Why go to all this bother just to stay alive? It takes time to get your evaluations going and to know just where you're going. *Suczek*

Some dialysis patients, of course, do choose death. They go off the machine, or—if stopped from doing that—they outwit their physicians and their families by some other method of ending their lives, as in the instance of a young man who, alone for 10 minutes, pulled out his shunt and bled to death. However sad such a story is, we can still understand and empathize with the choice. Harder still on the bystanders, kin, and health personnel alike is an election to die. In the words of the researcher:

> Johnnie was dying but slowly. In recent weeks, he had refused to do his postural drainage, and his mother had finally gone along with him. He has become progressively morose, and his mother has told the physician she couldn't stand it because he never smiled anymore. The physician thinks perhaps she feels guilty about having forced the treatment on Johnnie, and also for wanting him now to die.
> *Benoliel*

When likable children elect to die more quickly than they might, the health personnel can also be terribly upset, especially when they have known them before and have become very attached to them.

Let us return, however, to the more usual and happier cases where ill persons are trying to maintain relatively normal lives—a task that can only be controlled by the patient and/or his agents. It neither belongs to the health personnel nor can it be delegated to them, except during medical crises. They can only help in its solution if they are aware of its possible complexity. Every deleterious change in symptomatology, every item added to the regimen, every shift of social relationships in which the person is engaged will alter his and his family's task of organizing their lives satisfactorily, despite the symptoms *and* the regimen.

MULTIPLE DISEASES AND THEIR REGIMENS

Many people suffer from more than one chronic illness. This means they may be simultaneously on two or three or more regimens. To carry out each may take considerable juggling of time and effort. It is easy to see that some regimens may suffer in favor of others. Peak periods of danger or of bothersome symptoms will give priority to the corresponding regimens. What is not as obvious is that certain regimens may actually exacerbate the symptoms of another illness.

> Mr. Smith has both chronic bronchitis and a stomach hernia. For the first, he is supposed to do several minutes of daily postural drainage. But this enhances the probability that he will get heartburn from his hernia. Furthermore, if he attempts to reduce the probability of his hernial heartburn by using a high pillow while sleeping, that sometimes brings on pains, ordinarily quiescent, from a pinched neck nerve.

Patients may not always be thoroughly rational in how they decide among competing regimens, but decide they must. The choice is not necessarily as their physician would advise, if she or he knew—but the choice is theirs, not his!

SUPPLEMENTING AND SHOPPING AROUND

From much of the foregoing discussion, it can easily be seen that even when a patient thoroughly trusts her physician, she does not necessarily follow *only* the physician's instructions or commands. She may very well supplement those with additional regimen items learned, or searched out, elsewhere.

A study of how the Chinese and American-born Chinese in San Francisco utilize health services demonstrates that ill persons may supplement physician regimens with herbs recommended by a herbalist, the services of an acupuncturist, or foods and other items including drugs recommended by kin and neighbors.[3] Understandably, those who are more chronically ill tend to be receptive to multiple sources of regimens. Although non-Chinese usually do not have herbalists' counsel to draw on, they freely utilize the services of chiropractors, osteopaths, faith healers, and many other types of seemingly knowledgeable or experienced persons. They use their advice not only in lieu of but in addition to that of licensed physicians. Furthermore, when a physician's regimen does not seem to be working efficiently or rapidly, they will eventually search out another physician or another type of healer and switch to him or her.

For some types of illness, in fact, there are very inadequate medical technologies. So the sufferers—we use the word advisedly—in desperation go from one potential source of relief to another. Aside from visiting nonphysicians, they may visit a number of physicians in the same specialty who have, perhaps by reputation, different philosophies about regimens; they may even undergo a series of operations by different surgeons. They even go to different kinds of medical specialists, thinking that a different kind of expertise may at last help. Of course they may also go or be referred to different well-known medical centers. Their "shopping around" may last for years, as in the instance of arthritics who get either little or only transitory relief from one recommended regimen or another. Many amputees have multiple side effects from pain-killing drugs and experience "pain careers" that go on and on and on—as they seek unsuccessfully for relief from their excruciating chronic pain. In effect, like arthritics and back pain sufferers, they experience a kind of *technological limbo* feeling: that there is no technology (regimen) that can help ("*nobody* can help me"). Their shopping around is a direct reflection of the inadequacy of technological resources at anyone's command—or that few experts command—to manage their illnesses.

From the standpoint of the physicians, switching tends to reflect either an unjustifiable lack of faith or, in the case of patients with fatal diseases, search for the impossible cure. From the standpoint of the sick person, the physician is simply the source of necessary services. Among those services are the ones pertaining to regimens: what to do, what not to do, and access to the drugs, machinery, or procedures essential to the carrying out of the regimens. In short, to understand why patients switch, supplement, or at least only partly adhere to the physician's regimen, we must understand that his or her regimen or counsel does not stand alone but is only an element in a complicated pattern of living.

We will return to the further implication of that last phrase in the chapter dealing with family responses, but it is well to remember that physicians are neither the only nor the last court of appeal for incurable long-term illnesses. Furthermore, since so many of those illnesses cannot be controlled—either symptomatically or in terms of the disease process itself—it is entirely understandable that the sufferers turn to other physicians or to other types of healers. Indeed chronic illnesses are so intertwined with life's other problems—including the practical, emotional, occupational, and religious—that when the sick turn first and foremost to physicians, that is something of a miracle, both because of faith but also because of a belief that has its source in medicine's success in convincing people over the last two centuries of its effectiveness. Yet, ultimately, as some of the medical anthropologists remind us,[4] sick people the world over shop around for healers, as well as combine regimens—except that they do it differently in different societies, and for different diseases. As one of the anthropologists has put it, emphasizing as we have done here the active search for at least partly effective regimens, "In this kind of model the sick person is not seen as a passive 'patient,' the suffering object of the active therapist or as the determined occupant of a 'sick role,' but as an agent seeking health, engaged . . . in a 'quest for therapy,' in problem-solving, and manipulating the resources available in the environment."[4]

References

1. Chu, George: The kidney patient: a sociomedical study, doctoral thesis, Berkeley, 1975, University of California, School of Public Health.
2. Goffman, Erving: Stigma, Englewood Cliffs, N.J., 1963, Prentice-Hall, Inc., p. 91. Goffman is quoting from Orbach, C., Bard, M., and Sutherland, A.: Fears and defensive adaptations to the loss of sphincter control, Psychoanalytic Review **44:**121-175, 1957.
3. Louie, Theresa: The pragmatic context: a Chinese-American example of defining and managing illness, doctoral thesis, San Francisco, 1975, University of California, School of Nursing.
4. Worsley, Peter: Non-western medical systems, Annual Review of Anthropology **11:**315-348, 1982, p. 325.

CHAPTER 3

SYMPTOM CONTROL

The control of symptoms is so obviously linked with adherence to effective regimens that, having seen the complexity of that phenomenon, we are not likely to conceive of symptom control as merely a matter of medical management. Of course, the correct choice of regimens can be crucial for both disease and symptom control, and during medical crises the wisdom and care of the professionals may be absolutely essential. Yet the sick person spends most of the time away from the medical facilities, so he or she and the family must rely on their own judgment, wisdom, and ingenuity for controlling symptoms.

Different kinds of illness have different symptomatologies associated with them. This means that people who suffer from different illnesses will be faced with carrying out different tasks to control their symptoms (for example, alleviating pain, preventing nausea, husbanding energy), and they will characteristically use different means (regimens) for maximizing that control. Furthermore, some illnesses are much more variable than others: less stable, changing abruptly, moving downward or upward more speedily. All of this is associated with differential symptom control tasks. Undoubtedly, too, different illness tasks require different types of assisting agents: epileptics need protective agents, people prone to cardiac arrests need crisis agents, diabetics ordinarily find that others act as control agents even to the point of irritation, whereas immobile people need body movers. The illnesses do tend to share one feature: the total work required can scarcely be sketched out in advance, given both the uncertainty of detail attending most chronic illness courses *and* the external, to-the-hospital contingencies that inevitably bear on the illness work, whether the work is purely "medical" or only medically related.

A portion of the sick person's and family's need for judgment, wisdom, and ingenuity about symptoms is recognized by health personnel, but probably only a small portion. Physicians, of course, do indicate to a patient (with respect to certain diseases) that he or she must work out aspects of the regimen (such as how woozy one gets from a given amount of drug) and also discover the idosyn-crasies of one's own body to control symptoms more effectively. To a great degree, however, the sick person is alone insofar as he or she requires an intense body awareness, what it can and cannot do *now*, as opposed to before.

Of course, people with lifelong illnesses, and especially those who have no great ups and downs in symptomatology, have long since come to terms with their bodies, managing their symptoms with relative skill and sometimes with scarcely any awareness of management tasks, because they are just part of their daily life. A person who has just become aware of having a disease or symptoms, however, may discover that her body is a very surprising thing indeed. She will need to come to terms with it and develop new relationships with it. Thus a cardiac patient who now suffers from sudden losses of energy simply cannot ignore a changed body. The "cannot ignore" probably will involve coping not only with something phys-ically new but with something affecting one's sense of self:

> Richie, a stroke patient, has described how when awakening from sleep with a pain in his right side, he would carefully have to think through what to do. He would seize his upper right arm with his left hand, prying loose his right arm and hand "from wherever they had gone to be—I usually was sitting on my right hand." He felt that both his right arm and leg "behaved like strangers . . . the absence of touch was psychologically important. It meant that the limbs did not belong to me."[7]

How drastic the changes and the requisite adaptations can be is poignantly illustrated by the extraordinary movements of a patient with myasthenia gravis who had great muscular flaccidity. In the words of the research nurse who interviewed him at home:

> He lifted his pills into his mouth by using the sides of both his hands, and he lifted the cup by encircling his palms about it and lifting it to his mouth. This was not an easy operation for him. . . . As we talked he struggled to assume relaxed, conversational postures which he was not able to hold for more than a few seconds. His most comfortable position seemed to be one of having his arms resting and outstretched on the table. If he tried to bend his arms up from the elbow with the elbows on the table, in a moment or two the arms would fall down. He tried to cross his arms across his chest or cross his arms or rest the elbows on the table; but they would simply fall.
> *Davis*

Whatever sophisticated technical references there may be for symptoms, the person who has symptoms will be concerned primarily with whether there is pain, fainting, visible trembling, sudden loss of energy, shortness of breath, impairment of mobility or speech, or evidence of some kind of disfigurement. Aside from what these may signify to a person about his or her disease or life span, such symptoms can interfere with life and social relationships. How much they interfere depends on (1) whether they are permanent or temporary, frequent or occasional, predictable or unpredictable, and publicly visible or invisible, (2) their degree (as of pain), their meaning to bystanders (as of disfigurement), and the nature of the regimen called for to control the symptom, and (3) the kinds of life-style and social relations that the sufferer has hitherto sustained.

REDESIGNING LIFE-STYLES

Even minor, occasional symptoms may lead to some changing of habits. Thus someone who begins to suffer from minor back pains is likely to learn to avoid certain kinds of chairs and even discover, to her dismay, that a favorite sitting position is precisely what she must eliminate from her repertoire. Major symptoms, however, may call for the redesigning or reshaping of important aspects of a life-style. Thus the stroke patient quoted earlier has also written:

> Before you come downstairs, stop and think. Handkerchief, money, keys, book, and so on—if you come downstairs without these, you will have to climb upstairs, or send someone to get them.[7]

People with chronic diarrhea need to reshape their conventional habits like this:

> I never go to local movies. If I go . . . I select a large house . . . where I have a greater choice of seats. . . . When I go on a bus . . . I sit on an end seat or near the door.[2]

Major redesigning can involve moving to a one-story house, buying clothes that cloak disfigurement, getting the boss to assign jobs that require less strength, and using crutches or other aids to mobility. Some of the alternative possibilities are more unusual; they are based on the ingenuity of the sufferer or stumbling on a solution. Our interview with people who have colitis and emphysema are especially replete with examples of ingenuity through necessity—or desperation—like the mailman who lived "on a leash," having arranged never to be very far from that necessary toilet while on his job, or the emphysema sufferers who learn to use "puffing stations," where they can recoup from lack of breath while looking as if their stopping were normal.

In working out this redesigning of activities, friends, family, and health personnel may also provide the truly effective or inventive idea. (They are redesigning agents.) Some examples: a community nurse taught an emphysema patient how to rest while doing his household chores. A woman, in the absence of attentive personnel, taught her sister (afflicted with brittle bones because of a destructive drug) how to get up from the toilet, without a back brace, without breaking bones in her back. Another woman figured out how her cardiac-arhritic grandfather could continue his beloved walks on his farm by placing wooden stumps at short distances, so that he could rest as he reached each one. Unfortunately, relatives and health personnal can function in just the opposite fashion. For instance, a woman with multiple sclerosis had carefully arranged her one-room apartment so that literally every object she needed was within arm's reach. However, the public health nurse who visited her regarded the place as in a terrible shambles, urged less disorder, and proceeded to tidy up things a bit herself.

Some people are very inventive in what we term "devising," that is, working out physical arrangements that permit them to do things without undue discomfort or pain or drain on energy. Many arthritic individuals are very clever at devising to accommodate their partly disabled hands and feet. They find and use old-fashioned collar-button hooks to manage their otherwise recalcitrant buttons. (One stroke patient scoured the city of New York looking for an instrument that would solve the frustrating problem of managing his shirt buttons. He remarks caustically: "The doctors were at their blandest and most maddening here: not only did they have no solution, they pretended there was no problem."[5]) They also buy clothes with zippers instead of struggling with buttons. They fix faucets so they can be moved with elbows. Arthritic people with bad feet or cardiac sufferes who have little energy for mounting stairs very frequently make certain that two sets of eyeglasses and other objects in daily use are distributed upstairs and downstairs. People with low energy may devise ways, too, to avoid pushing open the heavy entry doors of public buildings, (including hospitals), for example, by falling into step behind people with more normal reserves of energy.

Perhaps the lack of inventiveness and social skills—quite as much as poor finances or few material resources—are what prevent people from not reaching some relatively satisfying redesign of life. The cancer patient with lessened energy who can ingeniously juggle her friends' visits and telephone calls can manage to sustain a relatively unimpaired social life. The arthritic farm women who can make arrangements with neighbors to bring in the store groceries can live on their farms during the summer, although they must move to town for the winter months.

> One sufferer of multiple sclerosis of our acquaintance (a student) not only has rearranged her apartment but has persuaded various people to do various things necessary because of her increasingly restricted mobility; she has had a veritable army of people come to her aid—the university architect redesigned certain of the public toilets for her wheelchair and also put in some ramps; the

handymen around the university help her up and down stairs daily, by appointment; they have also rebuilt her cupboards so that they are reachable from her wheelchair; and so on.

It is certainly worth adding—and emphasizing—that among those who are most advantageously placed to help as skilled redesigning or devising agents are the health personnel. They are apt to meet a great number of patients—say, those with arthritis—who share virtually identical symptoms necessitating redesigning strategies. If personnel are alert to how those patients have handled their problems, they might pass along very helpful information to each new patient. "You know, I talked with someone last week, Mrs. Jones, who. . . ." Alas, how many health personnel know neither what Mrs. Jones did nor what Mrs. Smith needs; and how many, even when knowledgeable, bother to communicate their knowledge? In our view, all health personnel should regard themselves as conduits through which such information flows from one inventive sick person to another. They should be active transmitters of that information, that is, intelligent transmitting agents!

FAILURE AT REDESIGNING

When the sufferer or his agents are unable to figure out how to ease or get around his symptom, or to have it discounted through some social arrangement, then he will have to pay for his failure. Sometimes he pays physically, sometimes socially. It is worth noting that the making of new or different social arrangements may not simply be a matter of intelligent solution or social skill but may be affected by moral considerations. Some patients with multiple sclerosis would not have been able to do what the student did, because they would have seen her activities as taking undue advantage of strangers or as showing a lack of pride in oneself. Certainly the social isolation attending multiple sclerosis[1] is contributed to by the lack of social skills and by the personal pride, but also by some failure of ingenuity by the ill persons, their family members, and friends.

Good solutions are also a matter of good fortune in having skillful or inventive friends and relatives who can help with the reshaping and reformation of social relationships pertinent to the management of one's symptoms. If, however, they choose to oppose one's own ideas for rearrangements, that can make symptom control more difficult. The situation is especially difficult, sometimes, when the rearrangement of others' lives is also involved. Thus an asthmatic woman said

Some of my friends simply don't understand that I am allergic to animals. They are so fond of them, they get upset that I can't have them about, and really don't believe me. They are so sensitive about their animals.

She also remarked that

> My friends now understand that during my worst periods I can't come to their homes unless the dust is minimized. So they will clean the day before I visit, and I'll wait for the dust to settle before going there.

Even when other people do not oppose the chronically ill person's ideas about redesigning but simply show poor judgment or lack of imagination about useful redesigning, symptom control is made additionally difficult. The point is illustrated on a large institutional scale by the relative lack of imagination in the redesigning of homes for the elderly, as anyone can attest if he or she watches these stiff-jointed or low-energied people either as they struggle to rise from sitting positions on low sofas and chairs, or as they carefully pick their way along highly polished corridors—without handrails.

INTERACTIONAL CONSIDERATIONS

The reshaping of activities pertains not only to items of life-style but, because of the potential or actual visibility of symptoms, to the crucial issue of interaction. There is need for a variety of judicious or clever maneuvers to keep one's symptoms as unintrusive as possible—to hide them, disguise them, minimize them, temporarily eliminate them, or at least help to change their public meaning.

Sometimes the tactics are very simple: a college teacher with bronchitis, whose peak load of coughing up sputum is in the morning, arranges his teaching schedule so that he can stay at home, or at least in his office, until after lunchtime. Another person, who tends continually to have a runny allergic nose, always carries tissue in hand when in public, so that she does not call more attention to herself by rummaging in her pocketbook for it. Another with a tendency to cough carries cough drops with him—especially requisite when he attends concerts. More difficult problems can arise. If someone cannot help coughing up sputum in public, then he is careful not to allow the offensive matter to show by completely covering his mouth with the tissue. And anyone who coughs much will need to explain persuasively or indicate that his cough is not infectious! An epileptic man or woman may have to persuade acquaintances that epileptic fits are not communicable! Emphysema sufferers learn to sit down or lean against buildings in such a fashion that they are not mistaken for drunks or bring themselves to embarrassing public attention. People with heart trouble need to explain that when they feel it necessary to lie down, that signifies merely a draining of energy and not that they are having another heart attack! The need for rather continual monitoring of symptoms—and so far more complex interactional tactics still—is illustrated vividly by colitis sufferers who must manage the potentially embarrassing situations attendant on their frequent diarrhea.

Notable in those all too realistic examples is the need to minimize or in some sense render a symptom invisible. This is different from keeping the disease secret. The symptom itself is sufficient to cause embarrassment, to destroy ongoing interaction, or even to make the person permanently stigmatized. The problem is illustrated in drastic form by a schoolgirl who always attempted to get herself to the clothing closet in time to hide her short epileptic seizures—a feat she was able to manage for some months. Toynbee, the historian, when a schoolboy at a boarding school, managed for much longer to hide from his schoolmates his difficulties in passing urine:

> Generally speaking, it was never a case of making water when I wanted to, but always . . . of doing so when one could. I felt it necessary to keep my disability secret . . . since the worst thing that can happen to a boy at his preparatory school is to be in any way "different"; so I went when they did to the school latrines, though nothing happened there but the increase of my envy. . . . I used various strategems. One was to ask to be excused during class, when the latrines would be deserted. Another was to stay awake at night and use the pot under my bed when the dormitory's other occupants were asleep, or at least when it was dark.[3]

For interactional management, agents of various kinds can also be useful: wives who scout out the terrain at a public meeting to find the least obtrusive spot and then pass on the information to their husbands in wheelchairs or on crutches. Spouses can also save the day: some even have prearranged signals with their husbands or wives so that when a symptom starts appearing (such as a runny nose), he or she will be apprised of it. A more dramatic instance:

> A husband, at a party, noticed his wife's temporarily slurred speech—a sign of her tiredness and pain from cancer symptoms—and since they wished not to have their friends know about this domestic secret, he acted quickly to divert her neighbor's attention and soon afterward manufactured an excuse so that they could leave the party without awkwardness.

When visible symptoms cannot be disguised easily, misleading explanations of their presence of occurrence may be offered. Fainting, for instance, is explained away by someone "in the know" as a temporary weakness from flu or some other reasonable cause. When a symptom cannot really be much minimized, then a spouse may attempt to minimize it by preparing other persons for the distressing sight or sound of the husband's or wife's affliction. The sufferer herself may do this, as when a lady with cancer who had lost much weight warned friends over the phone that when they visited they would not find her looking like herself at all—"I've lost a tremendous amount of weight"—and each friend who visits is very likely, in turn, to warn other friends what to expect.

All such tactics, it can easily be seen, tend to involve a considerable degree of personal and/or family organization so that they can successfully be carried off. Of course, a cooperative, tactful audience is also helpful. When there is failure on either side, interaction is badly disrupted and can end in consequences like epileptic individuals losing jobs because their convulsive fits frighten other employees, or persons ill from neurological disease withdrawing increasingly from daily interaction.

SYMPTOM CONTROL AND DISEASE CONTROL

A further issue associated with symptom control especially highlights the social rather than the purely medical aspects of that control. This issue involves the different relationships that exist between symptom control and disease control.

To block the downward course of the disease may contribute also to suppressing the symptoms, as when the chemotherapy that is used to check the spread of cancer is also useful in reducing the visible signs of cancer. Of course, sometimes symptom and disease control can be opposed to each other, such as when a physician chooses not to give medication immediately because this would suppress important diagnostic signs. Sometimes, however, there is not much connection between disease control and symptom control: for example, suppressing pain helps the arthritic person live more comfortably but does not really affect the disease. The same is true of the comfort care given in hospitals to a dying patient during the last days of life: hospital staffs have abandoned their attempts to save the person's life and are concerned only with giving care that will both keep him reasonably comfortable and help him to die with a maximum of dignity—and, not so incidentally, make their own work lives easier and, if they are involved with him, minimize the impact of his loss on themselves.

It is often said that when symptom and disease control are opposed or independent, then the patient leans toward symptom control and the health personnel toward disease control. That can happen, but sometimes it is just the reverse. The real question is, under which conditions will that first tendency appear, and under which conditions will the calculus be reversed or the parties actually be in complete agreement? The answers to that question are complex. We shall be content here with some pertinent commentary plus a few illustrations.

First, pertaining to complete "misunderstanding": an elderly lady who suffered from three diseases—including one that the physician considered potentially fatal (cardiac)—abandoned her digitalis because it tended to make her nauseous but continued taking pills for her two other illnesses. When, however, the patient is not afraid of his disease or even denies he has it (as with some patients with tuberculosis), then he is only concerned with the appearance and control of his symptoms, although usually his physician is much more focused on the disease. In diseases where symptom control is possible at least to some extent, but disease control is not, then physician and patient naturally will concur on the priority of symptom control.

When people are reminded that their disease *can* be fatal because of an occasional crisis, as are asthmatic or diabetic individuals, then they, as well as the health personnel, are likely to be very attentive to disease control, especially when daily problems of symptom control are minor. When a progressively deleterious disease is understood to be potentially fatal, then, like the health professionals, the sick person is likely to read the symptoms primarily as signs of her retrogression and is probably more interested in blocking, or at least slowing up, that retrogression than in mere symptom control. When, as in fatal cancer, there is no chance of doing this, then both she and the professionals can agree that symptom control takes priority—and not necessarily just for comfort but to maintain a more normal social existence while dying.

LEARNING ABOUT SYMPTOM CONTROL

To return again to symptom control (quite apart from associated questions pertaining to disease control), the really important point about it is that those afflicted have to learn, in detail, about the symptoms and their consequences. The sick person has to learn the pattern of his symptoms: when they appear, how long they last, whether he can prevent them, whether he can shorten their duration or minimize their intensity—and whether he is getting new ones. Nobody can entirely or accurately imagine, without that actual experience, what are the consequences for his bodily movements, his abilities, his work, his daily or weekly moods, and his social relationships.

That the body has the capacity for disturbing surprises is the lesson of every newly appearing disease and of new phases of old ones. This is brought out with sad vividness by interviews with the victims of multiple sclerosis and other neurological diseases; they are continuously surprised by their symptoms—their falling down suddenly, fainting, unexpected clumsiness, shakiness. As in some other illnesses, their symptoms often come and go, at least at first, a phenomenon that causes them still further surprise and that makes very difficult their assessing of "what's going on." Even when a person knows roughly what her trajectory will be, alas, her body can still provide some awesome surprises:

> Diana came in in a distraught state. She broke down crying. "What is happening to me," she repeated, "there is something terribly wrong here."[6]

Above all, the sick person must discover her limits, that is, how well and for how long she can carry on, temporarily or permanently, despite them. To carry on physically, even at reduced efficiency, means learning also to do many of the things discussed already, such as devising and redesigning. It means also the planning of activities. Having learned when symptoms peak during the day, one attempts to link up that physical pattern with the patterns of the working or sociable day. If a housewife with cardiac disease tires early, she will attempt to get her work done early. A colitis sufferer, working in a barber shop, has struck a bargain with his co-workers; he cuts hair during his relatively symptom-free mornings and does tasks such as sweeping the floor during his worst hours. One kidney transplant patient negotiated with his employer to come to the job late and to stay working until late, because that fit his daily symptom pattern. When patterns are uncertain, then it is much harder to schedule given activities. People with sudden losses of energy may have to warn their friends that appointments can be called off (as do cancer patients in late stages of illness).

An alternative is to seize the minutes or hours when they do have energy and use them for all they are worth. Persons with cardiac disease, in the months after their myocardial infarctions, for instance, may have to learn to do this, usually only after bitter experience, unless forewarned by another cardiac patient. Such individuals usually have to learn also that they are not much "good at sex" during late evening hours; in fact, in one of the few good articles on that subject, a cardiologist has urged persons under his care to have intercourse much earlier in the day.[4] As he remarks, the reticence of both ill patients and their physicians results in little communication between them on this worrisome but vital topic of sexual activity.

Having learned the symptom patterns, one still has choices as to how to handle them. A graphic illustration of this point:

> A sculptor had colitis. He found that going to the toilet and cleansing himself carefully was less important than the time and expense required to recast his sculptural molds. So, in his private studio, he often elected to defacate on himself and his premises rather than to interrupt his work.
> *Reif*

For most symptoms, one really does have options—and, of course, different people choose different ones. Thus some epileptic people choose not to go out at all, whereas others control the consequences of potential public seizures by always having protective agents with them when outside the house. Again, when one knows that sitting in soft chairs greatly increases the probability of back pains, one can decide to refuse the hostess' offer of "the best chair" or meekly submit to her invitation.

> One young man who developed ulcerative colitis chose to leave college and join a tolerant hippie commune, where he lived with his symptoms sans regimen. He did this after struggling for many months to control his symptoms through a regimen that took up almost all of his time.
> *Reif*

Thus the options chosen, whether temporarily or permanently, reflect personal values. And as noted earlier, those values may include dying quickly or "now," rather than struggling to control symptoms finally defined as unbearable.

References

1. Davis, Marcella: Living with multiple sclerosis, Springfield, Ill., 1973, Charles C Thomas, Publisher.
2. Goffman, Erving: Stigma, Englewood Cliffs, N.J., 1963, Prentice-Hall, Inc., p. 91. Goffman is quoting from Orbach, C., Bard, M., and Sutherland, A.: Fears and defensive adaptations to the loss of sphincter control, Psychoanalytic Review **44:**90, 1957.
3. Goffman, Erving: Stigma, Englewood Cliffs, N.J., 1963, Prentice-Hall, Inc., p. 89. Goffman is quoting from "N. O. Goe," in Toynbee, P., editor: Underdogs, London, 1961, Weidenfeld & Nicolson, p. 150.
4. Griffith, C.: Sexuality and the cardiac patient, Heart and Lung **2:**70-73, 1973.
5. Hodges, E.: Episode: report on the accident inside my skull, New York, 1964, Atheneum Publishers, p. 109.
6. Lowenstein, Prince Leopold of: A time to love . . . a time to die, New York, 1971, Doubleday & Co., Inc.
7. Ritchie, Douglas: Stroke: a diary of recovery, London, 1960, Faber & Faber, Ltd., pp. 63-64, 186.

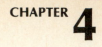

REORDERING OF TIME

From what has been noted so far, it is apparent that the symptoms, regimens, and crises of various chronic diseases lead to temporal disruption. Therefore this calls for and indeed forces changes in the daily management of time. Since we have already touched on the scheduling and timing problems attendant on the control of symptoms, those topics will not be discussed again. Two other types of temporal disruption and reordering are worth our notice here, because they can constitute such difficult problems for patients and their families. In the solution of these problems, it is questionable how much aid the health personnel actually give or perhaps could give under current arrangements for medical and health care. Patients and families currently seem pretty much on their own in handling their temporal problems.

TOO MUCH TIME

One that is all too familiar is too much time. That problem may only be temporary, as with persons who are waiting out the postcrises period. It can quite literally be a permanent condition, however, if the person is so disabled by the symptoms that there is little in the way of activity that he or she can engage in, or so discouraged by them, or not inventive in finding substitute activities for ones now impossible or forbidden. Some people may try very hard to be inventive and still fail, as with the woman who taught handicrafts. Now that her hands tremble she finds many crafts hard to do; she tried to invent new ones that she could do and teach, but could not imagine any.

Among the consequences of too much time are boredom, decreased social skills, family strains, negative impact on identity, and even physical deterioration. Some of the poignancy of "free-time blues" is expressed by one person who said: "It hit me so fast. I liked my work. I'm a worker! Now I have such an empty life. I can't go out. I can't work." Even those people ingenious enough—or with adequate physical or intellectual resources—to fill up empty time with new kinds of interests, still may find that time passes very slowly.

TOO LITTLE TIME

Just as common, but perhaps more subtle in its effects, is not enough time. The person's time can be sopped up by symptom control and by regimens acting in the service of that control. Agents who assist, caretake, and control may also expend enormous amounts of time on their particular helping tasks.

> Asked what kinds of activities she had of her own, the mother of a child with cystic fibrosis answered that she had none, and although she keeps telling herself "maybe next week" there never seems to be enough time.
> *Benoliel*

That particular parent's temporal deprivation apparently is shared with others whose children have cystic fibrosis, for according to one study:

> "They did feel deprived of time and energy to engage in leisure-time activities and in interpersonal relationships. Most important, they felt that there was a decrease in time and energy for self." Furthermore, the demands on their time meant a proportionate amount of time was taken away from being with the siblings of the sick child.[1]

Not to be totally engulfed, the agents may need to get other backstopping agents (babysitters, housecleaners, cooks) or call for a review of the family's division of labor (the burden of a sick mother should be shifted from one family member to another, or an elderly sick father should live for a while with another of his grown daughters).

Occasionally, the regimens require so much time or crises come so frequently (one sickle cell sufferer had been hospitalized dozens of times) that life simply becomes organized around those events—there is not enough time for much of anything else. As a nursing student describes a kidney transplant sufferer:

> Her life really did revolve around the necessity of the routines of her medical management. There was little room for flexibility because of the knowledge that a crisis could be precipitated by carelessness. She felt that she had to fit in whatever living she could between doctors' appointments and the daily pill routine.

Even just handling one's symptoms or the consequences of having symptoms may take so much time that life is taken up mainly with handling them. This can be seen very strikingly in talking with emphysema sufferers: the amount of time spent in resting by emphysema sufferers while in the midst of activities or tasks—with time fragmented or stretched out—is enormous. The same phenomenon is evident in observing the lives of those with colitis, but it is characteristically true of other diseases also. Thus a very bad dermatological condition caused one woman to spend hour after hour salving her skin; otherwise she would have suffered unbearably.

Unfortunately, the persons who suffer cannot just abandon their bodies, whereas it is quite possible for family members and other assisting agents to abandon them out of desperation for what the temporal engulfment is doing to their own lives. Abandonment, here, may mean shifting the temporal (and other) burdens to a nursing home or other custodial institution. Abandonment or not, certainly some family strain is the consequence of too little time left over for one's own pursuits.

TEMPORAL JUGGLING

The basic temporal problems—too much time, too little time, scheduling, and timing—involve patients and their agents (assisting, controlling, protecting, caretaking, and so forth) in a delicately balanced game of temporal juggling. We say delicate and balanced, because whenever there is a downward change in the symptomatology or a change in regimen, or virtually any change of personal or familial life-style, then the temporal arrangements are likely to be affected. A family member may spend more time at various functions: helping with the housework or with regimen procedures, or acting as a regimen control agent, or assisting with symptom management, or even becoming a protective agent. Changes in agential functions, necessitating that more time be spent, may come about as the disease progresses.

The strain of sustaining some of these temporal arrangements, as suggested here and in preceding pages, can be considerable. The strain can be measured imaginatively in a kind of mirrored opposite if one considers what happens during those periods termed "symptom free." Life, including its temporal aspects, then returns relatively to normal. The same relief occurs sometimes for family members, even during crises, when they are temporarily granted more normal schedules and more time by virtue of handing the sick relative over to hospital personnel. Relatives are granted that kind of temporary relief also when the sick one goes away for a visit or a vacation, or when they themselves can get away for even a short while.

> A mother of an asthmatic daughter is finally sending her away to a special school for asthmatic children, finding release that way from the burdens of caring for a patient who has been back and forth, from and to the hospital "100 times."
> *Benoliel*

Of course, it is not just time—or even events in time—that they are all juggling. In fact, to repeat an important point, they are juggling potentially fragile patterns of temporal arrangements that can be disturbed by changes in symptoms, regimens, the disease itself, social and family relations, and sometimes lessened finances.

Reference

1. Rosenstein, Beryl: Cystic fibrosis of the pancreas. In Debuskey, M., editor: The chronically ill child and his family, Springfield, Ill., 1970, Charles C Thomas, Publisher, p. 29; reviewing the actual study by Turk, J.: Impact of cystic fibrosis on family functioning, Pediatrics **34:**67, 1964.

CHAPTER 5

MANAGING AND SHAPING THE TRAJECTORY

In this and succeeding chapters, we shall use the concept of "trajectory" and its associated work (trajectory work) as a central notion for illuminating the experiences and problems of the chronically ill and of those who participate in their care.

First, it is necessary to draw a distinction between a course of illness and an illness trajectory.

The first term offers no problems to anyone, since we have all experienced an illness that did not merely appear but developed gradually over time, getting worse and then stabilizing or perhaps relatively clearing up. *Course of illness* is also a professional term, since to knowledgeable medical, nursing, and technical staffs each kind of illness has its more or less characteristic phases, with symptoms to match. In contrast, *illness trajectory* is a term coined by the authors that refers not only to the physiological unfolding of a sick person's disease but also to the *total organization* of work done over that course, plus the *impact* on those involved with that work and its organization.[3,6]

This trajectory work, as we have seen in the foregoing chapters, can be varied and taxing. In the hospital the personnel refer to the "management" of illness, but the highly problematic character of many chronic illnesses—with their many phases and contingencies, both medical and otherwise—challenges the very idea of illness (and trajectory) management. As a term, *management* does not catch anything like the full complexity of the work, its medical outcomes, or the consequences for all who are working at it. For that reason it makes sense to think also of problematic trajectories in terms of "shaping"—that is, handling the contingencies as best one can. That implies far from full control of the trajectory in all its phases.

CERTAIN AND UNCERTAIN TRAJECTORIES

For some diseases, the courses of illness are fairly predictable. We can anticipate their phases, and even the relative rate at which the phases will change. For other diseases, such as multiple sclerosis, both the phases and their rates are quite uncertain. Of course, for any given person who is ill, the sequential phases may be fairly predictable, but when they will appear and disappear can be most uncertain. This matter of certainty and uncertainty is of utmost importance, because the efficiency of social arrangements is so closely linked with the predictability of the trajectories. Uncertain courses of illness and their trajectories help to maximize personal and familial hardships.

If a given trajectory is relatively certain, then planning and preparation can be made in advance of each new downward phase—that is, provided people act rationally on that certainty. They may have had imaginary rehearsals, sometimes quite accurate ones, by virtue of speaking to or seeing people "ahead" of them on the same disease trajectory. They can move to easier physical terrain before their mobility decreases. They can, foreseeing early retirement, save for it. If they can foresee death they can prepare for it, as did one cancer patient who prepared his wife for independence by sending her to a nursing school.

However, if the rate of deterioration is unexpectedly speedy, then the prepared arrangements will be that much out of alignment. Paradoxically, even when the rate of deterioration is slowed there can be difficulties, as when expected caretaking or assisting agents die before their ill relative's really severe decline finally begins, or when funds have been saved for the expected bad days but inflation or some other contingency drastically reduces those funds.

Even when there are reprieves or partial recoveries—with uncertainty in rate of phasing or in "how far back" the recovery will go—then the reprieves or partial recoveries can cause considerable difficulty both in daily living and in the making of social arrangements. Sometimes the physician actually knows the extent of the expected recovery but does not convey it to the ill person; alternately, this information may have been conveyed but is not completely understood by either the person or family. Thus

> A surgeon who does kidney transplants said that customarily when pressed for estimations of how long after the transplant life will become relatively normal, he answers "2 years," although he knows that both his estimates of when and how normal are *very* approximate. One patient who took the surgeon's answer literally and went back to work full-time after 2 years "ran into trouble."

That phrase refers to trouble with social arrangements, of course, as well as to medical difficulties.

The same general issue was addressed by Fred Davis in his *Passage through Crisis.*[1] This researcher noted that for children stricken with polio two different perspectives develop in the posthospital period, "depending mainly on the rate and amount of functional improvement demonstrated by the child in the home setting." A child who makes significant strides in physical capabilities tends to generate in his family "an aura of achievement and a frequently unrealistic expectation of limitless improvements." By contrast, when he shows little or no improvement a

> moratorium psychology takes hold. The vague, overgeneral statement by doctors and others that improvement can occur within 18 months following onset of the disease is interpreted to mean that if improvement has not already taken place it might still do so all of a sudden and in one or two great bursts "before time runs out."[1]

We can easily imagine how difficult it is for both sets of families to make stable social arrangements, given their expectations of these kinds of illness trajectories.

One sees a poignant instance of this same phenomenon with people who are dying when there is a pattern of decline-reprieve-decline-reprieve-decline to death. Reprieves are certainly welcomed by kin, provided they are genuine and the dying person is not too much of a burden, but they certainly render the previous social arrangements unstable and are likely to call for considerable and hasty rearrangement.

> Illnesses associated with reprieve patterns . . . hinder full preparation. Reprieves spark hope, so that the family is never completely prepared for the death: they think the next reprieve may be complete, not temporary. Thus, even when the doctor announces a time of death, usually a few days ahead of time, the family members may feel that the "miraculous" return to life they have watched before might happen again. As one uncle said, "It was hard to fully reconcile ourselves since we've seen her revive before and she could do it again." When a pattern like this is established, the family may refuse to give up all hope even if the doctor tells them they must, which may put the family through many "tortuous" episodes—after each, wishing the patient had died. Further, the short notice he is able to give them is usually not enough to allow the family members time to reconcile themselves and begin preparations.[2]

Even when complete recovery from an acute disease is assured but rate of recovery is somewhat uncertain—as, say, in mononucleosis—the patient's social arrangements are rendered relatively unstable compared to those possible if the illness trajectory were more predictable in rate.

DIFFERENTIAL DEFINITIONS OF A TRAJECTORY

Because trajectories, as defined here, are not merely reflections of physiological happenings but are linked with people's definitions of what is expected of a disease, it follows that the ill person may define her trajectory differently than may other people. She might not see eye to eye with the physician, for instance, because the physician does not wish a patient to know all there is to know about her future. The reason for this may be that she does not really understand, or wish to understand, what the physician says, or that temperamentally she is optimistic and so cannot really conceive the worst, or perhaps has a tendency toward pessimism and so draws too dark an imagined future. There is a great deal of "shopping around" among the available physicians, not always simply in quest of more effective symptom control but often in a search for physicians who have alternative views of one's trajectory and so will try other means to alter it for the better. In the case of predicted fatal diseases, the shopping around is for a physician who will not give up.

> Linked with lingering and reprieve-pattern illnesses is the ever constant hope
> that medical researchers will find a cure in time: "They are working on it
> constantly." Some families travel from medical center to medical center and
> even make telephone calls to research centers all over the world to see how
> close "they" are to "the cure," adjusting their preparations accordingly.[2]

Whatever possible difference of definition exists between the ill person and the physician can be paralleled by similar differences between the ill person and friends and relatives. They may not really understand what the future is, either because they have not been told everything or because they have not had sufficient experiences with the disease to know about its course. Perhaps they overestimate the sick person's normality, but sometimes they are more pessimistic. They can even treat him or her as socially dead considerably before he or she is biologically dead.

At any rate, regardless of the disease trajectory's shape, the chronically ill attempt at every phase to place themselves somewhere on their trajectory. They seek cues that suggest whether they are moving into a new phase, carefully watching shifts of symptomatology. They may also wait anxiously for the next symptom to appear, debating whether it portends a new phase or whether its presence is only temporary. Sometimes the physicians cannot tell them with accuracy; sometimes they can, but then the sick may not accept the assessments.

Understandably, ill persons seek to impress on others some definition of their trajectory and their current place on it. They may attempt to give their own true definition, or they may give a false one that they do not really believe. They do the latter, for instance, when the truth might lose them jobs or status or "face." Sometimes the ill person has to work hard to convince some people that her condition is not so bad and will get no worse, if it is important to give them reassurance, because of their great anxiety or their overstating of the illness.

Ill persons may also have problems legitimizing others' views of trajectories, since some people will not believe they are really *that* sick. Husbands and their wives sometimes have to convince spouses who simply will not face up to the facts.

> One cardiac sufferer of our acquaintance wished to step down from an administrative position but had a rather difficult time convincing his associates, not merely that he had just had a myocardial infarction and therefore was unwell, but that he was unlikely to be able, for 3 or 4 years, to carry heavy administrative burdens and had to resign immediately.

Apropos of difficulties in legitimizing; certain diseases can be very painful or discomforting, but the people who suffer them are at a great disadvantage in not having visible symptoms to legitimize their condition. Unless x-ray examinations or other diagnostic procedures back up their assertions, other people are likely to think of them as malingering or maybe somewhat sick, but not *that* sick—or even as pretty neurotic. Sufferers from neurological diseases are often thought of as having "psychological diseases" before an accurate diagnosis is made. People who complain of unbearable back pain—which is notoriously difficult to pin down diagnostically, especially if they have been through two or three back operations—are quite often given short shrift by hospital personnel when they come in "once again." Faced with these patients' persistent claims to pain, the staff tends to assess them in a variety of negative ways: as "demanding," "clock watchers," "manipulators," "malingerers," or "crocks." The patient's attempts to convince the staff that he or she really does have "that much pain" frequently only reinforce and increase the staff's disbelief.[7]

Proper definitions of a trajectory by others can be a problem even when a person is clearly dying. Although most friends may believe it, others may refuse to confront the issue (and treat the person as if he or she were not dying), and still others may act as if the person were already nearly dead.

> A friend of a lady dying of cancer said sharply to another friend, who could not enter the sick person's house without a mournful and depressed demeanor, that she should "snap out of it. Sheila's not dead yet, and wants to be treated like someone who's all here."

TRAJECTORY PROJECTION

The preceding chapters suggest the complexities of trajectory management and shaping at home, which adds up to a much wider range of tasks, strategies, maneuvers, interactions, and solutions than those seen in the hospital setting. An additional consideration needs to be emphasized to appreciate fully the complexity of work at home. In the hospital, after a patient's illness has been diagnosed, the attending physician or physicians attempt to plot out the probable future course of the illness, as well as the medical interventions ("work") that will be made, along with the various resources necessary to carry out the interventions with maximum effectiveness. In short, they work out a "trajectory scheme" through which the staff hopes to manage or at least partly control the trajectory. By contrast, at home this trajectory scheme has an additional ingredient that derives from the following crucially different condition: the sick person, and close kin if there are any, are working out this trajectory over a *lifetime*—whether it runs only 10 days, 10 years, or over many decades. The significance of this for the trajectory work is understandably profound.

But how can this be phrased so that it is not just a trite statement that, from direct experience or by hearsay, everyone knows? The answer is bound to be very complicated and will depend on the nature of the specific disease. So next, we will look briefly at several cases illustrative of either different illnesses or different phases of their associated trajectories. This comparative scanning can begin to tell us something about the impact of the patients' and kin's temporal visualizations of trajectories—that is, their "trajectory projection"—on the actual trajectory work carried out by them.

Case 1. Trajectory projection impacts dramatically and drastically on present action when the ill person has been told he or she has only a short time to live: days or a few months. Quite aside from the announcement's emotional impact, what is the work to be done? That depends on "circumstances": Are there young children? Is the patient married or divorced? Are there many or few, elaborate or simple, business and financial matters to be settled? Are there many or few farewells to make before dying? Is the person old enough to be relatively prepared for death or young enough to have much identity work to do before dying? But there is so little time to carry out those immediately crucial tasks! Some persons are lucky enough to have adequate personal, social, economic, religious, organizational, and other resources for deciding on and doing much of that work; alas, others are lacking in those resources, and the means for getting those resources—quickly.

Case 2. At the other extreme are those illness conditions where future recovery is uncertain but possibly will be quite considerable. The road back may require much hard work—difficult regimens, much pain, and the like—but if the person and his or her family pull together, he or she will recuperate well. Characteristic of this phase of trajectory work, with light seen at the end of the tunnel, is concerted, persistent, shoulder-to-shoulder work. The work is directed mainly at "improving the illness status," while most of life's other tasks are held in abeyance. They will be taken up again later, to whatever degree is permitted by the amount of "comeback."

Case 3. Certain illnesses are loaded with potential for medical crises. Hemophilia, for instance, lies at the extreme end of a continuum running from continuously potential to only occasionally though drastically potential. Crisis prevention colors every day, and crisis action is frequent, in the lives of people with hemophilia.[4] All of the afflicted person's other activities, and those of his or her immediate family, are inextricably linked with the crisis work itself. Virtually no day goes by without the threat of potential death or at least great physical damage intruding, whether dramatically or implicitly. Peaks and valleys—unanticipated trajectory phases in the evolving symptomatology—inevitably link up with, affect, and are affected by life's other tasks. The family is *continuously* shaping its present to prevent a disastrous future.

Case 4. When a child is diagnosed as having cystic fibrosis, the parents are told that the life expectancy is at most not beyond 20 years or so, and might be considerably less; they are also informed that death could come speedily during any bout of lung illness. So, aside from all the crisis managing, the symptom monitoring, the symptom controlling, the carrying out of onerous regimens, the parents will carry a burden of rearing a child who bears an invisible death date on his or her forehead. That knowledge sets excruciatingly difficult tasks for most parents. Their basic problem of course is how to "raise" the child knowing that he will never reach full adulthood. By no means does that problem intrude on each day, but (quite aside from occasional real medical crises) from time to time the whole of parental existence is colored by it.

Case 5. Then there is the situation of a young couple, the husband having been rendered anxious about the crisis potential of his wife's diabetic condition, as evidenced during her pregnancy. Looming over him at least, although perhaps less for his wife, was the vision of future crises, one of which might carry her off. With such temporally organized imagery and behavior, the distant future medical events of her diabetic biography were discounted, put into a kind of temporal freeze. As the husband, who had assiduously studied the technical literature bearing on diabetes, put the issue: he knew his wife might later have many difficulties, even losing some of her eyesight, but somehow they would cope with that if they finally happened. Right now the potentially disastrous diabetic comas were of much more pressing concern, so that most of his trajectory work was directed at preventing and monitoring for any ominous signs of them.

Case 6. As sick people recuperate from severe chronic illness, regaining some or most of their physical powers, the cutback on many of their activities gradually decreasing, then inevitably they look forward to the time when still more limitations on their lives will be mitigated or even completely wiped out. Perhaps inevitably too, either they or their spouses will race ahead of each other in their anticipations of that happier time. One or the other is likely to begin planning, fantasizing about, or even making specific preparations, say, for traveling abroad. The other may concur and join in that work of imagination and planning, but he or she may silently think, or caution aloud, "Well, let's see what happens over the next weeks or months; let's play that by ear." Thus the principals in this particular drama have different trajectory projections, are marching to different temporal music. Their daily activities and trajectory work may not be appreciably affected, but insofar as the more optimistic spouse really believes in this pushing back of the limitations, a certain amount of preparatory work, whether mental or physical, will get done. If so, it enters into the totality of the family's or at least the more optimistic spouse's trajectory work. A varient of this phenomenon is when the ill person is cheerful about the future while the spouse or parent knows but is withholding information about the probable unhappy future. There may instead be mutual pretense, with both sick person and parent or spouse knowing that any future plans are highly improbable or impossible, but both carrying on as if there were a good future—or *any* future at all.[2,5]

COMING TO TERMS

So, whether dying or not, sick persons must come to terms with their trajectories and ask certain people who are significant to them to do the same. Others who may be equally significant may, as noted earlier, be offered other definitions by sick persons, because they want the others to consider them sicker than, or not as sick as, they believe themselves to be. An instructive and realistic instance of this differential presentation of the sick self is that of a young woman graduate student who was quite ill for a relatively long time from mononucleosis, an acute and completely curable disease. While still recovering, she presented herself as follows:

1. To people in general, she passes as not ill.
2. To her friends, she is "fine, but," since she hasn't come back all the way yet. The same is true for the faculty in a summer school where she is soon to teach, so they will not ply her with too much work too early.
3. To her parents, she says she's recovered, because she wishes to reassure them.
4. To her roommates, she still has "ill aspects," is "not all right yet," a presentation she nourishes, since it saves her from sometimes exhaus-

ting housework; but then again, they can see or sense that she's not yet fully recovered.

5. With the physician, she emphasizes her recovery, because she is bargaining for more activity than he wishes to permit.

6. With her boyfriends, she has perhaps the most difficulty, because they cannot deal realistically with her being ill. "You'll be better by tomorrow—or in a week." Because she sees them especially in the evening, when more tired, she finds herself drawing limits in activity—about how late she can stay up and so on. And they are disappointed. One boy hasn't been kissing her because of *his* ideas of possible contagion, and she has not been able to convince him that this idea is wrong!

At every downward step in a trajectory—if it is the kind that does not simply remain on a plateau—the ill person must reassess where she is and therefor what social arrangements are necessary to manage effectively her symptoms, social relations, daily life, and preparations for life in the foreseeable future. Of course, other people have to do the same for her, especially those in the immediate family. In a genuine sense, any chronically ill person who phases drastically down, or up for that matter, becomes a new person in the house. If he now loses his ability to walk or climb stairs, it is quite like having someone else there—someone who have to be given crutches or be put in a wheelchair, or who now presents a most awkward situation, because no longer can he climb up to his bedroom but must sleep in a downstairs room.

The same person is likely to become a new person to himself, too, in the sense that his body is no longer what it was, and so to some extent "I am no longer what I was." In reverse, it is very striking that when the ill get reprieves or have partial recoveries, they can barely imagine their recently very sick selves (without energy, for instance) as themselves. Thus

> One woman, dying of cancer, who had such a reprieve simply could not get over the Helen that was but who right now is not that person, although fully cognizant that she could become that Helen again, and rather soon. Yet, that recent energy-less self is not and was not "really" her.

And

> A man with cardiac disease remarked, now that he is 2 years beyond his myocardial infarction, that it is only during occasional bad hours that he can vividly recapture his "very sick self" who found even talking on the telephone demanded more energy than he could command.

CONSEQUENCES FOR PERSONAL IDENTITY

It should be obvious that a person's changing views of his or her trajectory, and the shifting social relations that may occur as it progresses, can profoundly affect the sense of personal identity. That, of course, is not news! What is worth underscoring, however, is that the instability of social arrangements brought about by a developing disease in turn feeds into the sufferer's self-image and his or her trajectory and into previous social relationships. Thus, with the multiple sclerosis trajectory, the phases and their rate of change are so uncertain that all social arrangements are rendered exceedingly unstable—therefore so are the sufferer's social relationships. His views of himself cannot remain unaltered; even if his sense of self does not become hopelessly unmoored and negative, his very efforts to maintain his social relationships relatively unimpaired and to build the new ones necessary to handle his new disabilities will contribute to a changed sense of identity. (The ingenious student with multiple sclerosis mentioned in Chapter 3 certainly has not the same self that she had when her symptoms were still mild, and not the same self either as before she began gradually to lose some of her eyesight.)

It would be much too simplistic to assert that specific trajectories determine what happens to a sense of personal identity. Certainly they do contribute and quite possibly in patterned ways. The identity responses to a severe heart attack presumably may be very varied, but belief that death can be only a moment away—and every day—most likely would have a very different impact on identity than trajectories expected to result in slow death, or in "leaving me a vegetable" or in "perfectly alive, but a hopeless cripple." Quite aside from dreadful last phases, certain illnesses can profoundly affect the identities of the sick person because the diseases, or their symptoms, are commonly regarded as stigmatizing. Leprosy and epilepsy are examples. People with such diseases are therefore likely either to have negative feelings about themselves or to develop psychological means for avoiding self-deprecation.

As for the various illnesses that are merely annoying or discomforting or somewhat intrusive into social relations, their identity impact is perhaps harder to predict. Such illnesses may not have any perceptible effect on self-conceptions. For instance, people who suffer from chronic sinusitis or mild bronchitis or diabetes may simply develop routines for handling symptoms and regimens, without deep involvement of their identities. As they grow older, however, they may encounter an unanticipated increase in their symptoms and develop changed trajectory projections; they then may have to come to new—and "deeper"—terms with their illnesses.

References

1. Davis, Fred: Passage through crisis, Indianapolis, 1963, The Bobbs-Merrill Co., Inc. p. 107.
2. Glaser, Barney, and Strauss, Anselm: Awareness of dying, Chicago, 1965, Aldine Press, pp. 170-171.
3. Glaser, Barney, and Strauss, Anselm: Time for dying, Chicago, 1968, Aldine Press.
4. Massie, Robert, and Massie, Suzanne: Journey, New York, 1976, Warner Communications.
5. McIvers, P.: Good night Mr. Christopher, New York, 1974, Sheed & Ward.
6. Strauss, Anselm, Fagerhaugh, Shizuko, Suczek, Barbara, and Wiener, Carolyn: The social organization of medical work, Chicago, University of Chicago Press. (In press.)
7. Wiener, Carolyn: Pain assessment, pain legitimation and the conflict of staff-patient perspectives, Nursing Outlook **23**(8):508-516, Aug. 1975.

CHAPTER 6

SOCIAL ISOLATION

Now and again in the foregoing pages, we have alluded to the loss of social contact, even extending to great social isolation, as a consequence of chronic disease and its management. It is entirely understandable that this should be so, given the accompanying symptoms, crises, regimens, and often difficult phasing of trajectories. Social relationships are disrupted or falter and disintegrate under the impact of lessened energy, impairment of mobility or speech, hearing impairment, body disfigurement, time spent on regimens and symptom control, and efforts made to keep secret so much about the disease and its management. It is no wonder that chronic sufferers themselves begin to pull or feel out of activity and communication.

The process may proceed very far, so that social contacts are maintained only by the slenderest of threads and with very few people, or it may be far less drastic and not permanent. In any event, we ought to regard pulling away or finding oneself out of contact as a tendency accompanying many chronic illnesses, linked with their trajectories and a variety of associated social contingencies. For our purposes it may be useful to dwell briefly on some differences between voluntary pulling out and involuntary moving out, as well as on tactics used by patients and others to combat the tendency toward social isolation.

THE SICK PERSON WITHDRAWS

As suggested already, loss of social contact is furthered by some of the symptoms and regimens themselves. Thus a loss of energy means correspondingly that much less energy to spend on friends. So choices may have to be made about with whom to spend less time or whom to cut out altogether. These kinds of choices can become especially acute during the last phase of a very ill person's life, as with one cancer patient who

> restricted visiting by friends to just a few with whom he could manage to sustain conversation—except during his three or four reprieves when he would feel the need for more varied contact and would reach out to a much wider circle of

friends. Because he was dying, the smaller circle seemed not, on the whole, to feel rebuffed during the reprieves, as otherwise they might have, since then they saw much less of him.

It is thus not difficult to trace some of the impact on social contact of varying symptoms, in accordance with their chief properties. A face disfigured with leprosy, as previously noted, along with the possibility of "being found out" leads many to stay in leprosy colonies; they prefer the social ease and normal relationships that are possible there. Diseases that are—or that the sufferer thinks are—stigmatizing are kept as secret as possible, and he or she "passes." However, it is with some relief that the sick person is able to talk about it with friends who may understand. Some may find friends (even spouses) among the fellow sufferers, especially during clinic visits or at special associations formed around the illness or disability (ileostomy groups, Alcoholics Anonymous). Some virtually make careers—sociability careers as well as work careers—doing voluntary work for those clubs or associations. People can also leave circles of friends whom they feel might now be unresponsive, frightened, or critical and move to more sympathetic social terrain. In the words of an epileptic woman who has used, or perhaps slid into using, a warning tactic plus moving to a supportive terrain:

> I'm lucky, I still have friends. Most people who have epilepsy are put to the side. But I'm lucky that way. I tell them that I have epilepsy and that they shouldn't get scared if I fall out. I go to things at the church—it's the church people that are my friends. I just tell them and then it is okay. They just laugh about it and don't get upset.

When symptoms and regimens begin to take their toll of social contact, ill people may make very considered choices between that contact and their willingness to put up with symptoms and even with their progressively advancing disease. One cardiac male, for instance, simply refused to give up his weekly evening with the boys playing cards—replete with smoking, beer drinking, and late hours—despite his understanding that this could lead to further heart attacks. Compare this with another man with cardiac disease who avoided the coffee breaks at work because everyone smoked then, and also avoided many social functions for the same reasons. Consequently, he believes that people probably think him unsociable since his illness, but he cannot figure out how to stop himself otherwise from smoking. Perhaps the extreme escape from—not minimization or prevention of—social isolation was exhibited by one lady with kidney disease who chose to go off dialysis (she had no possibility of getting a transplant), opting for a speedy death because all she could see was an endless future of dependence on others, inability to hold down a job, increasing social isolation, and her life now lacking in purpose. The physicians even agreed with her decision—her right to "opt for an out."

OTHERS WITHDRAW

Features of social interaction (when combined with symptoms, regimens, or trajectories) can also lead to very subtle forms of lessened social contact and social isolation. Thus dying friends are avoided or even abandoned by those who cannot face the physically altered person or even simply the torture of visiting. A friend of mine who was losing weight because of cancer remarked bitterly that a colleague of his had ducked down the street to avoid meeting him. Even spouses who have known great intimacy together can draw apart because of features of an illness, for example, the husband with cardiac disease who is afraid of the sex act, or who is simply afraid of dying and cannot tell his wife for fear of increasing *her* anxiety, but who feels slightly estranged from her because of his inability to tell her. One gets a sense that women with mastectomies feel somewhat isolated even from their husbands because of the awkwardness that grows up, not only about the surgical mutilation but also about talking of potential death. Furthermore, many of these women do not know how to get others to talk to them about their fears of dying from their cancer.[2] During the last phases of a disease trajectory, a virtually unbridgeable gap may open between previously intimate spouses. As one man has written: "This 'mystery of inaccessibility' to the quality of her experience and suffering was to me almost the greatest torment during the last weeks of her life."[1]

Quite aside from the question of death, interactional awkwardnesses appear that increase the potential for lessened contact and a sense of increased social isolation.

One stroke patient has written that when colleagues came to visit him during his recovery, he sensed their boredom with conversations that he could not sustain. "My wife, who was usually present, saved the conversation from dying—she was never at loss for a word."[3]

And

A cardiac patient hospitalized away from his home town at first received numerous cards and telephone calls, but then once his friends had reached across the distance, they chose to leave him alone, doubtless for a variety of reasons. He and his wife began to feel slightly abandoned, even though they recognized that if only one person telephoned daily, the news would be passed around among a dozen friends. The same cardiac patient later returned to part-time work, appreciating at first that his fellow executives left him relatively alone, knowing that he was far from recuperated—and yet, he felt considerably "out of things." This latter sense of isolation was difficult to combat; the former was partially countered by relatives who lived in the town where he was hospitalized, for they repeatedly emphasized that anyone who telephoned "surely is talking up a storm about you with everyone else."

Withdrawal from others can be furthered, however, by excessive demands and changed personality after a crises or as disease progresses. The most complete form of this, of course, is the abandonment of sick people. Husbands or wives desert or separate, and adult children place their elderly parents in nursing homes. With some kinds of chronic diseases, especially stigmatizing (leprosy) or terribly demanding (neurological or mental illness or advanced geriatric diseases), friends and relatives and even physicians advise the spouse or kin quite literally to abandon the sick person: "It's time to put him (or her) in the hospital or nursing home." "Think of the children." "Think of yourself—it makes no sense." "It's better for him (or her), and you are only keeping him (or her) at home because of your own guilt." These are just some of the abandonment rationales that are offered by others or that the sick person formulates. Of course, the sick person, aware of having become virtually an intolerable burden, may offer those rationales also—which does not necessarily lessen his or her own sense of estrangement. The spouse who does not choose to follow the advice of abandonment counselors runs the risk, in turn, of disrupting relationships between himself or herself and them.

SUMMARY

Lessened social contact and considerable social isolation are among the more pernicious effects of chronic disease. However, as we have noted, lucky contingencies or hard work and some skill at making suitable arrangements can counter the tendency toward social isolation. Again, it is worth repeating a point made earlier about those social arrangements: they tend to be all the more unstable for disease trajectories that are downward. In short, the worse the disease (or the worse its phase), then the more probability—other things being equal—that the sick person will encounter and feel increased social isolation. "Other things being equal" includes, however, concerted attempts by kin and friends and, sometimes, professionals to decrease that isolation.

References

1. Lowenstein, Prince Leopold of: A time to love . . . a time to die, New York, 1971, Doubleday & Co., Inc.
2. Quint, Jeanne: The impact of mastectomy, American Journal of Nursing **63:**88-92, 1963.
3. Ritchie, Douglas: Stroke: a diary of recovery, London, 1960, Faber & Faber, Ltd., p. 37.

CHAPTER 7

A BASIC STRATEGY: NORMALIZING

The chief business of chronically ill persons is not just to stay alive or keep their symptoms under control, but to live as normally as possible despite the symptoms and the disease. How normal they can make their lives (and their families' lives) depends not only on the social arrangements they can make but on just how intrusive are the symptoms, the regimens, and the knowledge that others have of the disease and of its fatal potential. If none of these factors is very intrusive on interactional or social relations, then the tactics for keeping things normal need not be especially ingenious or elaborate. However, when regimen, symptom, or knowledge of the disease turns out to be intrusive, then sick persons have to work very hard at creating some semblance of normal life for themselves. So may relatives, friends, and, sometimes, the attending health personnel. Furthermore, even when their normalization tactics are working well, various ups and downs of symptoms, new or additional regimens, and the hazards of the trajectory itself, combined with any changes of relevant social contingencies, all potentially threaten whatever arrangements have been established for maintaining a near-normal life and social relationships. Much in the foregoing pages bears on this uneasy equilibrium between what we may term the "abnormalization and normalization of life" (as does material in Part 2). In this section, therefore, the commentary will be confined to a relatively few points.

Many of the tactics discussed in the preceding pages can be read not only as measures for symptom control or regimen management, but as attempts to establish or maintain as normal an existence as possible—like the emphysema sufferer resting artfully at her puffing station, so that bystanders will not think she is drunk, or the man with low energy coaching his friends to expect rapid and unexpected collapse during conversations—they are not to worry, but to "carry on as usual," talking while he listens with eyes closed, until he has regained sufficient energy. Apropos of energy, one inventive child with a cardiac impairment, according to his pediatrician,

> used to be especially fond of playing cowboys and Indians. He was much in demand as an Indian because they were always getting shot and he could rest while he lay down and played "dead."[9]

However, consider even the mild symptoms exhibited by asthmatic individuals with runny noses or arthritic persons with mild pains. The former may explain her rhinitis as "just a runny nose" and watery eyes as caused by "a piece of dust or something in my eye." "They just accept what I say, they can't disagree with me." A man who has low back pain was asked if he did anything to prevent others from knowing about the pain.

> Yes, I do. I either consciously try to walk straighter and throw my shoulders back—or else I just ham it up and play the old man—like I say I had a hard night.
> *Wiener*

FATAL DISEASES AND THEIR INTRUSIVENESS

Perhaps a good place to start the discussion of normalization of intrusiveness is to note how difficult it is to keep relationships normal when people know that a disease soon will be fatal. We have touched on this several times earlier, but the general point is that even if the sick person can forget that he or she is dying, many other people find it extremely difficult to forget this dread fact, even momentarily. They do not realize that a dying person lives for 24 hours a day, 60 minutes an hour, and does not necessarily wish to interact solely as a dying person during every minute. This point is related to "identity spread," which is discussed later, but here we are only emphasizing the especially intrusive character of known fatality.

Particularly instructive in this regard are the experiences of parents with a child who is unaware that he has a disease that eventually will kill him (cystic fibrosis) or that he is actually dying (leukemia). In both instances, "closed awareness" ("don't let him know") and secrecy are the ruling principles of family life. Otherwise, one treats the child just as normally as is possible, within the limits of the necessary regimens and the possibility of fatal crises. Children with leukemia, however, present a much more difficult problem to parents who wish to keep things normal in the face of a much more imminent death. Futterman, Hoffman, and Sabshin have described the anguish of parents' private anticipatory grieving while they strive to maintain a front before the child himself.[3] For much of the time, the child actually may look quite normal and live quite a normal life—but the parents have to work very hard at *acting* normal, unless they can manage to keep the idea of impending death at the back (far back) of their minds. That is a very difficult thing to do. In contrast, parents of children with potentially distant fatalities need not work so hard to maintain an atmosphere of normality in their homes, except insofar as the child may rebel against aspects of a restrictive regimen that he feels make *his* life abnormal.[9] If, however, there is some possibility of a quick, fatal crisis, then the parents may oscillate between maintaining a normal family atmosphere and yet anxiously keeping an eye on the potential crisis.

INTRUSIVE SYMPTOMS

What about the intrusiveness of symptoms? Some, of course, are not even visible. Unless the sick person chooses to show or reveal them, they are exceedingly unlikely even to disturb anyone. Some symptoms are perfectly visible but are not accurately read by people who do not have eyes educated for those particular symptoms. For instance, signs of leprosy may be perfectly apparent to knowledgeable health personnel or to lepers but most frequently are misread (as arthritis, burns, and so forth) by people who, if they knew, otherwise would treat the leprous person quite differently.[4] Visible symptoms, then, are not simply a matter of physiological appearance but of learned perceptual capacities. Nevertheless, it is certainly true that, "other things being equal," symptoms such as twisted hands, limps, pollution smells, and slurred speech are likely to be noticed, and that certain symptoms are more likely to affect interaction adversely than are others.

Identity spread

So powerfully intrusive are some symptoms that chronically ill people often experience what may be termed "identity spread." That is, they undergo the experience reflected in the common complaint made by blind and physically handicapped men and women: people assume that they cannot act, work, or be like ordinary mortals. Blind and physically handicapped people are continually having to cope with people rushing up to help them do what they are quite capable of doing or being treated in other ways as only blind or only physically handicapped. The same is true for the chronically sick who happen to have visible symptoms. Nonsick persons, especially strangers, tend to overgeneralize the sick person's visible symptoms. These come to dominate the interaction unless the latter uses tactics to normalize the situation.

Normalizing tactics

In the section on symptom control, we have seen tactics similar to the following: one hides the intrusive symptom—covers it with clothes, puts the trembling hand under the table. If it cannot be hidden, then its impact is minimized by taking attention away from it—like the tactics of a dying woman who has lost a great deal of weight but who forces visitors virtually to ignore her condition by talking cheerfully and normally about their mutual interests. An epileptic patient quoted earlier chose church people as her friends, remarking that she had coached them so they would continue to talk during her seizures, and offer her a drink of water when she came out of it, but otherwise go on as usual.

Sick persons, then, use tactics to make or keep a symptom invisible or, if it is visible, to reduce it to a minor status. They work hard at keeping their poise. In short, they do their best to keep control of the interaction.

> A husband described his dying wife's control of her hospital situation: gets the nurse to adjust her correctly on a gurney, tells the nurse where to put the bowl in case she gets nauseous on the journey to the x-ray area, where to put her dark glasses which she needs now for protection against the light. "I heard later, how, racked with pain and frequently overcome by sickness, she had cooperated in the jests and never . . . lost her composure and dignity."[7]

In a further example:

> Another patient noted that he doesn't wish to make his girl friend "rack her brains to find comforting words." He thinks sick people do that, because the closer people "are to you, the more they endeavor to appease you and assuage your fears with unconvincing words of solace."[5]

A sick person may even control the interactional situation by making others come to terms with the reality of his illness while yet not letting that reality dominate. Describing her experience with a young professional woman who has multiple sclerosis, an acquaintance remarked on how

> She brings your focus smack down on her abnormality, underlining it . . . at . . . one and the same time addressing you in a manner commensurate with young professional women who are actively involved in interesting jobs and doing it well, and at the same time making you address yourself to the very aspect of her which places all other impressions suspect or in question.
> *Davis*

Failure of tactics

Among the sick people who have the most difficulty in keeping control of interaction are those whose visible symptoms are, by and large, frightening or repulsive to others. Their symptoms tend to "flood" the interaction, affecting it so much that its usual character is destroyed. Instead, awkwardness, embarrassment, and even cruel rejection prevail. Under such conditions, the sick person may elect to withdraw almost totally from ordinary interaction, as did one man who could not stand being out in public with his parkinsonian trembling. (An alternative to such isolation for a very few kinds of sick people is to live in the company of others just like oneself.) The more usual outcome of inability to control interaction, however, is that as much as possible one limits interaction to close family or to friends with whom one can feel maximally comfortable. These latter have learned to live with the visible symptoms without reacting too obviously, or at all, to them.

"PASSING" AND CONCEALING

When the sick person's symptoms are invisible or others are unaware of the disease, then he or she has the option of "passing"—that is, engaging in normal interaction because nobody will define him or her as nonnormal. Of course, if there is some possibility that the symptoms can be rendered visible (as with Toynbee, quoted earlier, who concealed his urinary disability), then the secret must be guarded carefully. Otherwise, one can see the consequences in such stories as that of a middle-aged man who described, still with some sense of shock, having fondled (20 years before) the breast of a seemingly unresponsive date who, alas, turned out to have had a mastectomy operation. After such operations, some women are very anxious about their first appearances in public and very concerned that they should appear as normal as possible.[10] The same is true of those who have had other disfiguring, if publicly invisible, operations. For instance, the author of a book on ileostomy notes and advises:

> The worst calamity the new patient can imagine is that the appliance will fall off. The second worry he has is that people will stare. One or two leaves of absence from the hospital for an hour or an afternoon are reassuring experiences which prepare them for the trip home.[6]

Two researchers have reported graphically on the problems of concealment frequently encountered by lepers in a society that fears their disease.

> Thus, at times, patients will go to considerable trouble to maintain their secret, disappearing from family and friends, elaborately disguising their whereabouts, remaining confined or hospitalized (colonized) indefinitely, restricting social contacts, and/or, less often now than in the past, assuming an alias. In the effort to conceal, individuals may also refuse to seek treatment where they suspect themselves of the disease or even know they have it.[4]

Whereas the person who successfully "passes" in the world of the normal reaps considerable benefits, sometimes the psychological costs can be high.

Those who conceal illnesses, such as various neurological ones, that they believe are discrediting or dishonoring have to carry the burden of anxiety that their concealment may be discovered. At the very least, that discovery may be embarrassing, but it also could be humiliating or destroy friendships or bring about unemployment.

The newly diagnosed leper who decides to "pass" needs to spend a certain amount of time and psychological effort at "working through" feelings about posing publicly as something he or she is not—that is, a normal healthy person. With leprosy, which can be potentially communicable, there is an additional psychological cost to the concealment: lepers then face such difficult decisions as to whether to marry and whether to have close contact with their children or friends. It is no wonder, as noted before, that many prefer to remain in leper colonies, thus avoiding any "risky encounters with normals."[4] However, persons who suffer from the usual run of chronic disease do not have such available colonies. They must decide either to conceal their illness most of the time and from most people or to reveal it fairly openly.

It is worth underlining that there can be severe financial penalties for failure to conceal some chronic illnesses, quite aside from the social penalties. Thus cardiac patients who find they cannot conceal their illness also discover how difficult it is to get back their jobs or, indeed, to get decent new employment: potential employers do not think them sufficiently capable of normal tasks. Worse yet, people who are diagnosed as having sickle cell disease need to be extraordinarily careful not to let insurance companies know of those diagnoses, else they will not obtain life insurance or may speedily lose whatever insurance they have. Becoming chronically ill while on the job and having too intrusive a symptom or regimen, or just having the disease known about, can cost the job.

> Mr. James, who had a job at a department store, expressed concern because now he's about to go on center dialysis and his boss may think he's not capable of holding down the job. He said: "How can I tell people? My boss? What are the people I work with going to say? They'll treat me like I was blind or had a hearing aid or something. I want to go back like nothing ever happened, but they'll say 'He's crippled. He can't do it.' "
> *Suczek*

DISCREPANT ASSESSMENTS OF NORMALITY

The possibility of disagreement between the sick person and others about the extent of her illness is, in fact, a rather general problem faced by all the chronically ill. The parties can disagree in two ways. First, the sick person can believe she is more ill than they believe. Examples would be when she chooses more invalidism than her condition, to them, seems really to warrant. Actually, she may be wiser than the physicians, as for instance when the disease has not yet been accurately diagnosed, so that her complaining is still discounted or partly, but erroneously, attributed to psychological factors. The consequences of such discounting include not just further potential deterioration but even moral accusations leveled against the integrity of the "not really sick" person. He is said to be avoiding work or responsibility, to be not facing up to reality, and so on. Aside from general disagreement about how generally sick he might be, after each crisis or peak period of incapacitating symptoms the sick person may find himself rushed by others, including his helping agents, who either misjudge his return to a state of improved health or simply forget how sick he might still be. Especially is this so if he does not evince more obvious signs of still being sick. All chronically ill people who have partial recovery trajectories or oscillating better-and-worse periods necessarily run the hazard of others discounting their quite possibly slow recovery. ("Act sicker than you look or they will forget quickly how sick you were and still are" was the advice given to one cardiac patient who, after his attack, was about to return to his executive position.)

Probably with more frequency, however, the sick person believes her condition is more normal than others believe. Friends and relatives tell her: "Take it easy, don't rush things." Her physician warns her that she will harm herself, even kill herself, if she does not act in accordance with the facts of her case.

> Two pediatricians report about children with rheumatic fever that: "Activity is a sign (to them) that they are like other children and will not die. Many times a child will go to extremes as soon as the . . . acute phase of his illness is past to prove that he is physically fit."[9]

It sometimes happens that the ill person has accurately assessed how she feels, but others are still thinking in terms of where she *had* been. According to the same pediatricians just cited:

> The difficulty in a large proportion of rheumatic fever cases is to convince the father and mother that their youngster is once again [after an acute phase] ready to lead a normal life. Overprotection can be as detrimental to the child's ultimate welfare as overactivity.[9]

Another instance:

> Mr. James had had a kidney transplant and eventually went back to work, where he found himself having to prove to his fellow workers that he was not handicapped—doing extra work to demonstrate his normality.
> *Suczek*

A rather subtle variant of differential definitions of normality is that the ill person may know how very ill she is but wish others to regard her as less ill and to let her act accordingly. A poignant instance is this one:

> A dying man was trying to live as normally as possible right down through his last days. He found himself rejecting those friends, however well intentioned, who regarded and acted toward him as "dying now" rather than as "living fully to the end."

DOWNWARD TRAJECTORIES AND NEW LEVELS OF NORMALITY

Since many chronic illnesses have characteristically downward trajectories—even if long plateaus intervene between downward changes—the sick person needs to come to terms with where he is now. Said another way, he is in trouble if he does not make arrangements appropriate to his current physical condition. If he continues to act and live as if that condition were only temporarily bad and will soon improve, then sooner or later his arrangements will prove inadequate.

The psychological acceptance of a new level of normality, when it does not necessitate radically new social arrangements, is illustrated by the squared-shoulder comment of a man with Parkinson's disease: "I can live with my symptoms"—implying that he could at least sustain most of his ordinary activities despite some body trembling and occasional dizziness caused by his drugs. It is precisely when the chronically ill cannot make the new kinds of necessary arrangements or cannot settle for the lower levels of functioning that are destroying valued life-styles that they opt out of life. When friends or relatives will not enter into new and more onerous arrangements, necessitated by lower levels of functioning, then they in turn opt out—by divorce, separation, or abandonment. Those who are ill from diseases like multiple sclerosis or other severe forms of neurological illness (or mental illness, for that matter) are likely to face this kind of abandonment by others. However, the chronically ill themselves, as well as many of their spouses, relatives, and friends, are remarkably capable of accommodating themselves to increasingly lower levels of normal interaction and style. They can accommodate themselves either because of immense closeness to each other or because they are grateful even for what little life and relationship remains. They strive valiantly—and artfully—to keep things normal at whatever level that has come to mean.

Of course, their successful accommodation to lower levels of normality—including the worst—depends on the willingness and creativity of all engaged in what is truly a collective enterprise.

The process is illustrated by what happened to one mother whose family accommodated by moving to a house without stairs, by her friends who shopped for her, by her husband accepting a house that is not as clean as previously, and his acceptance, too, of a wife who must now use a cane and cannot frequently travel or socialize outside her own home. Later, the symptoms became more incapacitating, and this woman's mother arrived, uninvited, and "took over." She managed the house, did the cooking, usurped command over the young children's discipline. All this resulted in the husband's withdrawal from household tasks (he could not tolerate his mother-in-law) and with a general breakup of the very delicate domestic arrangements made previous to the arrival of this intruding—if self-defined helping—agent.
Davis

However, the process of coming to terms with lower levels of normality is eased by the fact that symptoms and trajectories may stabilize for long periods of time or not change for the worst at all. Then the persons so afflicted simply come to accept, on a long-term basis, whatever restrictions are placed on their lives. Like Franklin Roosevelt, with his polio-caused disability, they live perfectly normal (even supernormal!) lives in all respects except for whatever handicaps may derive from their symptoms or their medical regimens. To keep interaction normal, they need only develop the requisite skills to make others ignore the differences between each other in just that unimportant regard.

References

1. Benoliel, Jeanne Quint: Becoming diabetic, doctoral thesis, San Francisco, 1969, University of California, School of Nursing.
2. Davis, Fred: Deviance disavowal, Social Problems **9:**120-132, 1961. Reprinted in Davis, Fred: Illness, interaction and the self, Belmont, Calif., 1972, Wadsworth Publishing Co., pp. 130-149.
3. Futterman, E., Hoffman, I., and Sabshin, M.: Parental anticipatory mourning. In Kutscher, A., editor: Psychosocial aspects of terminal care, New York, 1972, Columbia University Press, pp. 243-272.
4. Gussow, Z., and Tracy, G.: Strategies in the management of stigma, Unpublished manuscript, New Orleans, 1965, Louisiana State University Medical Center, Department of Psychiatry.
5. Kesten, Yehuda: Diary of a heart patient, New York, 1968, McGraw-Hill Book Co., p. 196.
6. Lenneberg, E., and Rowbotham, J.: The ileostomy patient, Springfield, Ill. 1970, Charles C Thomas, Publisher, p. 114.
7. Lowenstein, Prince Leopold of: A time to love . . . a time to die, New York, 1971, Doubleday & Co., Inc.
8. Mayers, Marlene: Coping with chronic illness—four persons' views, Unpublished manuscript, San Francisco, 1973, University of California, School of Nursing.
9. Merritt, D., and Davison, W.: Chronic diseases in children. In Wohl, Michael, editor: Long-term illness, Philadelphia, 1959, W.B. Saunders Co., pp. 625, 638.
10. Quint, Jeanne: The impact of mastectomy, American Journal of Nursing **63:**88-92, 1963.

CHAPTER 8

THE BURDEN OF RHEUMATOID ARTHRITIS

CAROLYN L. WIENER

In this chapter we present some characteristic problems facing people who suffer from rheumatoid arthritis. The discussion is meant to illustrate the point that each type of illness brings in its wake particular and specific difficulties, as well as raising the more general issues shared with other chronic illnesses.

RESOURCE REDUCTION AND UNCERTAINTY

Rheumatoid arthritis is a systemic disease affecting connective or supporting tissues. Its etiology is unknown, but the result is that the involved tissue becomes inflamed. When the disease attacks joint tissue, pain becomes the signal for patient and physician. In most cases, the onset is insidious, with ill-defined aching and stiffness. In about one fifth of the cases, severe multiple joint inflammation develops suddenly at onset.[4]

The victim of rheumatoid arthritis is faced with a reduction of personal resources—resources taken for granted by the healthy. More than one kind of resource can be profoundly affected. Mobility may be reduced because of the incapacitating effect of pain, and because weight-bearing joints are so deformed or acutely inflamed as to prevent the arthritic from wearing shoes and to make walking difficult or impossible. A reduction of skill may occur, attributable to increased

---

This case is a modified version of a paper. The burden of rheumatic arthritis: tolerating the uncertainty, *Social Science and Medicine,* 1975. Most of the patients in the study were chosen on a random basis from the files of the Arthritis Clinic of a major medical center and interviewed either in the clinic or in their homes; the rest were interviewed as inpatients in the orthopedic unit. Of the 21 patients seen, 16 were women, 5 men. The ratio and closure figure were determined strictly by availability; however, as reported in the *Primer on the Rheumatic Diseases* published by the Arthritis Foundation, medical studies of rheumatic arthritis affirm that women are affected three times as frequently as men.

pain, loss of dexterity, and loss of strength. Joints are not only swollen and painful, but have limited movement. A progressive disease, it can lead to dislocation of fingers and deformity of the hands. A weakening and then wasting of muscle may occur above and below the affected joint, causing a loss of strength. Pots become too heavy to lift, handbags too heavy to carry, doors too heavy to open. Finally, a reduction of energy can occur, caused by the metabolic effect of the disease (its attack on connective tissues) and also by the circuitous quality of pain (pain drains energy, and fatigue produces more pain).

Rheumatoid arthritis patients learn, along with their diagnoses, that the disease is not only incurable, but its specific manifestations are unpredictable. Often as not, they hear the physician say, "You're going to have to learn to live with it." The disease imposes a burden that many patients would assess to be a less "livable" condition than merely reduced resources, however, and that is its total absence of predictability. The disease does not often follow a strictly downhill course. Most cases are marked by flare-up and remission. Even in the most hopeful case, bad flare-ups may suddenly occur, just as the most severe case may suddenly and inexplicably become arrested. The disease has been referred to as a "rheumatic iceberg," in that the duration is lifelong even when so quiescent as to be no problem,[1] but quiescence and flare-up are themselves unpredictable.

The variability of progression severity and areas of involvement among these arthritics cannot be stressed enough.[1,2,5] For example, they may have reduced mobility but no impairment of skill, reduced energy but no interference with mobility, reduced energy one day and renewed energy the next day. Loss of skill will remain fairly constant if it is caused by deformity, but is variable if caused by swelling. The other resources (mobility and energy) can also fluctuate. Thus uncertainty pervades the life of arthritics: on any given day, they do not know beforehand about symptoms: (1) presence (if there will be *any* pain, swelling, or stiffness), (2) place (area of bodily involvement), (3) quantity (degree of disabling intensity), and (4) temporality (whether the onset will be gradual or sudden, as well as duration and frequency of flare-ups).

Pressing their claims on the arthritic in consequence are two imperatives: (1) the inner, or physiological world, monitored for pain and disability readings by the day, sometimes the hour, and (2) the outer world of activity, of maintaining what is perceived as a normal existence. Like two runners in a nightmare race, these two imperatives gain one on each other, only to be overtaken again and again.

When the physiological world gains a lead, the arthritic finds that severe pain is more easily endured by withdrawing from interaction: "I go off by myself . . . to cry, or swear, or both." If these flare-up periods increase, both in duration and frequency, the uncertainty problem will be resolved by the certainty of more bad days than good. The activity world, to extend the metaphor, will have lost the race. The arthritic will have become an invalid and will be increasingly isolated. However, the very uncertainty that makes the disease so intolerable also militates against acceptance of invalidism; there is always hope for another remission.

THE HOPE AND THE DREAD

All illnesses provoke theories of causation—circumstantial relationships as discerned by the sufferers—and rheumatoid arthritis is no exception. Part of their psychological tolerance stems from the hope that a remission can be correlated with something they can control, such as diet. Belief in dietary causal linkage may be sustained for a long period, only to be upset by another flare-up.

Hope is primarily directed, however, toward control of symptoms. Uncertainty as to how long a given flare-up will last makes an arthritic vulnerable to folk remedies suggested by friends, kin, and other patients, as well as by the arthritic's own reading of literature. Self-doctoring ranges from ingestion of celery juice or massive doses of vitamin E, to use of plastic bags filled with powdered sulfur and wrapped around the feet at night, or to a poultice of ginger root steeped in vodka and an alloy. The clinic provides a place where such ideas can be exchanged. In addition, there is a trial-and-error approach to the use of applied heat and change of climate, diet, and appliances.

Even if relieved, arthritics are haunted again by uncertainty, for the relief they have attributed to a specific measure may indeed have been an independent, spontaneous remission; still, they continue to hope until proven wrong. When a measure is believed to be providing temporary relief, as acupuncture is presently doing for some, the hope becomes extended: "Maybe some week the 2 days relief I'm getting will become 3." The reversal of the hope for remission (that is, the hope that the arthritis will perform "on cue") is of course less common, but that this hope can also be felt serves to emphasize the exasperating quality of the uncertainty. One patient reported she waited 6 weeks for an appointment with an acupuncturist, then was refused treatment because the disease was in remission and might be reactivated by the treatment. Even those whose deformities make their invalidism appear irreversible to others, have so often experienced the oscillations of flare-up and remission that they continue to hope. One man, almost totally incapacitated by his disease, had driven miles to the clinic and waited there 4 hours for what turned out only to be a refill on his prescription. He explained his patience to the interviewer, "Maybe if you're around when they find something new, they'll try it on you." Similarly, a woman who evinced almost total withdrawal from social contact still hoped to return to adult school "some day."

Countering such psychological tolerating is the fantasy of disease progression. An arthritic may hope for longer and longer remissions, but may simultaneously be dreading the possible course of the disease—the next place it is going to hit. As one expressed it, "I think of my body like a used car, waiting for the next part to go." In a clinic they see others who are worse off, and when they say, "I'm lucky it's not in my . . ." the implication is clear. All this leaves them constantly on the alert. Pain, when it hits in a new place, makes their uncertainty intolerable. Knowing the possibilities is one thing; having them occur is another. Arthritics must wait to see if the pain persists, and while waiting the uncertainty is heightened. They begin to worry that the new pain is not really arthritis but something even more serious, requiring professional diagnosis. They are inhibited by a selectivity when reporting symptoms: "If I tell the doctor about all my aches and pains, he won't be listening when it's really important."

The dread of a progressively worsened state brings with it a dread of dependency, expressed frequently as "I don't want to be a burden." Some fear dependency on kin so much that they will live alone at tremendous sacrifice. To illustrate, one woman, now 44, recalled the early onset of her disease, telling of her move then to an apartment and her struggle to continue working:

> It was harrowing. When I got up in the morning my feet were so painful I couldn't stand on them. I would slide out of bed and with my elbow and rump get into the bathroom. I learned to turn the faucets with my elbows.

For her, the activity world pressed on, in spite of the decreased pace of her physiological world, and in fact brought her through this early period into a long period of remission.

NORMALIZING IN THE FACE OF UNCERTAINTY
Covering up

Arthritics develop a repertoire of strategies to assist in normalizing their lives, that is, proceeding with the activity imperative *as if* normal. The principal strategy employed is that of "covering up," concealing the disability and/or pain. Variations of the following quotes appear throughout interviews with them: "If anyone asks me how I am, I say fine," "When I walk, I walk as normally as possible—if I walked like I felt like walking, I'd look like I should be in a wheelchair." Covering up does not constitute a denial of the disease, in the psychological sense of the word. As described by M. Davis, "it is the rejection of the patient of the handicap as if it were his total identity. In effect, it is the rejection of the social significance of the handicap and not rejection of the handicap per se."[3] Unsuccessful covering up invites the risk of interrupted interaction via offers of help, or questions ("skiing accident?"), or suggestions of home remedies ("Someone at work suggested I try alfalfa. I wanted to tell her I'm not a cow."). Interaction, thus interrupted, impedes the ability of arthritics to view themselves as they would prefer to be viewed by others.

There are various conditions under which covering up is impeded. An arthritic who is subject to sudden attacks, such as freezing of the back with resulting immobility, is a case in point. One woman who had such an attack while visiting her hometown found that she could only walk at a creeping pace—some of the time only backwards:

> People on the street would ask if they could help . . . the embarrassment was worse than the pain. I thought they would all think I was crazy or drunk.

Visibility—use of a cane or crutches, wincing when arising from a chair or getting out of a car—is another impediment to covering up. When the arthritic has the additional problem of deformity, the potential for covering up is further reduced. Inability to cover up leads to reactions such as those evinced during an interview by a young woman who had struggled to remove coins from her wallet with badly deformed fingers. She said poignantly:

> I have just become aware of how uncomfortable people get around me. They don't want to be reminded of sickness; they are fearful for themselves, just as young people don't want to be around old people.

If covering up is successful, a price may be paid, however, because this strategy can drain the person's already depleted energy. ("Do you know the stress you put your body to trying to walk straight so people won't see you can't walk?") Concomitantly, there is increased awareness of pain and stiffness once within the confines of the home. Patients report that after situations in which they "toughed it out," they give in to their fatigue and nervousness, dumping their irritability on close family members.

Keeping up

Armed with their strategy for covering up, and lulled by their good days, arthritics struggle to keep the activity imperative ahead in the race, through efforts at "keeping up"—keeping up with what they perceive to be normal activities (preparing a holiday meal for the family, maintaining a job, participating in a family hike). They may carry through with an event successfully, then suffer increased pain and fatigue; yet that risk is taken precisely because such payment is not at all inevitable. Keeping-up efforts may also continue—despite their seeming irrationality—to maintain self-images. To illustrate, one woman, who had a period of relief as the guest of her daughter, not being allowed to use her hands even to open a car door, suffered another painful onset the first day home when she cleaned her sink and bathtub, because "I hate dirt."

Another keeping-up problem occurs for those who have mastered the art of raising their thresholds of pain toleration. They may be slow to read the signs of body dysfunction, as with, for example, one patient who for a month walked around with a broken leg, thinking his pain was arthritic.

Some engage in excessive keeping up—supernormalizing—to prove a capacity, or to deny incapacity, or to recapture a former identity. Hence pain-free and energetic days invite frenetic activity or catching up. The result is often (but again uncertain) that time is really lost through increased pain or decreased energy the next day. Supernormalizing further ties in with the uncertainty of ascribing causes, as with a patient who knows her condition worsens during the summer, but is unsure about whether it is exacerbated by the weather or by her increased activities in her garden. Furthermore, some engage in supernormalizing as a device to distract themselves from pain. This too may bring increased pain, increased fatigue and sometimes fever.

Justifying inaction

Successful covering up and keeping up can even turn out to be a mixed blessing. Although their relationships generally remain normal, when arthritics cannot get by they then find it harder to justify inaction. Again this is related to the uncertainty of their physical condition: they cannot legitimize their current abnormality, because sometimes they are normal and other times, although hurting, they were covering up or keeping up. This difficulty increases when others have stakes in their remaining active, as with a young mother whose condition worsened when she tried to keep up in sports with her husband: "My husband really doesn't understand. He is very healthy and he thinks there is some magic formula that I'm not following—if I would just exercise, or have people over. . . ." Accusations may not always be so overt, but others' stakes are nevertheless troublesome, as with a tennis pro who found it necessary one day to cancel a lesson only to be observed out playing the next; he began to worry that his club members were suspecting him of malingering.

Paradoxically, arthritics who attempt to present a normal image to the world nevertheless are perplexed when not taken seriously by others. There is a longing for understanding, for a sensitivity by others, that goes beyond their justifying of inaction. An arthritic may be proud that "nobody knows" and yet wish that "somebody cared." The same person can boast of a mastery of covering up ("If I went around looking like I feel, no one would want to be with me") and still say, "I don't think anyone has any idea how much pain I have." As expressed by another:

> Pain is essentially private. Sometimes you wish for someone to understand and be patient with your pain. To allow you to have it!! I do not mean sympathy or pity.

Pacing

Accompanying the use of the various normalization strategies is the really main one of "pacing"—identifying which activities one is able to do, how often, under what circumstances. Since these activities are what lead one to view oneself as normal, pacing is the means arthritics have of maintaining an uneasy equilibrium between the abnormalization and normalization of their lives.

Arthritics know it takes them longer to complete daily tasks. For example, they allow extra time to get dressed, since putting on hose and tying shoe laces can be agonizingly painful. "I dress a little, lie down and cry a little, and dress a little more." They decide if they can work a 3-day week, or do housework for an hour; they know if they shop they may not be able to cook. Housework is not spontaneous, but planned around periods of respite. During remission, the arthritic may have resumed activities or assumed new ones, but then be forced by a flare-up to cancel some or all of these. Again the uncertainty factor operates: pacing is not a static decision but necessarily fluctuates with the monitoring of the physiological imperative. Along with pacing decisions run all those problems mentioned earlier in relation to justifying inaction.

Decisions on activities (which ones, how often) are also affected by the time that is lost when resting between activities. Rest is prescribed, but not always honored, for symptom control; however, when pain and stiffness are bad, patients find they have no choice but to lie down. For some, rest becomes a ritualized part of the daily regimen—an anticipatory device for coping with pain and decreased energy. Time expended in rest results in a further cutback of desired activities. It also may lead to a contingent existence. Since covering up and keeping up have become an integral part of their mechanism for coping, many arthritics prefer to rest and then make a fresh assessment of the physiological imperative rather than suffer the embarrassment of cancelling plans.

RENORMALIZING: THE ADJUSTMENT TO REDUCED ACTIVITY

Renormalizing—that is, lowering expectations and developing a new set of norms for action—is directly related to the frequency and duration of flare-ups. This means, for example, settling for half a window being clean when an arm begins to hurt in the middle of the cleaning, or, as one put it, "Sometimes I cannot open a jar; I'll bang it on the sink, and finally say damn it, put it away and have something else."

Renormalizing can have serious import if rheumatoid arthritis strikes early in life, as it did with one young woman who, instead of pushing to the limits of action, decided to redefine those limits. She recalled her decision:

> At one point I was struck with fear. If I got interested in a guy I'd have to be on the go and I knew I couldn't go out one night and then the next day. Maybe I set up enough blocks, so it didn't happen.

Increased frequency and duration of flare-ups will spiral renormalization into lower and lower expectations. New coping mechanisms replace old mechanisms for tolerating uncertainty. For example, when constant use of a cane made covering up impossible, one man adjusted with a substitute philosophy: "this cane opens many doors."

Eliciting help

Part of the step downward, of renormalization, is the accepting of help. Arthritics in fact may have to elicit help—to be dressed, cooked or shopped for, helped in carrying out tasks at home and at work. If they live alone they may have to ask a neighbor for help with zippers and buttons. Once the need to ask extends beyond the immediate family, the act is weighed for importance. For example, one may consider asking a neighbor to unscrew the cork from a wine bottle but decide to forgo the wine; however, when pain and stiffness make public transportation a forbidding prospect, one will ask to be driven to the clinic.

Eliciting help threatens the arthritic's psychological tolerating, for it reinforces the dread of dependency. Here is perhaps the most extreme illustration: one woman stood without moving for 2 hours, when her back froze while she was visiting a friend in a convalescent home. She would not ask for help but waited until she could walk home, one mincing step at a time. Throughout her interview she expressed her fear of "being a burden."

Hesitation in eliciting help also stems from the fear that others may not be responsive. Problems of justifying inaction surface again when others have stakes in action. One patient, who is supposed to wear braces on her hands at night and sometimes forgets to put them on, said: "It's too much of a strain to pull up the light comforter I use, let alone get out of bed and get the braces." Yet, no mention was made of eliciting help from her husband. This was the woman referred to earlier, who feels her healthy husband "really doesn't understand." Within their own families, arthritics have preferred certain helpers because of this matter of differential responsiveness. For example, one will only accept help from her son. His role was merged with his growing up. At onset of her disease 13 years ago,

> My son was then 5 years old, and *he* had to take care of *me*. I'd sit on the side of the bed at night and he'd put my legs up, *he'd* tuck *me* in. Many times he had to dress me from top to bottom. My older daughter and sisters have tried to help me but I don't feel comfortable having them do for me.

Eliciting help decreases the arthritic's potential for covering up and keeping up. A case in point is the woman who took a leave of absence from work because she could no longer perform to her own satisfaction; she could not lift the heavy robes on her sales job and could not stand having other workers do it for her, since, "after all they're being paid the same thing as I." Deprived of her strategies for normalizing, she could no longer view herself as self-sufficient and capable, as she wanted to be viewed by her co-workers. Lastly, awkward or embarrassing situations may occur when eliciting help, and these only serve to highlight dependency. One man, for example, was forced to ask a stranger in a public toilet to zip his pants up; his fingers are closed to the palms of his hands, and he had left his trusty buttonhook at home.

Since eliciting help is a tacit acknowledgment of the gain that the physiological imperative is making on the activity imperative, an additional strain on psychological tolerating stems from the identity problems that arthritics suffer when their eliciting of help results in a role reversal. Thus a young mother described her distress at being unable to pick up her baby. As he got older he learned how to clasp his legs around her. Now 5 years old, he must open milk cartons for her. She is anguished at her reduced capabilities as a mother: "My son wants to play games and I have to rest; I call him and he runs away, knowing I can't run after him." Male arthritics who have lost their dexterity must rely on wives to carry heavy objects or open garage doors. Women frequently complained of their diminished role as homemaker, using language like this:

> I liked being a housewife and keeping the house immaculate. The house is my responsibility, and now my husband (and children) have to do much of the work.

Role reversal may result in a permanent change in the household's division of labor. Helping out has now become a new job. Then, tolerating the uncertainty has lessened, and dependency need no longer be a dread, for it is all too clearly a reality.

BALANCING THE OPTIONS

When tolerating the uncertainty, arthritics are ultimately engaged in the precarious balancing of options—options somewhat limited because of their already reduced resources of mobility, skill, strength, and energy. Indeed, a balancing is involved in all of the pacing decisions (weighing the potential benefit of acupuncture against the climb up two flights of stairs "that will just about kill me," or the potential withdrawal from church activity against the loss of social interaction). The options are constantly presenting themselves, each to be met with an ad hoc response: whether to keep up and suffer the increased pain and fatigue, whether to cover up and risk inability to justify inaction when needed, whether to elicit help and risk loss of normalizing.

At the same time, another very worrisome balancing can be in operation. Arthritics may be put on strict drug regimens: the drugs hopefully provide control—to help the arthritic normalize. Patients with long histories of frequent flareups often undergo sequential trials of potent antirheumatic drugs, all of which can have adverse side effects.* Some have difficulty in recalling the sequence of these trials; frequently they were not told what was in their injections and did not ask. For them, the balancing was weighted in favor of relief at any cost: "When you're hurting like that you have to do something." Even after an accumulation of drugs, and faced with total hip replacement due to drug-induced osteoporosis,† one arthritic attested she would have taken the drugs even if she had known the results: "I'm glad to have had those years of life."

There is a varying degree of knowledge among arthritics as to specificity of possible side effects. Usually the specific realization only follows an actual occurrence; even then, direct causation is not always fully comprehended. One patient who suffered from cataracts, which is acknowledged to be a side effect of corticosteroid therapy, referred to her eye problems as "arthritis in the eyes." She was indeed also suffering from iritis, a recognized accompaniment of rheumatoid arthritis, but she did not appear to have made a connection between the cataracts and her 8-year ingestion of corticosteroids. Some persons, when warned of the potency of their drug, purposely do not ask for specifics: "If you know what to look for, your mind overpowers you." They are avoiding the potential strain of balancing.

Knowledge of the specific possible adverse effects of a drug heightens the psychological tolerating by placing an additional responsibility on the arthritic. ("I cut down on the Butazolidin when I have a good week. Recently when I had a flare-up of neck pain I had to increase it again."; "I know when I take more than 16 aspirin a day my ears start to ring.") Pain increases vulnerability—an arthritic may rationally resist starting on a drug with known side effects, but when the pain becomes intolerable such resolution is tempered by the uncertainty of duration:

---

*Soluble gold salts, antimalarial compounds, phenylbutazone, indomethacin, and adrenocortical steroids—generally, but not exclusively, in that order.

†A loss of bony substances producing brittleness and softness of bones, likely to be particularly severe during the course of corticosteroid therapy.

"When the pain is this bad you feel like you'll never come out of it." The psychological burden is increased further by another uncertainty. What "works" (that is, keeps inflammation and pain controlled) for one day or one week, may not work the next.

Balancing decisions are therefore constantly being reassessed. One must decide what the options are, must decide between them by calculating consequences, must face the consequences whatever (with uncertainty sometimes) they actually turn out to be; furthermore, one cannot rest easily or for long on previous definitions and decisions about options. Thus, about balancing there is at best only temporary certainty. This, too, the arthritic must learn to live with.

References

1. Bland, John H.: Arthritis: medical treatment and home care, New York, 1960, The Macmillan Co.
2. Bunim, Joseph, editor: Symposium on rheumatoid arthritis, Journal of Chronic Diseases **5**(6):609-778, 1957.
3. Davis, Marcella Z.: Transition to a devalued status: the case of multiple sclerosis, Unpublished doctoral dissertation, San Francisco, 1970, University of California, San Francisco Medical Center.
4. Primer on the rheumatic diseases, New York, 1964, The Arthritis Foundation.
5. Walike, Barbara, Marmor, Leonard, and Upshaw, Mary Jane: Rheumatoid arthritis, American Journal of Nursing **67**(7):1420-1426, 1967.

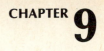

THE FAMILY IN THE PICTURE

All through the foregoing pages, we have seen how ill persons' attempts to manage their medical crises, regimens, symptoms, diseases, and social relations have been abetted—and sometimes hampered—by kin, especially those of the immediate family. Although physicians and other health personnel are perfectly aware that family members are "in the picture" and can be useful or harmful in conjunction with their own professional efforts, nevertheless what happens in the home is mostly over the horizon, is partly or completely invisible to them. *That* is the "family's responsibility." To the extent that the family fails, that is *their* problem. Today health workers do engage in more teaching of patients and family about procedures, regimens, and so forth, but they do little actual monitoring or evaluation—except through medical inspection itself.

At any rate, what is involved in managing chronic illness at home can be very complex and, as always, involves far more than the strictly "medical" aspects of illness management. The illness impact on the family (especially the spouse or parent) is often the key factor in how successful is the trajectory management. In this chapter we will touch on that interaction, although the main emphasis will be on the types of work performed and on the conditions and consequences of that work both for the control of the illness and for the personal identities of family members.

TYPES OF WORK

In the preceding chapters we reviewed various types of work done by relatives as well as by the ill, including crisis, symptom management, regimen management, time management, and body resource work. In Part 2, in chapters on hospitalization, others will be emphasized, especially clinical safety work, comfort work, and psychological work. All of those include subtypes of work, for example, preventing crisis, handling crisis, rectifying crisis. Anyone who has been through a diagnosis of an unusual or even just severe chronic illness knows—as the autobiographical accounts by those who have written about their suffering tend to highlight—the tremendous amount of work often involved in obtaining a reliable diagnosis and "running down" options to the treatments initially suggested, as well as in getting the physicians to "talk straight" during succeeding phases of the illness. An appropriate term for all of that is "information work."

At home there is an additional problem: how to coordinate the various kinds of illness work with the ordinary "home work" that is entailed in keeping a household running. That includes (1) house provisioning, cleaning, and repairing, (2) all the tasks involved in feeding family members, and (3) keeping the family afloat financially, as well as actually doing the chore of keeping payments on bills current. Since all of those tasks must be done *and* the symptom, regimen, and other illness tasks must be done also, it follows that ways of handling both types of work—simultaneously and sequentially—must be arranged, maintained, and then rearranged when contingencies or new conditions arise that call for their alteration.

THE BURDEN OF WORK

Rather obviously the burden of work when an adult is ill falls on spouses, especially when the children are too young to help much or are old enough to have left home. Unless the family can afford nurses, housekeepers, and other helping agents, it will fall to the spouse to do all the things that the ill person cannot manage but that need to be done—not only the medical activities such as helping with monitoring symptoms and carrying out regimens, or with medically related activities such as cooking the right food for diet—but doing those necessary mundane things that the sick person can no longer do (lifting objects, fixing the plumbing, carrying the groceries, driving the car, even shaving).

The arithmetic of time and energy for all those tasks can total up to quite an exhausting, even crushing burden. Here is the treadmill of a wife whose husband has Parkinson's disease; she had to retire from her job to care for him:

> I have been lifting him (with my bad back) and turning him and all that. In a hospital, you have a person doing the trays, another doing something else, and someone else doing something else. In the home, you are doing the cooking, the serving, the trays, the housecleaning, the wash everyday, because you have to strip their beds everyday, you have to keep their bed fresh. I do everything. I have learned to cut hair. And shave him. Another thing: your time has to be the patient's time. No matter how you plan it, it never quite works out like you would like it to, because you find yourself having to rest when they are resting, and that doesn't always work out. When they are resting you are doing something else. How do you get this rest? . . . . A typical day? Well I don't go to bed until 1 in the morning. That is when I get a little bit of rest. At 4 in the morning, I get up and give him his medication. About 6 a different medication is

due. After that is the bathing. Then I wash. Sometimes I have two washloads full. Right after the bath comes breakfast, because they have to have their meals at a certain time because of being on medications. I make it easy for him. Like if we have watermelon, I take all the seeds out. I cut up his meat. Before you know it, it's time to do housework, then it's time for lunch. I eat at the same time. I better or I won't get a chance later.

It is worthwhile to note that this wife does not even report on the more complex problems of domestic interaction but essentially only on how she substitutes for the physical failures of her husband and the extra work of caring for his failed body.

Even when a sick husband is perfectly capable of doing a great deal of work around and for the house, and takes full responsibility—indeed pride in the responsibility—for his regimens and symptom monitoring, the crisis work and events during the crisis itself can add up to enormously stressful work and devastating cumulative impact on the spouse. The wife in question is not only on the lookout to save her diabetic husband from shock and coma, but

> whether it is insulin shock or diabetic coma I don't know. He will regress back into the war and I am a Jap and he is going to get me. One time he beat my chest until it was just black. The last insulin shock he had his undershirt around my neck before you could snap your fingers. I said now Fred, let me go; it is my voice that calms him. To this day he won't believe me that this happened. It is a constant vigilance with this man, and yet as a wife you have an obligation. At other times you feel like, oh my gosh if I could just wash my hands, but you don't and can't. I've told the doctors help me, I need some help with this man. I can't get it. It is tearing me down. My doctor says "I can give you pills to calm you down but it is your problem." He is tearing me down because you are always on the lookout. How he is, does he need something? What can you do? You can't leave him. I can't get doctors to help. At the stress clinic they told me either leave or it is your problem. And he is getting worse.

TRAJECTORY WORK AND THE DIVISION OF LABOR

As in all households, couples share the work, however unequally, in some fashion, including now the medical and medically related tasks. The latter set of tasks is related, of course, to what kind of illness the couple must manage, as well as to its phasing. How they share the ensuing work will, in turn, be affected not only by the degree and kind of physical impairment, by the kinds of financial or other resources they can use as physical substitutes, and by what ailments or illnesses the caring spouses may have—but also by a multitude of other considerations. These latter include especially the kind of affectional bonds existing between husband and wife, the degree of ready or easy communication between them, the perceptiveness and willingness of the sick person to do his or her own identity work as well as help to sustain the spouse through the trials, tribulations, and ordeals of requisite trajectory work.

Thus the ways couples can divide tasks between them, although unspecifiable in general, can be well understood in light of the contextual conditions that affect the shared (and joint) domestic division of labor. To make that point graphic, here is a brief description of one young couple's management of her diabetes. She takes responsibility for carrying out her regimens and for monitoring her own symptoms. Also, both wife and husband talked separately to the interviewer about her ability to exert self-control in the face of temptations like tabooed food. Yet because her diabetes had gotten out of control when she was pregnant, to the point where he actually saved her life by rushing her to the hospital, the husband has become quite anxious about future crises. So he has become much more of a regimen control agent than previously, warning her when he thinks she is (or is about to) overexert herself, go beyond reasonable physical limits. Nevertheless, he leaves the ordinary symptom monitoring and daily regimen management entirely to her.

Another instance is the wife of a man with Parkinson's disease who leaves the medical activities to her husband, who is perfectly capable of doing them; yet she finds herself drawn into doing work (acting as a behavioral control agent, essentially) that she believes entirely necessary. This work entails cautioning him against and preventing his engaging in activities that she believes he can no longer do without strain—or without damage to his self-conception if he fails—such as taking on too many graduate student tutorials, traveling to distant conferences, or continuing to make appearances, as an authority in his field, on TV panels, since he has tremors and has somewhat slurred speech now.

How unanticipated the division of labor can be in doing the total trajectory work (neither one of the couples just described could have dreamt of what tasks they might be called on to perform) can be further drastically illustrated by the poignant account given in *Death of a Man* by Lael Wertenbaker.[9] Her husband had decided to manage his dying, and living while dying, of cancer in his own way, using physicians as little as possible. All went reasonably well including his control of increasing suffering, until the last extremely painful and lingering days when in desperation he decided to end his life. His first attempt at suicide failed; the second succeeded, but only because she aided him.

There is one type of outcome of illness that we term a "comeback trajectory," where the stricken person recovers at least some measure of functioning. Here the spouse's work is especially visible. The comebacks are variable not only in degree but in rate of recovery and in amount of help required from others during the various phases of comeback. In general, though, we cannot emphasize too much how important are the spouses (or other kin who have either much commitment or can spare time, like mothers and sisters) in the comeback process. The kinds of work needed are very varied—depending on the symptoms, regimens, and the psychological states of the ill. Also, the sick person cannot do many of the tasks either alone or at all, especially when still in or just over the acute phase of the illness. As the recovering person progresses further along the comeback trail, the balance of work in the division of labor will shift away from the helping agent toward him or her. However, retrogressive days or weeks—a not infrequent happening—bring about a rebalancing, again, in seesaw fashion. In those chronic illnesses where acute phases tend to reappear periodically, there will be many comebacks, some retrogressive from further back and others from not so far back, so that the division of comeback labor will tend to change in tandem, periodically, as well as in rhythm with the phases of recovery.

PSYCHOLOGICAL WORK

It will come as no surprise to the reader that among the most important work that a caring spouse does for the sick wife or husband is "psychological" work—the tasks running all the way from relatively uncomplex ones (like "bucking him up when his spirits are low," doing diversionary work to fill in his or her empty hours, helping to keep composure in tough physical or social situations) to those that involve very complex maneuvering. Often the maneuvering is kept secret from the other—like a wife throwing tasks his way so that he can still feel "like a man," or making other subtle moves that sustain the ill one's sense of identity. In those instances, a spouse is not merely a substitute physical resource but a facilitator of the stricken one's impaired action and a sustainer of important facets of his or her identity.

What is not so evident perhaps is that the sick person may also be doing psychological work for the hard-working and hard-hit spouse. Some of that work may not be evident to the spouse and may indeed be kept under cover; otherwise it would not be really effective. Yet, a striking feature of some couples' relationships is that the work is knowingly reciprocal, as each sustains the other in ways small or large. These couples stand in stark contrast to those who draw further apart while managing their lives under the gun of a debilitating or otherwise terrible illness. The former couples tell the interviewer that the illness has in fact brought them closer together, as shoulder to shoulder they fight the illness and its consequences. Among the potential consequences, however, are widening or narrowing of what can usefully be termed "the marital gap." A great deal of work goes into trying to keep that gap from appearing, widening (or widening further if it is already present), or becoming, eventually, marital disaster. Adding to that possible eventuality is the propensity of either sick person or spouse to keep his or her feelings from being expressed to the other—if only mistakenly to protect the other, although sometimes that is really necessary for physical or psychological health reasons. This kind of secrecy work can be exhausting but manageable, but it also can be maritally disastrous.

Yet the expressive and other types of sharing can be so intense that, during phases when the sick person is feeling better or has come finally out of the worst period, the healthy spouse may experience great difficulty in "letting go" (to use the poignant term of one of them). Letting go means not only that she or he need no longer stretch to the limits to extend the ill one's boundaries of activity, or even that they can get back to the more normal styles of domestic life; it also means the well spouse's getting reengaged with his or her own more independent life whether it be the occupational or social aspects. Hence this solemn, binding, and eloquent statement by one wife to her husband, now relatively well after a long recuperation from congestive heart failure: "You have to promise me that you will be very careful. Then I can do my thing and not have to worry. So that you can do *your* thing—and I can do *my* thing. So we can have what *we* want."

Her statement represents negotiative work of the most complex and certainly the most intense order. Even so, the letting go—the return to more normal personal lives—requires the fuller cooperation of spouses who not only mind their *p*'s and *q*'s, but sustain in a variety of expressive and complex ways the voyage back to normalcy. Also, the admonition, "promise me that you will be very careful," can serve to remind us that work is going on—and is going to go on—rather than being merely a reflection of domestic relationship. The work of the ill and their spouses bespeaks "travail," a French noun that has two appropriate meanings: "work" and "suffering."

OVERLOAD

When the work becomes almost unbearable, spouses speak in terms of being overloaded, of having stretched the limits of their energies and their tolerance. They may continue to "bear it," but not without recourse to using outside resources—psychological or physical—and not without being able to get away for respite. They "take off" for some days away from home, or they make arrangements for weekly or at least occasional getting out of the house—to visit with friends or just to be alone. The spouse may elect to work, not so much for the money as to get relief from both the work and the situation at home. Some cannot manage to get away, either for financial or for psychological reasons; perhaps they have no close kin who can spell them in their work, or at least not for long, and so there builds up in them a feeling of "no exit." This can strain the marital relationship so much that they reach the point of decision. Divorce or separation is the

most common solution, although sometimes the couple may despairingly con-
clude that a nursing home is the only sensible solution. Understandably, the principal conditions leading to the overloading—carrying a maximum burden—of the
spouse include a great deal of work endangered by the illness, an unsympathetic
or uncooperative sick wife or husband, a poor marital relationship to begin with,
and a greatly unbalanced sharing of the division of labor. Despite all that, some
spouses' sense of obligation is so strong, or their memories of past marital closeness still so pervasive, that they hang on until the very, and often, bitter end.

BIOGRAPHICAL WORK

Among the most consequential and difficult personal tasks—for the sick
and their spouses, as well as for their children—are those concerned with their
respective identities. Biographies and autobiographies written by the ill or their
spouses or parents make quite clear how much work they must all do in facing
what is happening to themselves, in figuring out psychologically how to come to
terms with what is happening.

Let us look at the ill person first. A series of interrelated elements enters
into his or her coming "to terms" or failing to come to terms. To begin with, there is
now, and perhaps to some degree forever, the failed body: a body function, a body
part, or several of them. This failure results in a changed conception of the body.
As a victim of multiple sclerosis said after the disastrous onslaught of her disease:
before, she never thought about her body because it could do everything she
wished, but now it bound her irrevocably to the house and virtually restricted all of
her movements, so that she was almost completely dependent on other family
members for everything she wished or needed.[2] Some sick people, perhaps especially stroke victims, make a distinction between mind and body, with the mind
able to do everything while they are trapped in their immobile bodies. Agnes de
Mille, after suffering a bad stroke, wrote about her injured brain and the incapacitation of one entire side of her body, but also wrote at length about her unimpaired and still creative mind.[5] People who write or talk about dying from their
cancer can have an initially paradoxical body conception: for a while after the
diagnosis, they have a perfectly healthy-looking body, but inside they know that a
fatal disease is destroying this body.

As the foregoing instances illustrate, body conceptions imply linked conceptions of what we have termed "biographical time." This is evidenced in
thoughts of expressions such as, "I am trapped in this body forever," or "I am
crippled forever," or "I *will* make this comeback, if I work hard enough at this
regimen and all it entails." When Cornelius Ryan, the well-known author, was
diagnosed as having cancer, he decided that his primary goal was to write a last
and important book (*A Bridge Too Far*) for which he had already done several

years of research—and he must complete it, not only for financial reasons (to leave sufficient money for family support after his death) but also for his own self-esteem.[8] In fact, he decided against being treated for his cancer at Stanford University, treatment that might possibly have prolonged his life, because he could not possibly take all his research materials to California. Since nobody knew how long he would live, his next 3 years became a tense race against time: would he finish before he died or would he not? As his body became increasingly wasted, his body conception changed accordingly, and understandably, too, his sense of "not much time" increased in tandem with both changes.

In the course of working out who one is, who one can be under altered circumstances, the sick person also grapples with physical and social limitations. Coming to terms with, living with, those limitations can take a great deal of "psychological" work. It is not always easy to give up activities that have brought great meaning to one's life; yet it may be necessary to do so, either in part or totally. Sick people may work through this grave problem by finding substitutes: if I cannot play tennis any longer, then I can learn to paint pictures or become an expert and successful stamp collector. Alternately, the physically immobile person may simply continue to do more of what he or she did in a minor way before, such as writing poetry and reading books. However, coming to terms in the deepest sense with a failed body, or with dying itself, necessitates much wrestling with self. In our interviews with the ill, and in published autobiographies, we have noticed various biographical processes: reviews of past experiences apparently necessary for "letting go" of aspects of self, reviews that sum up or take into account lists of one's capacities that can be used in the future, reviews that represent closures on life before death, and imagining future events, so vividly sometimes that they can be prepared and planned for. Coming to terms in this deep sense is not necessarily a for-once-and-forever process: it may be done repeatedly as a disease worsens and new limitations are forced on oneself.

What should be immediately apparent is that the spouse, and often the children, go through some of the same processes. They too have to face limitations forced on themselves because of the sick family member's incapacities or potential death. Not only the physical incapacities are involved, however. The sick may withdraw into themselves, and so marital or parental relationships change drastically.[3] A wife may begin to doubt her femininity when her husband can no longer make her feel like a woman, either sexually or through ordinary social intercourse. The healthy spouse, too, can engage in what we may term "biographical projection"—working out in imagination and thought what the future looks like in light of the partner's illness. Thus the impact of a severe chronic illness is felt not only in terms of increased physical labor, altered financial status, and family mood, but also in the profoundest sense in terms of altered identities.

Identities are not necessarily altered for the worse, since people do discover aspects of themselves quite literally because of the illness, working out correspondingly satisfying new modes of existence. Indeed, one of the more remarkable moments in sick persons' and families' lives is if they transcend a sickness and its more dreadful consequences. Again, autobiographies and interviews point to certain moments or days when lives rendered discontinuous by the illness—shattering the body conceptions, time conceptions, self-conceptions—are somehow brought together into a new and transcendent better *self,* permitting even dying persons to face their last days with a sense of integration and fulfillment. Although a great deal of this biographical work must be done by the person himself or herself, we do not mean to suggest that all of it is necessarily done alone. Again, family members sensitive to each other will help each other with their biographical problems. The saddest tales are when one or more of them fail each other, and so tend to fail themselves as well.

CHILDREN IN THE FAMILY

What of the children in the family? How do they work? How are they affected? How are the parents especially affected by a sick child, as opposed to the effect on a spouse of the partner's illness? These are difficult questions to answer because of the current lack of research bearing on them, but a few comments here should prove useful.

Although there are surely many similarities between the existential and work situations of the children and the parents, there are also some differences. Pediatricians pick up some of them empirically.[4] Thus for cystic fibrosis:

> Maintaining this therapeutic regimen puts a tremendous burden on the resources of the family—in most instances a burden borne almost entirely by the mother.

Also:

> There are many families where there are two or more affected in the family. The overwhelming burden inherent in caring for [more than one affected child] needs little elaboration.

For children with congenital heart conditions:

> Parents are tortured by guilt about prenatal cigarette smoking, x-ray therapy, tranquilizer use, even exercise.

> Many parents, often with adequate incomes, never go out together, as they fear leaving their baby with a sitter.

For the nephrotic syndrome:

> Anxiety and guilt are apparent to some degree in almost all cases, especially in the parents. . . . Was it the cold remedy I gave him? . . . Did I neglect the early symptoms? Many parents . . . are seriously depressed and must be supported and encouraged. . . . Family conflicts may be created. Parents, especially the mother, may become over-permissive and overprotective toward the patient. This may exaggerate sibling rivalry.

More systematically, we can note the characteristic features and impacts of having an ill child in the family as follows:

1. The very young child can have no conception of his own illness course or how it must be managed—that is, no trajectory projection. The parents do have such a projection and act on it, but of course the burden of managing the work and the psychological burden of the projection both fall squarely on them.[7]

2. In many families, the work falls unequally on one parent or the other. Frequently, as the pediatrician has noted, the mother is the primary worker, fitting all the illness work in and around her other work; with great frequency, however, parents will spell each other or divide up the labor in sensible or convenient ways. Thus the husband may do much of the searching for information or some of the heavier physical agentry, whereas the mother checks out special schools and ferries the child back and forth to the physician's office.

3. However, more or less tension may arise over the parental division of labor, and for a variety of reasons. In consequence, the marital gap between parents may increase—to the point where one or another proposes divorce or just leaves. The strain of dealing, over a long period of time, with certain child illnesses (cystic fibrosis, for instance), in terms of work and undoubtedly in psychological terms too as well, results in a high proportion of divorce and separation.

4. The phase of life cycle in which parents find themselves when their child develops, or is born with, a severe chronic illness can also make a great difference in how they are able to manage, and how successfully, the child's illness. Regimens can be costly, and parents only recently married may have no savings; illness in an offspring during the late teens and the psychological impacts on him or her can be very difficult for parents who themselves are in the midst of their own life cycle strains.

5. A particularly difficult problem faces parents of children with illnesses like cystic fibrosis or certain genetic cardiac conditions, where relatively early death is almost certain. The problem is how to "raise" the children: how does one juggle the calculus of rearing them in a normal way, giving them a normal conception of themselves, as opposed to confronting the reality that this may actually

increase the child's medical hazards and lead to a much earlier death? Also, the more abnormal a life the child is guided into, the more psychological problems may perhaps develop for the child.

6. The issues raised in paragraph 5, of course, also relate to the issue of parental control, which is intensified when a child has to be kept on a medical course that is as safe as possible through strict adherence to regimens and careful monitoring of symptoms. When the ill child has siblings the control problem becomes compounded, since he wants to eat what they eat, do what they do. Often additional problems develop when the special treatment given the ill child—or so it appears to the siblings—makes them in turn more difficult to "manage," either equitably or at all!

7. Other major roles for a parent may be those of crisis agent and protective agent. Understandably, the control agent activity feeds into that and can make for much tension between child and parent and between parents themselves, as well as for the siblings, as noted earlier. Protecting the child may also involve protecting him psychologically against the actions of the outside world, reducing the possibility of stigma, keeping the child out of social situations that may be wounding, and so on. This can sometimes amount to "picking up the pieces" with the child—doing identity work—when the wounds go deep.

8. The child's developmental phases and risk taking are another feature of the management of childhood illness trajectories. As Jeanne Benoliel has noted, diabetic children, for instance, pose changing illness and psychological problems as they develop physiologically and socially. Each developmental change can shift physiological responses, so that regimens must be altered. But life cycle developments also mean that the child moves from a school nearby to one more distant, moves into a phase when sports are important, when dating is important. At each juncture, having diabetes (or other illnesses) can have major psychological and social impact. The impact is of course mainly on the child, but the parents may be directly or indirectly—and profoundly—affected themselves, as may the siblings.

9. All of the factors just outlined point inevitably to the potentially great consequences for parental biographies and identities. The parental guilt discussed by the pediatrician quoted earlier is one consequence when the illness is genetic, or when the causation is unknown but parents define it as their own negligence. Bearing the burden of being the child's chief all-around agent, including standing between the child and death or poor development of unlimited other threats cannot help but have an impact on parental identity. The impact is not always for the worst, however, since bearing that burden can give joy, be challenging, and provide fantastic rewards. Growing along with a child who is growing up successfully and could not do so without those extra and sometimes heroic

efforts expended by oneself, can be among the most soul-satisfying of experiences, as some of the autobiographies written by these parents make quite clear.

10. Finally, the work and psychological impacts of a child's illness spill over, as already touched on occasionally to the lives of siblings in different ways than parental illness.[2,6] Thus siblings may enter into the division of labor by baby-sitting, monitoring for symptom control, and acting as control agents. They may feel guilty if they fail in those jobs. They may feel lonely during the ill child's medical crisis when parental attention and physical presence vanish over the horizon. They may resent being part of the illness regimens, as when they must share the diabetic diet imposed by a one-kind-of-meal mother. No doubt they are profoundly affected when a sibling almost dies or actually does die, not only in the sense that they mourn, but also that they imagine their own mortality. Probably we know less about the impacts of illness on the siblings than that on the parents; about both, however we are still in the realm of relative terra incognita.

References

1. Benoliel, Jeanne Quint: Childhood diabetes: the commonplace in living becomes uncommon. In Strauss, Anselm, and Glaser, Barney, editors: Chronic illness and the quality of life, St. Louis, 1975, The C.V. Mosby Co., pp. 89-98.
2. Birror, Cynthia: Multiple sclerosis, Springfield, Ill., 1979, Charles C Thomas, Publisher.
3. Colman, Hila: Hanging on, New York, 1977, Atheneum Publishers.
4. Debuskey, M. editor: The chronically ill child and his family, Springfield, Ill., 1970, Charles C Thomas, Publisher, pp. 40, 41, 63, 184-85.
5. DeMille, Agnes: Reprieve, Garden City, N.Y., 1979, Doubleday & Co., Inc.
6. Ipswitch, Elaine: Scott was here, New York, 1979, Delacorte Press.
7. Massie, Robert, and Massie, Suzanne: Journey, New York, 1976, Warner Communications.
8. Ryan, Cornelius, and Ryan, Kathryn: A private battle, New York, 1979, Simon & Schuster.
8a. Strauss, Anselm, Fagerhaugh, Shizuko, Suczek, Barbara, and Weiner, Carolyn: The social organization of medical work, Chicago, 1984, University of Chicago Press.
9. Wertenbaker, Lael: Death of a man, New York, 1957, Random House.

CHAPTER 10

THE SOCIAL ARRANGEMENTS OF DIABETIC SELF-HELP GROUPS

David Maines

Self-help groups are among the more amazing phenomena of the last two decades. They are now very numerous, many of them organized around the chronic illness concerns of their members. Some groups are linked officially or unofficially with the medical specialty associations, although others keep their distance from the physicians and their associated institutions. The self-help groups have received some serious study,[1] but they have not been closely examined in terms of how they appear to, and what they might do for, their participants. For that reason we have included in this book a case illustration written by David Maines, a sociologist who is currently studying a number of diabetic self-help groups whose members consist mostly of young adults. His account is revealing in that it gives us some idea of what these groups may be doing for their members. It would be wise to keep in mind, however, that although all chronic illnesses create common problems for their sufferers, each type of illness also brings specific sets of problematic issues to the foreground, depending on such factors as prevailing symptomatology and whether death looms in the background. What is much needed for future understanding, both of these self-help organizations and of the problems of their members, is a considerably broader array of types of groups that are focused on different kinds of chronic illness. Meanwhile, David Maines's chapter will help us to understand some of what young adult diabetics are struggling with, as that "what" bursts out in the group sessions.

WHAT IS A SELF-HELP GROUP?

Contemporary writings about self-help groups, or mutual aid groups as they also are called, sometimes have a faddish quality about them. These groups currently are a "hot topic" among human service professionals, partly because the recent proliferation of such groups can be seen as confirmation of the dehumanization of health care agencies and institutions about which those professionals have been so critical. Self-help groups, vast numbers and varieties of them, are regarded by some as part of the human potential movement or as an offshoot of the consumer's movement. They might well be that, but as Katz and Bender[1] point out, the concept of self-help as well as various forms of helping organizations goes back many hundreds of years. The Middle Ages saw a number of loosely organized extrafamilial helping systems: the Friendly Societies of England (there were 191 such societies before 1800) gave help to the poor, sick, and old; the early guild system of Europe and later the unions of England and America were formed on the principle of mutual support; in addition, religious and ethnic community organizations in large urban areas as well as the multiplicity of voluntary organizations across the country have functioned to neutralize the depersonalization of mass society. In this historical perspective, modern self-help groups are merely a recurrent form or expression of the people with common interests or problems seek to take some measure of control over their lives.

Recent studies of self-help groups have been concerned mostly with three problems: defining what a "true" self-help group is, assessing the outcomes of participation in self-help groups, and identifying those factors that characterize the self-help process.[2] The first problem, in my opinion, is a misguided one, and is reminiscent of those early, sterile efforts in the study of occupations and professions to distinguish a profession from a nonprofession. The latter two problems are more important because they seek to understand the basic mechanisms through which such groups operate and whether in fact the groups improve the quality of life for their participants. We need information on these matters. They pertain to how people organize themselves with respect to their problems, how involvement is perpetuated, how group-generated solutions can be used in daily life, and how group participation fits in with other sources of help or treatment. The phenomenon in question, in other words, is multidimensional. It involves (1) the persons themselves who must handle their emotions and experiences, (2) patterns of participation in work, family, and community life, and (3) the interorganizational linkages of helping organizations that form the matrix of care delivery.

Whereas investigations at any level of analysis or scale can provide useful information, studies of self-help groups must to some extent maintain a focus on the persons for whom these groups and organizations are arranged to help. In addition, they should maintain some focus on the processes and activities that constitute self-help. Unfortunately, few investigations have successfully held both these foci. As in most studies of small groups, we typically find reports in the literature of the variables (such as empathy, group solidarity, reinforcement, catharsis) that are thought to characterize self-help activities rather than of the actual practices of empathizing, reinforcing, constructing, maintaining solidarity, and so forth. Accordingly, there is a corresponding loss of viable perspective on the persons who have no choice but to deal in some way with extremely troublesome conditions—cancer, heart attacks, diabetes, alcoholism, and so on.

The list is an extensive one, but I will concentrate here on diabetes only. This chapter will provide an account of the diabetics and their self-help groups that I have studied and come to know recently. I will first locate them in the general activities of the American Diabetes Association, address the question of how these groups came into being, and comment on the processes of group formation. The sharpest focus, however, will be on the self-help process—that is, on how diabetics, by getting together and trying to help one another, attempt to cope with their lives and their diabetes. The imagery I want to put across perceives the encounters and events of everyday life as flowing through the self-help group and thereby constituting its substance. Problems at work, parental relations, pregnancy desires, vacation plans, going to school, the flu—the stuff of life for all of us—become exaggerated for the diabetic, and that "stuff" becomes the very content of the group process. Chem strips, seeing a physician, trying to maintain a normal blood sugar level, establishing and maintaining a proper diet—the activities and concerns that are mobilized by the disease—become very specific areas of attention and discussion among participants. The shifting varieties of dialogue of the self-help process (explaining, badgering, describing, denying, listening) are thus "filled" with the events, relationships, and emotions that occur outside the group and between the meetings. The meetings can be thought of as an attempt at living one another's experiences and reliving one's own experiences. In this sense, one of the goals of the group process is to enable participants to become observers and healers of their own and other's inner mental lives and styles of living. The "external" and "internal" aspects of that process merge into a flow of substantive themes and topics. By focusing on that flow, I hope to convey a sense of the ordinary lives of persons with diabetes and the way those lives are expressed in and through the self-help group.

THE CONTEXTUAL ARRANGEMENTS AND INCEPTION
OF DIABETIC SELF-HELP GROUPS

The diabetic self-help groups in Chicago have been organized through the efforts of the Northern Illinois Affiliate of the American Diabetes Association. Non-ADA groups have been started in the past, but they rarely have lasted long, and some exist in name only. It therefore is important to examine the ADA's activities and to identify within this organization those mechanisms through which interest and energy have been mobilized and coordinated.

The Chicago ADA covers the 20 northern counties of Illinois and has a membership of 5000 people. In terms of Tracy and Gussow's classification,[3] it is a Type II self-help group. These types are foundation-oriented, with the "emphasis on promoting biomedical research, fund raising, public education, and legislative and lobbying activities." The Chicago affiliate is engaged in a range of such activities. It provides a number of educational programs for individuals with diabetes, school personnel, nurses, dietitians, physicians, and the general public. In 1981 the affiliate sponsored four symposia on diabetes that focused attention on the newest information concerning research and treatment. The affiliate also provides a summer camp program for children with diabetes. This program involves a 3-week stay that entails education, recreation, and camping activities not generally available elsewhere for these children. In 1981 the affiliate awarded about $40,000 to young medical researchers in northern Illinois for investigations of diabetes. Of great importance as well are the free diabetes detection tests provided through the affiliate. Approximately 12,000 such tests were given in 1981, and of these, about 10% of the recipients were found to have abnormal blood sugar levels.

The mechanism within the ADA that has organized nearly a dozen self-help groups in Chicago is the Family Relations Committee. It is composed of several professionals (nurses, counselors, social workers) and ADA personnel who focus mostly on problems of outreach. In 1982 they organized a 2-day leadership conference for diabetics interested in being trained as self-help group leaders. Out of that conference emerged the current groups. The leaders are lay persons, nurses, and clinically trained social workers, and the groups meet in a variety of settings, including churches, ambulatory care centers, hospitals, and private homes. The groups are organized primarily on the basis of age; thus there are groups for adolescents, young adults, and senior citizens. Groups also cater to needs based on circumstances, such as being parents or spouses of diabetics. Roughly 6 months after that first conference, a reunion was held for the group leaders, once again organized by the Family Relations Committee. The purpose of this second meeting was to discuss the problems and successes of each of the groups. Issues of group composition, management of disruption, development of trust among group participants, and recruitment dominated that meeting. It is expected that such reunions will become a common feature of the monitoring and communication processes of the affiliate.

While the ADA is linked to the self-help groups through these sponsoring activities, it is clear that the linkage is a weak one. At the most, guidelines are recommended (for example, groups cannot suggest medication and should not use personal solutions to problems for other members' problems) and suggestions are made for recruitment, format, and group process issues. The groups exist under the auspices of the affiliate, but there are no charters and chains of command, and few rules and monitoring processes exist. Once formed, the groups appear to be very autonomous, and they come to value that autonomy a great deal. The affiliate in effect becomes only one of several resources for group members to use as they see fit, and there is a wide distribution of sentiment among members about exactly how useful the affiliate actually is. These groups exist as pure examples of Tracy and Gussow's Type I classification[3]—"truly mutual help organizations." That mutual help, and the problems inherent in it, can be explicated with information gathered through interviews with members of the group for young adults and my participation in several of their meetings.

THE YOUNG ADULTS GROUP: PROCESSES AND PROBLEMS

It is important to realize how difficult it is for diabetic self-help groups to form themselves into functioning entities. The ADA provides the leaders only with minimal training and resources. From then on, it is up to the participants themselves. The group formation can be characterized as one in which an aggregate of strangers, who have in common only their age and their diabetes, come together and attempt to create group trust, collective empathy, and a range of practical solutions to the everyday problems of living as a diabetic. In the process of this transformation, the rules of public life must not only become suspended, they must be reversed. Displays such as crying, divulgence of private life, and expressions of fears, all of which one is expected to suppress in public life, are now expected to become normal features of the group encounters. Few people are prepared for these new expectations and stylizations of self. It is little wonder, then, that the first few meetings focused primarily on very concrete issues involved in being a diabetic: diet, shots, dosage, symptoms, exercise.

By the time I had become acquainted with the group, it was well into the transformational process of becoming a more self-revealing group and one in which greater interpersonal risk was being taken by the members. An important aspect of that process was the emergence of "core members"—those who attended the biweekly meetings regularly and whose participation pushed the dialogue toward the interpersonal, emotional, and life situations that disrupted their ability to control or manage their diabetes. The themes of the dialogue represented ongoing concerns and dilemmas that are embedded in the selves of the participants and the sets of relations that shape their lives. Before discussing those theories, let us look briefly at the issue of turnover in group membership: who leaves and who stays.

Staying and leaving

The composition of the self-help groups changes as people enter and leave them. In the course of 3 or 4 months, for example, the young adult group changed from being predominantly male to being predominantly female. It also changed in size: at the beginning there were about 15 members, and now the membership has stabilized at around 8—a number that, according to Jim, the group leader, is the maximum for effective group results. Those who have left the group seem to have had in common the search for easy or quick answers to their diabetes-related problems or an intolerance for other's disagreements with their thinking. One woman left after the group in effect told her it was not alright for her to cheat on her diet periodically; another left when she encountered group resistance to her decision to take off weight rapidly instead of integrating a weight reduction program into her diet. A man who had developed a personal treatment regimen based solely on taking vitamins (which was based on his elaborate theory of the etiology of the impairment of the pancreas) left after group members began probing how he felt emotionally about having diabetes. Clearly, self-help groups are not for everyone.

Two features appear to characterize the core group members. First, some are in the process of forming friendships with one another that extend beyond the group itself. These friendships are not defined so much by patterns of recreational or sociability relations as they are by a caring for the quality of one another's lives. They are bonds of concern. Second, each participant gets something from attending the meetings that is meaningful in terms of his or her life situation. Kevin, for instance, rarely says anything during the meetings, but he finds a predictable form of association that has been absent in his life since his youth. Bill, whose diabetes is out of control and has not significantly improved, finds a sincerity of caring that he never received from his family. Jim is in very good control, has a stable and fulfilling occupation, and is working on forming a circle of friends. His health and personal stability, however, depend on his participation not only in the diabetes group but also in Alcoholics Anonymous, Narcotics Anonymous, and individual counseling. The core group members, as illustrated by these three examples, clearly bring different life situations to the group occasions, and group processes become meaningful parts of those situations. At the juncture represented by that meaning, the group and the forms of relations "outside" the group become inseparable. There is a uniqueness and a complementarity of personal meaning and group participation that must occur if involvement is to be ongoing.

Embedded in these processes of staying and leaving are the substantive issues dealt with by the group. Here are some of the more persistent ones.

Dealing with physicians

It is incumbent on all diabetics, especially those who are insulin dependent, that they establish good working relationships with their physicians. That relationship has been called a "partnership" by some to indicate how closely the two must work together on issues of diet, life-style, and medication. Yet dealing with physicians can be extremely problematic, and matters such as emotion, mood, style, gender, work, and relationships with others feed very directly into that problematic issue. This process was evident, for example, in one of the group's sessions, which will now be recounted.

Kate, a high school biology teacher, got the flu, which resulted in wide variations in her blood sugar levels. Her husband and father both became quite worried and kept asking her when she was going to see her doctor. When Kate finally made an appointment, in her words, "I began screwing up my diet because I lost the fear. The doctor somehow will take care of me so I won't have to take care of myself." Her physician, Dr. Smith, is a strict one. "He doesn't baby his patients, and insists on strict conformity" (from an interview with Jim, also one of Dr. Smith's patients). Many patients, unlike Jim, can't deal with this physician's unyielding standards. Kate remarked, for instance, "I really don't want another doctor who will tell me what I want to hear. Dr. Smith is okay, but I still don't get along with him. I don't like his attitude. He'll say 'what are you doing now that you weren't doing before' in a very condescending way."

A long discussion followed that statement, about milk and meat exchanges, about grades of fattiness in meats, and about substituting cheese for eggs (which Jim said were the wrong substitutions for Kate). Dr. Smith, Kate said, insisted she was not following her diet, which she insisted she was, and she told him she did not want to discuss it anymore. In an almost pleading way, she told the group she cannot have merely a physician-patient relationship with him. "He wants more of a father-daughter relationship. He has his rules and he's very dogmatic and won't accept any variation." Kate paused, looking at each member, and the group paused along with her. "He talks at me, not to me. When I spoke up, he yelled at me and told me not to come back." Ruth said that Kate needs to have a relationship where she can express her individuality. "Go and find another doctor," Ruth advised, and recommended a physician who was lower key and a better listener. "I'm so easily intimidated by authority," Kate responded, "which is strange for a teacher in charge of 30 students!" Jim responded by offering the observation, "but you keep going back for more aggravation." Kate replied that she is also seeing a nutritionist who is giving her different advice about her diet. "She says that Smith is all wrong, and I've chosen to listen to her." Ruth broke into the discussion by saying, "I know what you mean. I know the situation you're in—I've been there. I mean, you're the only one who knows how you feel, and you have to make the choices." That empathic response kept Kate going a while longer with more complaints about the physician. "I paid $52 for a blood test and 5 minutes of yelling. He won't even tell me about the studies he told you about (referring to Jim) and I'm a biologist!" Bill responded, "It's your choice to go to the doctor you want, and I wouldn't go there." Jim interjected that the American Diabetes Association can provide a list of physicians but would not recommend anyone in particular. "Well, that's all useless," Kate replied, "because they won't give information about a specific doctor unless it's in writing, because I wrote and I've been waiting for 3 weeks. So there. The ADA isn't much help."

The choice of a physician and the working relationship with him or her is a complex one. It is widely recognized that diabetic treatment regimens must be individually tailored, but it is less widely recognized that physician-patient relationships likewise must be individualized. Diabetes is extremely sensitive and can become easily imbalanced, especially for people like Kate and Ruth, both of whom are physiologically unstable. Kate felt trapped in the relationship with her physician and could see no viable way out. The group conveyed an understanding for that sense of entrapment and told her that she had alternatives. The group recommended some concrete choices. The solutions were only beginning to emerge, however, and the dialogue about Kate and her physician continued in subsequent meetings.

Badgering or caring?

It always is difficult to convey in written form the intensity and emotional complexity of some interactional episodes. Such episodes obviously are not planned—nor could they be. While certain topics might be predictable, the emotion that carries the participants through them can flash unexpectedly, sometimes catching even the most "tuned in" members by surprise. Such intensity was displayed in two related episodes occurring in back-to-back meetings. They primarily involved Jim, who is trim, clean-cut looking, and articulate, and who possesses an unalterable conviction of the necessity of good diabetic control, and Bill, who is underweight, whose face and neck show the red blotches of past and present boils, and who is chronically out of control. The episodes pertained to what the self-help group sees as the bottom-line diabetic reality: are you going to live or die? The forms of the episodes shifted in the moving and intertwining themes of badgering and caring.

> The first episode emerged from Bill's discussion of his losing his job and how his control had become somewhat worse since then. Jim asked Bill if he had gone to see his doctor to get his regimen adjusted, and Bill said that he had not. "I can feel when my sugar is up a little," said Bill. "It's up a bit right now, maybe 200 or 300." Jim challenged Bill. "I bet it's higher than that." "Well, it might be, but, you know, I don't know," replied Bill. "Well, let's test it," Jim persisted. Bill wavered, saying it was not necessary because he knew his blood sugar was a "little bit high" and that was all he needed to know. While Jim persisted further in trying to get Bill to test himself, Claire took some Chem strips and an Auto-lite out of her purse. This was not a planned act, as testing often occurs during group meetings. "Look, I'm not trying to badger you," Jim insisted. "It's just that I care. I care about you!" With a shrug, Bill eventually agreed to test himself. There was a period of light talk about taking tests at work and with friends ("they like to watch me shoot up," Ruth said) while each person drew a blood sample, timed the Chem strips, and matched the colors against the chart on the Chem strip bottle. Jim's was 110, Claire's was 120, and

Bill's was 500! There was no victory dance. Bill sat with his shoulders hunched over and his head down. Jim put his hand on Bill's shoulder and said forcefully, "Maybe I am badgering you, man, but you gotta take your shots and follow your diet. If you don't, you're gonna die!" "Well, I'll pay more attention—maybe" (Bill frequently ends sentences with "maybe"). "You don't have to bargain with us," Claire said. "Don't bargain with us. You're not making a contract. It's up to you to make a contract with *yourself*." Bill sat there, listening to Jim tell him not to make promises he cannot keep, because it will just lead to guilt trips. At that moment, the only thing Bill could do was to sit there. He was unable to argue with the Chem strip.

The second episode occurred just after Kate's series of complaints about Dr. Smith. Jim turned to Bill and said, "You said to Kate it's your choice to choose a doctor. What doctor are you going to?" "To the same guy I've been seeing the past 13 years. A family doctor," Bill replied. "You need a specialist, an immunologist or a diabetologist," Jim said, and then went on to describe how the knowledge of diabetes has changed and the resulting need for specialization. Bill shrugged. "Are you afraid to see someone with more knowledge of diabetes?" Jim asked. For the first time, Bill became animated. Typically, he slouches in his chair, conveying minimal involvement. This time, however, he sat upright on the edge of his chair and leaned toward the others. "The doctor wants you on a perfect line, like this," he said, and with his hand made a straight line in the air. "I'm like this," he then said, making a wavy line in the air, indicating compliance but not strict conformity. "No," Jim retorted, "you're like this!" and made a zigzag line in the air. Their exchanges were rapid-fire. "I can tell when I've got some sugar," Bill responded. Kate interjected that Bill's conception of accuracy might have been satisfactory 15 years ago but is unsatisfactory today, and that Bill is conforming to outmoded standards. Then Kate said, "I don't think we should harp on Bill. We told him what's good control and now it's up to him. We shouldn't badger Bill." Jim started to respond to Kate, but Bill interrupted, saying, "Everything just has to be so perfect. I'm not in perfect control. I know it!" Almost simultaneously, Jim and Ruth said that each little act adds up to a lack of control. Bill responded, "I'm not going to force myself. I don't eat breakfast sometimes because I'm not hungry," to which Ruth responded, "You don't know what not being hungry means. You might have a blood sugar of 600 at nine in the morning! Of course that wouldn't make anyone hungry if you had a blood sugar that high!" Kate jumped in again. "The only thing we can tell Bill is what is right and the rest is up to him." Jim responded, "But there's a technology now. Twenty years ago we didn't know what we know now, and the better we get to the norm the better we have a shot at normalcy." A brief discussion occurred about complications, and then Kate said, "Bill has to realize that next year he might have to be on dialysis or have his toes amputated!" Ruth interjected, "I've lost the train of thought" as Bill was saying, "Well, hell, I might get all fouled up!"

The discussion continued for another half hour at the same pace and level of intensity. The group was convinced that Bill was killing himself. The dialogue included mention of Bill's diabetic grandmother whose leg was amputated, Kate's grandmother who cried when Kate was diagnosed, and Jim's father who had diabetes for 20 years and never took care of it. At one point Bill insisted that he could do 30 push-ups to demonstrate that he was really healthy. The group rejected that offer of a display. Bill and Jim never really communicated, as symbolized by comments made toward the end.

> Bill: "I'm tired of taking tests. I'm tired of being a diabetic, and those charts and tests are always reminding me." Jim: "I'm not going to be a self-fulfilling prophecy, which is what Bill is—a walking self-fulfilling prophecy." Kevin sat silently through it all.

The issue was never resolved. Later, talking with me, Ruth said that she came out of that session feeling worse than when she went in. Jim confided his frustration, both with himself for becoming angry and with Bill's rigid noncompliance. The intensity of interaction bred that frustration, as well as an apparent tenseness. Ruth kept reminding everyone that it was alright for them to show anger and that the group should develop trust, and Kate was moved after the meeting to explain herself to Jim. She was only trying to keep Bill from not coming back. "Well, if I was harping on Bill," Jim told her, "I'm going to continue to, because it's a crime not to use knowledge and do the best you can." The intensity as a property of the group, dissipated, but the frustration was carried into the parking lot with each individual as they all went to their cars.

The life situations of group members

All of the foregoing dialogue and emotional display, with the urgings, denials, and negotiations, was rooted in the real-life situations of the persons involved. These situations are formed by each person's past, in how those pasts are currently interpreted and understood, and in the sets of relationships in which they are now involved. These situations establish the standpoints of the dialogue and are the contexts of the personal meanings that members bring to the group occasions. These situations thus must be understood if the dialogue and emotional displays are to be adequately comprehended. Consider the following.

> Bill grew up in what he called a "crazy house"—his family. His father was an alcoholic and was very belligerent toward everyone. He bullied his family and periodically had to be "locked up." All of Bill's brothers and sisters have left home as a result, and his mother is now seeking a divorce. When Bill was growing up, he avoided his family and its stress and instability. He would come home from school, get his bicycle, and stay away from his house as much as possible. After being diagnosed as a diabetic, he was made to feel as if he did not have long to live and was treated as a cripple. "You're a goner now," his

mother had said to him. His grandmother had been a long-term noncompliant diabetic and had had her leg amputated when Bill was 10 years old. That was part of what Bill described as a general "I-don't-care" attitude of the entire family. "I've still got that attitude," he said. "I don't think about the future." In that attitude, Bill actively lives his fatalism.

Jim's father was diagnosed as a diabetic when Jim was 7 years old, and after that he and his two sisters were served the same diabetic diet that his mother served to his father. Jim resented the "little bit of this and little bit of that" meals. He had his first glucose tolerance test when he was 11, and was found to be borderline diabetic. The meals he so resented as an adolescent thus probably postponed the onset of his disease. His father became increasingly absorbed in self-pity and his illness, to the point that there was little time or energy to spend with Jim. Jim resented that as well, and their relationship deteriorated to the point of fistfights and Jim's alienation from his family. Jim graduated at the top of his high school class and was admitted to Northwestern University on an academic scholarship. "Then I was free. I was into instant gratification to the max—bound and determined to make up for the times I could have only two cookies. You know, I'd sit down and have 2 pounds of Oreos and a half a gallon of milk and just pig out." He also became heavily involved in alcohol and drugs, soon lost his scholarship, and dropped out of school. Eventually, he joined AA and NA, but acquired the life-style of working excessively—100 to 120 hours a week—which itself was destructive. "I bought a house, but my house wasn't getting attention. And *I* wasn't getting any attention. Nothing was but my work and my bank account. I knew things weren't right. I could be driving home and all of a sudden have to go the bathroom and not be able to make it." During a 3-week hospitalization after diagnosis, he inquired about support groups for diabetics, and when the ADA leadership conference was held, Jim attended. His conscious approach to his diabetes is referenced by his now-deceased father's approach: "I don't want to deal with my diabetes the way my father did. I don't want to kill myself that way." Jim also does not want to oppress others with his diabetes the way his father oppressed him with his, and thus he seeks every means to achieve stability in his personal life. He compulsively seeks that stability.

Ruth comes from a stable Jewish family—a loving family, as she characterized it. She was diagnosed when she was 14 years old, and for about 5 years she was "real good about it—a real martyr." Her parents were supportive, making sure Ruth always had the best cut of meat, giving her injections, sending her to camp, and so on. Ruth said they were overly concerned and that her mother was always trying to protect her. Her first physicians were older family doctors, and her "regimens" were established through rough trial-and-error processes. Her insulin was not effective enough, and she started developing muscle atrophy from her shots. The physicians were patronizing when she started having episodes in which she would pass out. In her late 20s, she went to Joslin's Clinic in Boston for a "kind of drying out period. They really charted me." By that time, however, she was quite labile, and her diabetes now requires very close management. She works for the Social Security Administration, and she can "feel" the daily stresses affect her blood sugar levels while at work. She has a problem with her boyfriend, who does not fully understand that she *must* have certain *kinds* of food, in certain *amounts*, at scheduled *times* of the day. It makes staying at his apartment for the weekend problematic when he forgets to buy the food that Ruth needs. She has previously participated in encounter groups and says she has some experience in dealing with emotions. That process does not intimidate her as it used to. She has come to realize that she cannot be normal like a nondiabetic; she can be normal only *as* a diabetic. "You have to do the best you can to have the best quality of life you can have," she said during one of the group meetings. She punctuated her point with the story of her nondiabetic older brother who drowned a year ago. "He didn't take care of himself and he's dead and I'm not. But my parents always said how we have to be careful of Ruth because she's the one with the physical problems. Well, that's not always true, because we all have to accept our conditions and deal with them the best we can."

These three life situations—although many of the events that constitute them occurred long ago—are part and parcel of the self-help group. They are the often unspoken dramas that shape the substance of group dialogue. Occasionally they become the very substance itself, at which point persons are encouraged to try dealing with their own life situations. That process can vary widely. The dramas of one's life situation sometimes can be used as a justification for denial and poor control; sometimes the members will obsessively depict the details of their lives and thereby sorely try others' patience; sometimes someone's eyes will fill with tears as self-insight is gained. It is all part of the self-help process, as the participants attempt to make their way through their lives and to help one another the best they can in the self-help process.

CONCLUDING REMARKS

At this particular historical moment, the growth of medical self-help groups such as those for diabetics are linked to the increasing prevalence of chronic illness as well as to the acute care orientation of medical institutions. The long-term nature of chronic illness, the recursive effects between its physical and psychosocial factors, and its penetration into the very nature of participation of family, work, and community life require a wider based response than that currently provided by professional institutions and agencies.

People want to have a "say" in their lives. Beyond that simple and fundamental human condition, however, diabetics *must* have a say in theirs. That imperative was one of the dominant themes of the young adult self-help group. Sometimes the choices made were not especially in the best interests of good health, but to the participants, even for those who left the group, there was no debating that they *would* have a say in their treatment. However, a second theme was that the members must develop a skill, knowledge, and discipline to make choices that would result in increased health and postpone or forestall complications. This was seen not only in the badgering of Bill but in the concern over whether Kate would resolve the conflict with her physician. It is in the latter theme that so much of the drama is seen.

In using the term "drama," I wish only to convey how intertwined the self-help processes are with the symptoms of good and bad control and the life situations and contingencies that these young people face. Those intertwinings have their own scripts and plots. Bill's grandmother, his red blotches, his elevated blood sugar, and his unemployment and binge eating form the plot of fatalism, and he currently can find no other script except "I don't think about the future." The group members are earnest in their attempts to provide Bill with a new script, but they first must help him to envision a happier ending. Certainly that process is affected by the scripts and plots of Jim's life situation. He, along with Kate, Claire, and Ruth, can share much of Bill's attitude. They have all held it themselves before, but they can not fully understand it, and in their insistence that they will help Bill to help himself, the process of empathy is revealed as a fragmented and partial one. Self-help in that sense becomes a very individualized process. The group cannot "do it" for the individual, and on that score, Kate is right. Empathy is a tool that allows the participants both to enter into one another's experiences and to escape the feeling of terminal uniqueness. Having escaped, however, the person must assume the identity of the main character in the self-management plot. The reinforcing, sharing, tolerance, and trust that are thought to define the self-help process are revealed as problems rather than variables. They wax and wane with shifts in concern and mood, and the group must remind itself of what it as a group is about. It is free to do that, given its autonomy, and it must deal with its own collective mistakes and successes.

Sometimes those mistakes and successes are hard to define, however. Jim told me recently that Bill has stopped attending the meetings. He will probably come back, he had told Jim. Bill may have been "badgered out." He may be struggling with a new plot for which he has only a partially written script. Indeed Bill must learn to talk about himself in a new way. Bill gave the group a chance to penetrate his life situation, but whether he comes back or not is not the measure of the group's success with him. Either way, the two young men are as inseparable now as they were when Bill was attending.

References

1. Katz, Alfred, and Bender, Eugene: Self help groups in Western society: history and prospects, American Journal of Applied Behavioral Sciences, **12:**265-282, 1976.
2. Lieberman, Morton, and Borman, Leonard, editors: Self help groups for coping with crisis, San Francisco, 1979, Jossey-Bass, Inc., Publishers.
3. Tracy, George, and Gussow, Zachary: Self help groups: a grass roots response to a need for services, Journal of Applied Behavioral Sciences **12:** 381-396, 1976.

THE EXPERIENCES OF PATIENTS IN HOSPITALS

The preceding chapters have focused on the experiences and work of sick persons and their families at home. In this part of the book, we turn to the work and experiences of the same sick persons (patients) and their kin in the hospital. Many sick people are hospitalized at least once, and quite a few, alas, require rehospitalization from time to time.

Hospitals today are increasingly technologized: the care given there involves specialized machines, batteries of drugs, complex surgery, and complicated procedures—as well as highly trained physicians, nurses, and a variety of technicians. Contemporary diagnostic and treatment technology has been aptly dubbed by a governmental commission as "halfway technology," since it actually cures few in the (increasingly sick) hospital population, although certainly it may improve a patient's functioning and keep him or her alive. Like the technology, the care, and the staff's skills, the organization of the care—of the hospital itself—is becoming increasingly complex. All of that bears significantly on the work that goes into giving care to patients as well as on the experiences that patients have while hospitalized. Moreover, as we will be at pains to point out in the following pages, the triad of technology, chronic illness severity, and complex hospital organization bears also on the patients' work while in the hospital—for work they assuredly do. They had better, in order to obtain effective care, and sometimes, even to stay alive.

To illustrate these contentions, the next several chapters will emphasize both the work that patients do and how it links with the staff members' work. This chapter will give an overview of the patient at work. In the following chapter we will touch on two features of the kin's work. Chapter 13 focuses on the giving and obtaining of comfort, that is, "comfort work." Chapter 14 is concerned with the tasks that help to maximize patients' safety, or "clinical safety work."

CHAPTER 11

THE WORK OF PATIENTS WHEN HOSPITALIZED

An observant person can see hospitalized patients working to ensure their own comfort, working to catch staff's errors as with drugs and intravenous infusions, and working hard, too, at maintaining composure while undergoing procedures or as they make decisions about whether to go through another operation or to die. Patients can be seen monitoring the dialysis machines and other equipment. However, since they are not employees of the hospital and have no status as health professionals or as other kinds of health workers patients are not easily perceived by the staff as actually working—certainly not as a literal part of the division of labor in managing and shaping their own trajectories.[2] Indeed, much of their work is quite invisible to the physicians, nurses, and technicians, either because that work is not actually seen (is kept secret) or because, although seen, it is not defined as work but just as patients' activity or general participation in their own care. Ironically, patients are expected to be "cooperative," to use common hospital parlance, while the staff is working hard on their care: this means not merely that patients should be passive or pleasant but that they should actually do the things they are supposed to do in the service of their medical and nursing care. Doing the things they are supposed to do certainly can involve putting time and effort into the requisite acts or activities: in short, the sick do work, but their work is not necessarily conceived of as more than acting properly or decently in accordance with the requirements of their care by professionals and assisting personnel.

The relevant questions about the patients' work include:

1. What types of work do patients do?
2. How does that work relate to various trajectories and phases?
3. What is the relation of that work to staff work?
4. Under what conditions is the work visible or invisible to staff?

5. Under what conditions is the work appreciated or not appreciated by staff?
6. What are some consequences of patient work for staff work, for trajectories, and for the patients' own medical and biographical fates?
7. How does patient work at the hospital relate to the trajectory work done at home?

SOURCES OF PATIENTS' WORK

The classic picture of the patient—whether painted by a discerning Dutch realist or more recently described by Parsons[7] with "sick role" imagery—is of an acutely sick person, hence temporarily passive and acquiescent, being treated by an active physician and helped by equally vigorous caretakers. That is hardly an accurate depiction of chronically ill persons, of course, except when they are rendered helpless during the most acute phases of an illness. Although interrupted by occasional or even frequent acute episodes, much of the business of their lives is transacted in and around whatever symptoms bedevil them, and whatever regimens they must manage.[3] The chronically ill become very knowledgeable about the interplay between regimen technologies and their own unique body reactions; often they become very skilled in managing those reactions. Only they can possess, even earn, this specialized knowledge. Then, when they become very acutely ill or need a more complicated technology, they may enter a hospital. However, they do not leave any of their experiential knowledge behind them, even though the staff often regards them as medically innocent.[4]

In the hospital, patients are expected to act appropriately while the personnel go about doing medical interventions and the other acute care activities called for by the illnesses. Since traditional acute care philosophy still lies embedded in the medical-nursing care given in hospitals, this assumes a patient in a state of illness that renders him or her relatively helpless and dependent on trained professionals and technicians, who through their resources and skills will sooner or later effect improvement in the patient's condition. The latter's job is simply to cooperate with the personnel to whom responsibility for care has been delegated. So there is the paradox in which chronically ill persons, whose heads and often hands are respectably well endowed with experiential knowledge and skill, now become wards of the health personnel, presumably delegating all responsibility and caring tasks to them. Actually, of course, every medical intervention involves the possibility, often the probability, that the patient will have to do something, hence not be completely inert during the intervention. Given the organization of hospital work, it is easy to see that these knowledgeable patients may sometimes attempt to prevent or at least catch staff members' mistakes, seeking to have those rectified, or rectifying the mistakes themselves. They may enter into the articulation of tasks whose sequences might otherwise go awry, and they may provide some of their own so-called continuity of care through the daily three shifts and in the face of staff rotation—and so on. To reiterate, patients find themselves in a paradoxical—even ironical—situation wherein they do delegate responsibility for care to the staff, but—it simply is not as simple as that.

PATIENT WORK: EXPLICIT AND IMPLICIT

Some work done by hospitalized patients is explicitly recognized as genuine work, primarily because it duplicates or supplements the staff's similar work. On dialysis wards, nurses expect patients, unless very sick or inexperienced, to monitor both the machines and their bodies during most of the repeated dialysis session.[11] On physical rehabilitation units, the therapists recognize fully the work that patients do to endure and carry out the sometimes painful or otherwise difficult exercise. Furthermore, when teaching patients how to manage regimens and machinery just before discharge from the hospital, the work that must now be done at home is perhaps quite likely to be recognized as genuine work.

Associated with this explicit recognition of patients' work may be a quite clear and even elaborate staff philosophy about how much and what kinds of work the patients are allowed or requested to do. One particularly striking ideology that places special emphasis on patients' efforts is the Simonton method advocated for people suffering from cancer.[10] A central idea in this fairly complex philosophy is "visualization therapy," in which the person visualizes his or her internal body, the cancer itself, and the immunity system.

On the other hand, most patient work goes unrecognized: it is taken for granted. Among the unrecognized tasks are nonmedical ones pertaining to personal housekeeping: going to the toilet, putting out the bed light, combing hair, getting out of bed if ambulatory, feeding oneself. There are certain other things everyone assumes that patients, unless infants or nonsentient, can and will do, for example, giving information during the entry and diagnostic interviews. Patients are also expected to report discomforts and untoward symptoms or bad reactions to drugs. There are also demands made of them during various tests, as when cardiac patients are put on the treadmill and are instructed to report when angina appears. Certain other patients are instructed how to do necessary things and then are expected to do them: an example would be to cough postoperatively. Other tests require patients to put out considerable effort so that their performance levels can be measured; indeed the staff member may encourage the patient to perform to his or her utmost, often giving approval for successful efforts, as with someone who is having respiratory outputs monitored. In addition, of course there is much informal and even recognized teaching of patients on how to monitor machines or bodies. When they are deemed responsible and experienced they are more likely, naturally, to be trusted with the monitoring itself and with the reporting of its results.

Still other body work done is not so easily recognized as work, either by the staff or by the patients. It may involve expenditures of effort, even resolve and courage, especially if the patient is very ill or in severe pain—even though it is taken so much for granted that it slips by relatively unnoticed. Body position is an example. The x-ray technician asks the patient to turn now to the right, now to the left: the patient moves his or her body as requested. Immobilized patients or infants must be positioned, as they cannot be expected to follow orders to position themselves. Again, the physician, nurse, or technician says, "this procedure will hurt but it is necessary," and the adult or older child is assumed to be capable of refraining from any interfering movement. Children and occasionally adults who refuse to follow requests about body movements or lying still may be forcibly positioned or restrained.

Then, too, there are a few body tasks that require patients to do other things with their bodies: they must swallow barium, or "take a big breath now and hold until I say let it out," or "hang on to this rail with your right hand and walk, but keep up with the treadmill," or "blow into this as hard as you can." Even when it is necessary that the patient hold something so that the technician can do something and the latter literally says "help me," thrusting an electrical connection into the patient's hand, that does not necessarily mean the technician is thinking of the patient's work as anything more than just cooperating. Finally, there is another kind of body work familiar to us all: the giving on request of various body substances: urine, feces, sputum. Patients who have just gone to the toilet may conceive of this as work, but surely the staff does not!

Referring now to a point touched on earlier: the staff expect patients to be cooperative during procedures or other interventions. Cooperation refers often to behavior that involves endurance, fortitude, self-control in the face of discomfort, pain, or potentially humiliating medical intervention. Persons who are "normal," intelligent, and self-disciplined ought to be able to restrain their impulses to scream, shriek, pull their bodies away, refuse to undergo anymore of a procedure or take anymore of a drug. When somebody breaks the staff's implicit, although sometimes clearly recognized and explicitly stated, rules about these matters, the staff will attempt to get him or her to adhere to them. The staff may cajole, tease, scold, empathize, but insist on obedience, thus attempting to persuade the patient. Alternatively the staff may attempt to negotiate: "If you endure it then we will do it as fast as possible"; "Only one more time"; "Let's skip the drug (or procedure) for now but do not skip it next time, okay?" If the patient remains recalcitrant, or worse yet persistently recalcitrant, then a negative reputation will rapidly build up. These staff judgments about cooperative or uncooperative patients very often have a strong moral coloration, insofar as they involve not simply someone's capacity to endure but whether he or she chooses or has enough character to endure, or to lie still, or whatever action is being judged in a positive or negative mode.[3,6]

We are especially interested here in emphasizing that patients are being judged on their carrying out of *tasks*. These are not usually conceived of by staff as tasks (or jobs, or work) but in terms of patients' participation in the staff's work—contributory actions, rather than work, that have an implicit moral code. Patients, too, many morally evaluate their own actions, and themselves as actors, being proud or ashamed at their endurance or fortitude. Ordinarily, however, they do not conceive of their actions as work, in contrast, say, with their monitoring of equipment, which is obviously work.

There are more subtle kinds of patient work that if not done, or not done properly, get patients into trouble with the staff. An instance of this would be the complex situation that can arise when the staff knows that a terribly ill person now knows he or she is dying. The patient is, in our terminology, expected to do certain (unrecognized) work involving maintaining reasonable control over reactions that might be excessively disruptive of the staff's medical work as well as of its composure, and perhaps even disruptive also of other patients' poise.

> Once a patient has indicated his awareness of dying, the most important interactional consequence is that he is now responsible for his acts as a *dying* person. He knows now that he is not merely sick but dying. He must face that fact. Sociologically, "facing" an impending death means that the patient will be judged, and will judge himself, according to certain standards of proper conduct. These standards, pertaining to the way a man handles himself during his final hours and to his behavior during the days he spends waiting to die, apply even to physically dazed patients. Similarly, certain standards apply then to the conduct of hospital personnel, who must behave properly as humans and professionals. The bare bones of this governed reciprocal action show through the conversation between a nurse and a young dying girl. The nurse said, "Janet, I'll try as hard as I can"; and then when the youngster asked whether she was going to die, the nurse answered, "I don't know, you might, but just keep fighting." Patients known to be aware of death have two kinds of obligations: first, they should not act to bring about their own deaths. Second, there are certain positive obligations one has as a dying patient. . . . People are supposed to live correctly while dying, providing they understand that they are dying, but Americans have no clear rules for their behavior. . . .
>
> Nevertheless, in our hospitals staff members do judge the conduct of dying patients by certain implicit standards. These standards are related to the work that hospital personnel do, as well as to some rather general American notions about courageous and decent behavior. A partial list of implicit canons includes the following: The patient should maintain relative composure and cheerfulness. At the very least, he should face death with dignity. He should not

cut himself off from the world, turning his back upon the living; instead he should continue to be a good family member, and be "nice" to other patients. If he can, he should participate in the ward social life. He should cooperate with the staff-members who care for him, and if possible he should avoid distressing or embarrassing them. A patient who does most of these things will be respected. He evinces what we shall term "an acceptable style of dying," or, more accurately, "an acceptable style of living while dying." . . .

The contrasting pattern—what the staff defines as unacceptable behavior in aware dying patients—is readily illustrated. For instance, physicians usually honor requests for additional (or consultants') opinions, but object to "shopping around" for impossible cures. . . . Other types of unacceptable behavior emerge vividly from our field notes. Thus the next quotation involves a patient's serious failure to "cooperate" in his medical care, and it shows the extremes to which a physician will go to get such cooperation:

> The patient had been moving his arm around a lot so his intravenous needle was in danger of coming out; he is very testy at all such rigmarole. The doctor got irritated, apparently, at his lack of cooperation and said that if he took that needle out of his arm, he'd die. The nurse: "that's what the doctor said to his face—that this is what is keeping you here; you pull it out and you'll die."

. . . Patients who do not die properly . . . create a major interactional problem for the staff. The problem of inducing them to die properly gives rise, inevitably, to a series of staff tactics. Some are based on the patient's understanding of the situation: staff members therefore command, reprimand, admonish and scold. . . . These negatively toned tactics . . . are supplemented, and often overshadowed, by others through which personnel attempt to teach patients how to die properly.[5]

In short, patients are expected to do, and certainly often do, a great deal of implicit work, especially psychological or identity work, while dying; conversely the staff, whose medical-nursing and composure work is often shattered by patients who break the rules of dying, can be thus induced to engage in the additional and mostly unwanted work of persuading or teaching conformance with those rules.

PATIENTS' WORK: VISIBLE OR INVISIBLE, LEGITIMATE OR ILLEGITIMATE

Another condition for the nonrecognition of patients' work is when it is not visible to the personnel. Sometimes the work is done when they are not present. Sometimes, although a staff member and a patient are together, the latter's work is literally invisible, as with some kinds of comfort or psychological work. In either event, the patient may elect not to tell what he is doing or has done. Patients may not indicate their work for a variety of reasons: because it could be defined as illegitimate or as incorrectly done, because it involves criticism of the staff (as with monitoring of their competence), or because it is altogether too personal (as with much identity work), and so on.

Some of this work, may be discovered but not defined as such, even perhaps by the patient. If then regarded as legitimate, it may be responded to variously: with gratitude, dismay, amusement, empathy, indifference. If defined as illegitimate—as when a patient in pain takes medication carefully secreted away—then the staff will attempt to prevent future transgressions.[4,12]

If the illegitimate work seems foolish or crazy—as when a patient in pain keeps elaborate records of when pain medications were given—then the staff may merely scoff at or denigrate the patient among themselves. The last illustrations suggest, of course, that patients and personnel can hold very different definitions of legitimate and illegitimate work done by the patients (again not usually defined as work)—which is all the more reason for a savvy or suspicious patient to keep the work hidden.

Here is a complex and frequently occurring instance that involves both the issue of legitimacy and that of visibility: a patient defines some activity as necessary (perhaps as work, even), but the staff disapproves, never dreaming of the patient's definition but only perceiving that he or she is disobeying instructions and refusing obligations. An example of this is when a rather anxious patient who a few days ago suffered a myocardial infarction is now required to be ambulatory but is carefully working at "resting," as insisted on previously by the same staff. It is possible that the nurses may see the patient's immobility as an overcautious precaution, but they are more likely to view this silent work as a flagrant disobedience of the doctor's orders, prompted by an overly generous dose of anxiety.

One additional and rather special condition for the invisibility of a patient's work is when the staff is working on a main trajectory while the patient is doing subsidiary work on other trajectories. Then the staff's focus hinders their noticing the patient's work or makes it less probable that they will discover this work when he or she chooses not to reveal it, and if it is revealed the staff still may not recognize it as work in the service of another trajectory. Here is an instance of the lengths to which such work can go, in this case involving a daughter as well as the patient, but also what we would regard as the staff's contributory comfort work:

A very elderly woman came in for a standard cataract operation, ready to stay for 3 days. She and her daughter "came prepared," because she had arthritis and also easily became cold because of circulatory problems associated with her age. They brought the patient's own pillow, also special underwear and blankets to keep her warm. Nevertheless she became cold, so the daughter explained to the nursing staff that her mother was extraordinarily cold. A heating pad was then brought. Everybody worked hard, also, at only removing her clothing when absolutely necessary, as for the ECG: then the woman herself put her clothing back on, assisted by her daughter. Since there was no official restriction of her movement, she could get in and out of bed at will, something she needed to do because her arthritis made it difficult to remain long in one position.

TRAJECTORIES, DIVISION OF LABOR, AND PATIENT WORK

The work that patients do is trajectory work, in the service of managing and shaping aspects of their trajectories. So the details of their work, quite like the staff's, must necessarily relate to the specific trajectory in which they are so unfortunate as to be caught up. The patient's work is also connected with trajectory phasing. For instance, a young woman informed by her internist that her breast biopsy showed some malignancy and that she would require a mastectomy operation engaged then in phased work. Aside from being plunged into composure work and some initial identity work about dying and a disfigurement, she systematically sought information that would allow her to make intelligent decisions about the next steps. What kinds of operations were possible and feasible? What were the rates of success and failure for each? What were the alternative modes of treatment? What was the reputation of the surgeon to whom she was referred? Who could tell her? To whom should she go for another consultation? Who would be the anesthesiologist, and had that specialist and the surgeon worked much together? What would be the impact of the various therapies on her life? Unless a prospective patient is extraordinarily passive, he or she will ask some—or even more—of those questions; if as active and searching as this particular woman, they will be expending much time and energy to get reasonable answers.

As the trajectory moves along, the work will be different: in the hospital after her mastectomy, this woman decided not to take any pain medication, developed modes of minimizing body discomfort that came in the wake of the operation, refused to have her blood drawn by an untidy and fumbling technician, complained to the head nurse about that incident, and also worked at keeping her "cool" when a friend anxiously inquired about the operation. Once at home, there would be still different tasks in accordance with the next phases in trajectory management. Some who have had mastectomies confront the specter of cancer recurrence and possible death, which precipitates plenty of identity work that physicians seem loath to share with them—and husbands as well.

If it is true that hospitalized patients as well as staff enter into the work process, then there is posed for us an important question. Just what, then, is their part in the total division of labor concerning trajectory management? It should be clear enough by now that there is no simple answer to that question. Undoubtedly hospital personnel tend to believe the bulk of patient's work—definitions of "work" per se aside—would consist of handling composure and coming to grips with identity problems associated with the illness. If pressed they would agree that patients do share in getting some of the more strictly medical tasks done, and that they obviously also have to make some of the big decisions about surgery and other drastic procedures.

Answers to the foregoing question would have to include at least the following notion of types of patient engagement in the trajectory process. First, some of their work is the *mirror image* of the staff's work: patients give urine, and the staff takes it away to send to the laboratory for testing. Patients obey commands to position themselves, whereas staff members give the commands and then do the procedures. Second, some work by patients is *supplementary to*, but not exactly the mirror image of, staff's work—like maintaining composure in the face of procedural tasks. Third, work by patients may *substitute* for work that staff did not do but either were supposed to do or the patient believes they were supposed to do. Fourth, the patients may do work that they believe is *necessary*, although the staff would disagree (if it knew), like monitoring for potential error or incompetence. Fifth, the patients may *rectify* staff errors, directly by themselves or by reporting—or complaining—to responsible authorities. Sixth, patients may do the work that *staff cannot possibly do*, meaning not only their identity work but more medically tinged actions like giving information about allergies to certain drugs or explaining they have other chronic illnesses whose symptoms may interfere with the staff's working on the main trajectory. Seventh, patients may engage in work that is *outside the range* of what staff may conceive of as the locus of their own work, such as coping with highly personalized, deep identity problems precipitated by the illness, or other work that staff may eschew even when aware of the patient's "problem"—as when women who have undergone mastectomy struggle with disfigurement and fears of impending death.

These various types of work, of course, can match, supplement, and fit in with staff work in very diverse ways, including temporal relationships—timing, pacing, sequencing—as well as spatial ones. Combinations of staff and patient work are equally diverse, as are the relative complexities of their respective tasks. These points are illustrated in the following cases.

Case 1. The first situation is very subtle and complex. Immediately after a treadmill test—completed when the patient developed fairly severe angina symptoms—he was moved to a prone position under a nuclear tracer machine, which for the next half hour or more would be recording his heart's performance. The attending physician occasionally asked, "how are you doing?" and the patient responded "Okay." He was in fact all right, except that he was uncomfortable because of his angina, which caused him to burp from time to time. In turn, the burping soon gave him heartburn, but he contained his dis-ease. Soon, too, his neck began to hurt somewhat, because he had a somewhat severe back condition, and the position in which he was lying aggravated it. That discomfort he also contained without moving or saying anything about it.

From time to time the technician moved the recording part of the machine, so that the patient found himself protecting himself by slightly moving his head to avoid the machine or to get away from its mild but discomforting pressure. All of those tasks were technologically induced, if essentially minor. A more difficult and more important job was that he had to prevent himself from coughing; not an easy task, since he had bronchitis, and this happened to be precisely the time of day when normally and involuntarily he coughed up much phlegm. Just once he gave way, properly warning the technician beforehand; then he returned once more to his concerted control. Except for the body positioning, none of this work was visible to the technician, physician, or nurse—and ordinarily they would not become aware of it—but it was all relevant to the success of the machine's accurate recording.

Case 2. Turning now to staff and patient work done during dialysis sessions, we describe a very complex interaction: after repeated dialysis sessions, a patient learns and is taught how and when to work. Patients may be involved in setting up the machine and in connecting themselves to it. (Some centers have self-care philosophies, so patients are expected to do much of this.) Some take great pride in tending the machine, setting it as well as monitoring its performance. Men especially take pleasure in their knowledge of mechanics and can fiddle successfully with the machine when it is not working quite properly. Patients may also prepare the solution used in the treatment. During the periods immediately after getting on the machine and getting off, the nurses are much more in evidence, doing their tasks around the machine and in relation to the patients. The long in-between period involves much monitoring by the patient of both machine and body responses, since body and machine are in such potentially delicate balance. Patients are also monitoring each other, and they will call the staff if they see or believe another patient is "in trouble." Personnel may put forward a philosophy of patient participation, prompting even reluctant patients to do more for themselves during the dialysis session; however, the more experienced and "responsible" are trusted more by the staff, who can then be engaged in other work at the nursing station or with patients who need greater attention.

It goes almost without saying that dialysis patients do compose work: during the early weeks of being "on the machine" some, at least, need to muster their courage to get through the sessions, their anxiety levels being high. In addition, other more experienced patients are often engaged in abetting the nurses' composure work with new dialysis patients. Yet anxiety may never be quite eliminated in some patients: for example, one man told the researcher that he simply did not trust most nurses during the "dangerous period" just before the end of the dialysis session "when the bubbles that can kill you can appear if it isn't done right," so during this time at every session he does his self-defined most important work, watching the nurse's handling of the tube and machine like a hawk! Thus, while nurses are judging the patients' competencies, patients are also monitoring and judging them. In sum, although there is great variation in the amount of work done by these patients, we can appreciate the remark of one woman who jokingly said that "MediCal should pay me—I do all the work!"*

Case 3. A third illustration will bring out the interplay of staff-patient work in a negative sense: the patients are doing collaborative work in the absence or failure of staff's work. For instance, a patient hospitalized for an eye operation noted both her own work in others' behalf and that of patients acting as a group. Being more "awake" than some of her roommates, she was the one who called the nurse to point out oversights, such as when the eyedrops for a patient with glaucoma had been overlooked. "Occasionally three patients would consult with one another about the best strategy for handling a problem: whether to complain to the nurse or wait for the physician. It was a sort of lame-halt-and-blind collaboration. There was definitely a 'we' group feeling. Consultations among them often centered about IV monitoring; did the others think the drip was too fast, too slow, solution getting too low, time to call the nurse, does the nurse on duty seem to know or care about what's supposed to be happening?" The strategy of the patients in a situation like this may be to ask for a particular nurse whom they regard as responsible, to complain to the physician when she or he arrives, or to ask a family member to talk to either staff member.

•   •   •

To summarize this section then, there are unfortunately no simple answers to the seemingly straightforward question: what is the patients' part in the division of labor? The principal reason is that the question is perhaps wrongly—if conventionally—posed. The question should be: how do the various types of patient work fit in with the staff's work, and in relation to their mutual shaping of trajectories? Undeniably, however, there is an official division of labor and some reality to this official version, since there *is* physicians' work and nurses' work and various technicians' work; some of it overlaps, but some is rather distinct. The patient too has a status, all too often felt as constraint or powerlessness. Nevertheless, to achieve a realistic perspective on the division of labor issue, one must focus on the actual interplay of the work of the persons who embody those various statuses. In

---

*Our thanks to Barbara Artinian, who is studying dialysis patients, for this quotation.

hospitals—whatever the staff, patients, kin, and even the critics of the medical scene believe—this interplay of work is a many-splendored thing. The more aggressive, fortunate, and knowledgeable patients surely understand that phenomenon, even though they may be surprised at the analysts' contention that they do not merely react but work in their own behalf.

EXPECTING, DEMANDING, INVITING, NEGOTIATING, TEACHING

The various illustrations of patients at work suggest different modes of patient immersion in a ward's division of labor. The most obvious mode is that the staff *expects* patients to work (whether staff calls it work or not). Reluctant or recalcitrant patients are subject to the demand that they bear their responsibilities; furthermore, they are scolded or otherwise punished when they will not do their jobs—as with patients who fight the respirator or rehabilitation patients who will not "put out." Patients who honestly attempt to do their tasks but have difficulty— as with one who kept ruining a breathing test on a respirator machine by choking up and coughing—may eventually arouse some annoyance, but at least they are trying to do their best.

Patients are sometimes also *invited* into the division of labor, tasks being proffered for a variety of reasons: the nurse might be called away and have to leave temporarily, or is very busy, and the task proffered has lower priority; or the nurse wishes to avoid a bit of work, or would rather not do that particular task; or the nurse believes that the patient will feel less depersonalized, less "worked on," or perhaps more secure, if he or she does something. As we have seen, the patient may be invited to do something on explicit ideological grounds—whether the philosophy is a professionalized one or is derived from a wider social movement like "patients' rights."

Of course patients may *offer* to do something, fix something, move something, watch something, without waiting to be asked or persuaded. They also may *demand* to do one or another of those things. Another mode of entry by patients into the sharing of labor is through *negotiation,* where something is offered for something else in exchange. One sees this with the personnel's handling of young children, where rewards are given for cooperative behavior (composure work, body positioning work) in enduring painful, discomforting, or frightening procedures. The rewards may be tangible (one of the authors, when quite young, was promised and later given an ice cream cone and a quarter for enduring an operation). The rewards may also be more subtly symbolic, as when a physician warns a child of what he is going to do next, asking permission to work on her, showing solicitude, politeness, friendliness, generally acting "like a good guy"—trading all that for the young patient's cooperation. (We call this negotiation rather than persuasion because of the trade-off.) Persuasion refers more to "talking into, convincing" directly, as when a child reacts to a portable x-ray machine, crying because "of the needle," but then is persuaded that there *is* no needle. Both explicit and implicit negotiation transpire around patient work, and either staff or patient may initiate the exchange. Some types of cooperative work—as in rehabilitation exercises, with or without machines—are greatly facilitated by open and generous exchanges by both parties: yes, the staff member agrees, we can have a shorter session today providing you continue doing so well for the next 10 minutes.

TEACHING THE PATIENT: SOME ISSUES

"*Teaching* the patient" is translatable into getting the patient either to work or to work more effectively in his or her own behalf, largely through negotiation and persuasion. (Demanding, manipulating, and coercing that work are rarely appropriate to genuine teaching, at least by themselves.) The increasing complexity of drug and machine technologies and the complex regimens with which patients are faced as they go home literally force on everyone the concept of the patient-as-technologist.[1,9] In some part, surely, the rise of the liaison nurse (who bridges hospital and home) and the generally increasing emphasis on teaching the hospitalized patient express the response of the profession to the increasing prevalence and difficulties of managing problematic chronic illnesses and to the complex technology related to that management. One of our research assistants, a nurse-sociologist, expressed that point in a field note after her interviews and observations at a university medical center:

> One of the things that struck me in conversations with several nurses was their emphasis on patient teaching. A few years ago, commitment to patient teaching was primarily a preoccupation of nursing educators. Now, I was immediately struck by the preoccupation of the practitioners with this activity. What is more, it has become highly formalized and organized here, often with written protocols. It seems unrelated to the educational background of the nurses I interviewed: a nurse who was a graduate of Massachusetts General and who described herself as very technically and procedurally oriented, told in detail how she visits her patients prior to open heart surgery or major bowel surgery and instructs them. Another thing nowadays is the complexity of these machines: on 8 West they use aortic balloon pumps, Swan-Gans catheters, A-Lines, you name it. The patient cooperation (even when very ill) is still helpful, even critical to working with them on these machines. So this is very complex and increasingly tricky work that the nurses have to do, and they need all the help they can get. If they can't get the patient's help, they feel better off if the patient is "out." So if patient teaching gets the work done better, they do it.*

---

*Our thanks to Roberta Lessor for these observations and our use of them.

The old but now increasingly important function of the nurse-as-educator partly represents a turning away from a predominantly "medical model" of care, because staff members recognize the necessary social and psychological aspects of care.[8] The current teaching emphasis, however, also represents a more strictly technical focus on teaching patients and kin the basics of technology (whether drug, machine, or body monitoring) whose use is essential in home care. Without this teaching and its implementation by patient and kin, relapse may occur, the patient will be returning sooner to the hospital, and speedy death may even result. While much teaching is targeted at home care, increasingly nurses and other personnel (dietitians, physical therapists, and others) are teaching in the hospital, either informally or with more official accountability.

The teaching perspective does have some weaknesses, when conceived in terms of the policies and potentialities of patients' work:

1. Basically, the teaching perspective—regardless of the specific teaching model utilized—assumes the staff member is the teacher while the patient is the learner. Of course the contemporary models emphasize there is room for sharing, for learning together; yet they assume that the primary flow of information is from teacher to student.

2. There is a tendency to focus on formal teaching; this does not exclude informal teaching or teaching in situ, but formal instruction tends to be given priority.

3. The teaching perspective often focuses too narrowly on the medical, technological, and procedural aspects of illness management, omitting or underplaying important sociopsychological and biographical aspects of chronic illness trajectory management.

4. The teaching orientation tends to employ a language of "evaluation," "assessment," and "goals"—all probably reinforcing the teacher-learner axis per se, and giving the former a hierarchically superior position in relation to the patient while also emphasizing unduly those aspects of the teaching-learning situation that can be clearly assessed or measured (that is, the more "medical" and procedural aspects of the teaching-learning).

5. The teaching perspective does pay attention to certain features of the hospital or ward setting that create impediments to teaching and learning, but the perspective tends to embody a relatively incomplete grasp of the hospital as an organization and what that implies for staff's care and teaching, patients' work and learning.

6. The teaching orientation tends to emphasize both the patient's "needs" and what the patient needs to know. On the one hand, the focus is on the teacher responding to presumed or known needs, and on the other, the

patient is required to learn certain necessary things. Teachers may attempt to balance between those two poles *or* move toward one or the other. Meanwhile, a teacher can forget that her or his own needs and judgments about the requirement to teach specific materials can muddy the interactional waters, thus preventing deeper understanding of what is transpiring between oneself and the patient.

7. Finally, the teaching perspective does not specifically emphasize the implications of prevalent chronic illness for the teaching-learning process itself. A steady focus on chronic illness allied with the teaching perspective would literally demand that the teachers seek sources for their own learning in patients' experiential work at home and in the hospital.

PROBLEMATIC ILLNESSES AND DECISION MAKING

Problematic illnesses can involve patients in decision making. Patients enter into that decision making, whether by invitation, by their own assertiveness, or because contingencies make for facing the options directly. This would be true even if the "patient power" movement were less of a force, because so many trajectories are quite problematic. We also need not assume that each patient necessarily wishes to participate in decision making, or that, being a longtime sufferer, he or she knows a great deal about the options and their implications. The very open-mindedness of many trajectories ensures that patients will do the decision-making work. Sometimes this involves making choices on small operational matters; other times, of course, the choices are genuinely major ones.

Most options faced by patients are neither so fateful nor anguishing as in the case of the woman who hesitated between another operation and dying. The options consist rather of choices that patients elect to make or have forced on them, at virtually any point along their trajectories. However, problematic trajectories beginning to get out of hand typically involve some very difficult choices. Thus, a woman being treated for severe lupus developed an ulcer in response to medication (should she be operated on for this or not?), developed great anger at the staff and physician (should she be seen by a psychiatrist as "suggested" or not?), developed. . . . We have termed this kind of evolving situation a "cumulative mess trajectory," not because anyone is to blame for it but because virtually everything, medically and organizationally, eventually goes awry. Patients then have to be brought into the decision-making work that needs to be done at the critical junctures (let alone during the minor episodes) during these highly problematic, chronic illness trajectories. Much of their actual decision work is then explicit and highly visible to the staff, but not all of it—and sometimes not until after it is completed, as with unanticipated signing out from hospitals or even attempts at suicide.

We end this chapter by underlining the point that chronic illness trajectories flow from home residence into and through hospitals, and out again back to the home. When we consider such repeated cycles, it becomes apparent that patients are, as remarked earlier, working technologists too, not only at home but in the hospital. They may overestimate their own expertise, but most have earned and use it. In future years, not to recognize this reality is likely to bring a considerable increase of conflict between patients and hospital staffs. The very rise of self-care groups signifies the current gradual increase in recognition by groups of patients and kin of their respective expertise. (This is reflected in the words of one arthritic who exclaimed when given the informational teaching pamphlet put out by a hospital's arthritic center: "It's so skimpy!"). The future is very likely to bring an increasing challenge to hospital staffs by these patients over getting more of a share in the management of their own illnesses. Researchers like the authors wonder whether hospital staffs will recognize the source of patients' rising expectations: will staffs wait until the challenge becomes overt and the tempers impossibly high?

References

1. Benoliel, Jeanne Quint: Childhood diabetes: the commonplace in living becomes uncommon. In Strauss, Anselm, and Glaser, Barney: Chronic illness and the quality of life, St. Louis, 1975, The C.V. Mosby Co., pp. 89-98.
2. Davis, Marcella Z.: The organizational, interactional and care oriented conditions for patient participation in continuity of care: a framework for staff interaction, Social Science and Medicine **14**:39-47, 1980.
3. Duff, R.S., and Hollinghead, A.B.: Sickness and society, New York, 1968, Harper & Row, p. 24.
4. Fagerhaugh, Shizuko, and Strauss, Anselm: The politics of pain management: staff-patient interaction, Menlo Park, Calif., 1977, Addison-Wesley Publishing Co.
5. Glaser, Barney, and Strauss, Anselm: Awareness of dying, Chicago, 1964, Aldine Press, pp. 82-83, 86, 90-91.
6. Lorber, J.: Good patients and problem patients: conformity and deviance in a general hospital. In Conrad, P., and Kern, R., editors: The sociology of health and illness, New York, 1981, St. Martin's Press, pp. 395-404.
7. Parsons, Talcott: Social system, New York, 1951, The Free Press.
8. Redman, Barbara: The process of patient teaching in nursing, ed. 3, St. Louis, 1976, The C.V. Mosby Co.
9. Reif, Laura: Ulcerative colitis: strategies for managing life. In Strauss, Anselm, and Glaser, Barney: Chronic illness and the quality of life, St. Louis, 1975, The C.V. Mosby Co., pp. 81-88.
10. Simonton, O.C.: Management of the emotional aspect of malignancy, Symposium of new dimensions of rehabilitation for handicapped, Department of Health and Rehabilitation Services, University of Florida, Gainesville, June 14 to 16, 1974. (Mimeographed.)
11. Strauss, Anselm, Fagerhaugh, Shizuko, Suczek, Barbara, and Wiener, Carolyn: The social organization of medical work, Chicago, 1984, University of Chicago Press.
12. Strauss, Anselm, and Glaser, Barney: Anguish: case history of a dying trajectory, San Francisco, 1970, The Sociology Press.

CHAPTER 12

THE WORK OF KIN IN HOSPITALS

Throughout the industrialized world, the antibiotic revolution that culminated in the triumph of "antiinfection technology" essentially nullified the hospital's rationale for discouraging contact between patients and their kin. Since that time, there has been a gradually accelerating trend toward relaxation of visiting rules in hospitals, and the presence of visitors on wards has become increasingly common. Today even intensive care units admit visitors, some units having gone so far as to adopt "open ward" policies permitting close family members to come and go pretty much at will. Still, there seems to have been no radical change in the status of kin in terms of their relatively unrecognized work in hospitals, except of course, "psychological work" and work on pediatric wards. With a few exceptions here and there—as when family members are encouraged to help with feeding a patient—kin are not given an explicit part to play in patient care, nor does it seem to occur to many staff members that they may be a valuable but untapped resource. No matter what part the family may play in caring for the sick at home (and everyone knows that part is considerable), within the hospital it is still the prevailing assumption that the really necessary work is done by the hospital staff, a definition of the situation that kin do not as yet seem inclined to challenge directly. Staff members, on the whole, go about their business more or less oblivious to the presence of the outsiders, maintaining the flow of ward work around, among, and despite them.

But what about the kin's work? Do they actually do anything in the hospital besides their occasional physical comfort work and admittedly important psychological work? In this chapter we will discuss three kinds of *kin work,* each of which is profoundly affected by the nature of contemporary chronic illness, the technology for managing it, and the organizational features of that "management." The three types of work are (1) working with a sick relative "psychologically," (2) doing

143

necessary legal-administrative work, and (3) engaging in crucial decision making. Let us look at features of each, in the order listed.

THE SENTIMENTAL WORK OF KIN

Kin are known and expected to help the patient endure (keep composure) whatever happens while in the hospital, as well as to handle whatever identity problems are brought about by the illness while in the hospital. We have elsewhere referred to this psychological work as "sentimental work," using the latter term to refer to work that has its source in the elementary fact that any work done for or on human beings may have to take into account their response to that instrumental work (as with medical work); indeed their responses may be a central feature of that work.[2,3]

In medical situations a sick person is reacting both to the illness and its symptoms—with anxiety, fear, panic, depression—and to medical treatments that can frighten, wound sensibilities, and even threaten self-esteem. Sentimental work done under the changed conditions of today's prevalence of chronic illness, plus treatment is technologized hospitals, is something quite different from old-fashioned sentimental work. Staff and kin (and patients, too, of course) engage in this kind of work. For the staff, such work either is instrumental to getting technical tasks accomplished—like helping the patient maintain composure—or occurs because a staff member is empathic, sympathetic, or in other ways interacting with the patient as a human being rather than merely as someone with "a condition."

The sentimental work of kin can be quite intertwined with the technical work of the staff. The complexity of that interwining can be shown via two cases, which will be described through field observations made by one of the authors of this volume.

> A very sick 9-year-old girl, with renal disease plus complications, is lying flat on her bed, a nurse working over her, bright and alert, while the mother is holding the child's hand. The nurse has marvelously gentle hands. The work has been going on probably for some time. Both nurse and mother are cuing the girl about "another thing" yet to be done—perhaps they even said what that was, but I could not hear. Nurse begins to pat the girl's chest with a cupping instrument, to loosen phlegm, doing this gently but persistently. Child evinces pain, mother tells her they must do the procedure. Mother holds her hand tightly. Tells girl to take her hand away from her chest. Explains that although she has been spitting up the phlegm, she must now throw it up. (The child had been relatively nonsentient for many days, and this is her first day of sentience.) After about 10 minutes of the cupping procedure, the child is exhausted but asks for her book. Mother props it up in front of her almost closed eyes.
>
> After a minute or two, both women tell her that now the tube must be put down, explaining its necessity and agreeing that it will hurt. Nurse carefully measures the tube, threads it through the girl's nose and down into her

gallbladder. A physician appears and, with the nurse, pumps a vile-looking green liquid from the tube, examines it, and pumps down antibiotics. During the threading scene, the mother is intensely holding her daughter's hand: this is the peak miniphase. The mother cannot watch the threading of the tube (later I learn that she knows this procedure can be dangerous, creating possibly even an abscess). Mother kisses the child's hands, her head down, during the time required to insert the tube.

Meanwhile the patient has exerted immense control over herself, not uttering a sound or a complaint or moving unduly. The mother is intensely involved in promoting the girl's self-control. The nurse's gentle overall presence also must help, creating trust. She makes no abrupt, potentially frightening movements.

To my consternation, two nonward personnel have moved a huge bed scale into this small ward, and are now waiting to weigh the child. They lower the vertical table, moving it to the bedside, and mother and two nurses now move the child to the scale. The girl says, "it's cold," and the nurse nods agreement. Now they move her back to her bed, making encouraging noises ("we know it hurts"). One additional point: during the giving of antibiotics, the mother was called to the telephone; I overheard the conversation and talked with the mother afterward about it. Her daughter had been told she would be in the hospital, alas, during Halloween, but that there would still be "trick-or-treat" there. So the girl had asked for an elephant mask, and the mother was saying to whomever was on the phone that she had a job for him or her: to find the mask that she had promised her daughter.

In sum, the nurse's gentle presence seems vital to the accomplishment of her medical work, being sustained by careful tactile and body handling of the patient, continued fulfillment of the implied promises that she will not hurt the child more than necessary and that only needed procedures are being performed, in addition, she cues and explains every action. All of this sentimental work overarches every phase of the medical work. The mother is also "presence," and never more so than when she is sharing her daughter's worst moments during the painful tube procedure. The mother is also doing much explaining and alerting the girl to the next steps of the procedures. Maintaining her own composure, she is also working hard to help her daughter maintain her composure too. Her unspoken but clear signals to the child to be courageous, to endure the necessary suffering, involve more than an expectation of the child's situational bravery, going deeper with an appeal to and expectation of appropriate behavior from a "brave girl." If that is so, then the girl is doing more than simply maintaining her composure: she is surely doing identity work with herself.

The next case especially reflects the need with children or infants to pace all the tasks throughout the session as well as how the sentimental tasks (also paced) are allied with the standard work "roles."

Grandmother is playing with an infant boy in the crib. She carries him over to a scale so that he can be weighed. Two nurses are waiting there. Grandmother puts him gently on the scale, caresses him, stands aside. The surprised infant sees his mother peering over the scale, wiggling her fingers at him. She records his weight in her own book, while the nurses record his weight in the child's chart. Grandmother then carries child back to the crib, where the mother diapers the child, with grandmother helping to move the child's body and diverting his attention with a toy. A physician appears and performs a stethoscope examination as quietly and unobtrusively as possible over the mother's shoulder (she is now holding the child). Glances are exchanged between physician and mother, and a word or two. The physician next takes out an instrument with a built-in light and makes a toy of it for the infant, passing the instrument before the child a couple to times; the physician then peers through the instrument at the infant's eyes from a distance and again unobtrusively, the others having turned the infant's face in the proper direction.

Next there is a convergence of bodies. The nurse moves to hold a soon-to-be squirming infant down, the grandmother the same, but making frequent caressing movements while holding him down. Mother bends to the infant's face and "makes faces" at him. The infant is yelling because the physician is poking the lighted instrument into his ear and looking through it. Examination soon accomplished, we are then back to grandmother-mother and child interaction, playing, with his toy near him.

To summarize, sentimental work has aided in the skillful handling of silent procedures, highly invasive procedures, and an expected difficult miniphase. Kin presence and gestures are necessary to accomplish weighing and examination tasks. Kin work in periodic and frequent, and of course intense during the expectedly difficult examination time. Placing of toy near child is "familiarization work."* At the cost of much kin work, there is a relatively smooth flow of medical tasks and minimal disturbance to the child. Note the clear division of labor, which is quite explicit although not "planned."

In short, the two cases bring out how, along with the main procedural jobs to be done involving as they do a sequence of tasks, the sentimental work is interwoven with these jobs. Sometimes the workers are quite aware of their sentimental work, sometimes not. This work may become such an integral component of a staff member's style and the kin's relationship with the ill person that possibly he or she is not always self-reflective when doing the sentimental work. At any rate, during procedural work the sequential interlacing of different types of work done by kin and staff can be very complex.

---

*We are indebted to Christa Hoffman-Riem of the University of Hamburg for both the observation and the term.

LEGAL-ADMINISTRATIVE WORK

When patients cannot act for themselves and have no family agents to represent them, problems are created for everyone concerned, including administrative personnel charged with the task of maintaining bureaucratic order by seeing that proper documents are signed, financial arrangements agreed to, informed consent formalities observed, and so forth. The lives of patients in highly technologized medical settings have become increasingly punctuated by rituals of contractual agreement that are, in turn, a direct consequence of legal and organizational complexities created by the introduction of more and more high-level technology into hospitals. Hence it has become a matter of institutional necessity that someone who can represent the patient be readily available to legitimate the order of business and facilitate the flow of scheduled events. In the context of a complexly interlinked, time-intensive system, delays of any duration occurring at one point can adversely affect schedules at far-flung points throughout the hospital. The consequences range from mild localized inconveniences to problems of more general scope and gravity—as when expensive instruments (like the CAT scanner) are left standing idle, thus depriving the institution of revenues needed for amortizing the equipment or even for subsidizing other less remunerative units and services.

So an interplay of technology-related factors, including a higher and higher incidence of very sick patients unable to act in their own behalf, has increased the reliance of the hospital on family members to traverse the already numerous and constantly emerging legal checkpoints. Many of these have presumably been designed to protect the hospital's clients, but often they seem to be pro forma devices to protect the hospital against legal action and charges of negligence. In any event, the kin have, in their legal function, become an important adjunct to hospital administration in a situation that is daily more entangled in organizational and legal complexities.

MAKING CRUCIAL DECISIONS

Leaving aside the identity work and the clinical safety work in which spouses and parents engage, none of all the various tasks that kin do is so intellectually and emotionally demanding, so difficult to pursue, so fateful in its outcome, and yet so little understood by staff, as the work that goes into crucial decision making. We are not now speaking of decision making in its older acute care sense in which, once a diagnosis has been made, a clear directive for action is possible.

In the case of chronic illness trajectories, decision making can be quite another matter. As noted earlier, advanced stages of chronic illnesses tend to be characterized by any or all of the following: fragile trajectories prone to destabilization, more frequent and more serious crises requiring medical intervention and intensive care, added complications that are introduced when diseases and disabilities are cumulative, and increasingly problematic and/or experimental options for treatment. Under several such circumstances, the work of deciding which options to choose in stabilizing a trajectory is, in its uncertainties and perils, not unlike steering a course through a mine field.

When a chronically ill person becomes so critically ill that he or she is hospitalized for treatment, the kin are often well aware that difficult choices will have to be made among less-than-perfect options. Between their concern for their sick relative and their own stake in the outcome, family members are highly motivated to find out everything they can about available options.[1] Many, especially the more sophisticated and assertive, will insist on the right to take an active part in any decisions. This insistence is not always met with professional favor and cooperation. There are frequently strong sentiments, especially among physicians, that professional judgment based on medical knowledge, skill, and experience should unquestionably prevail. Increasingly, however, the physician's unquestioned authority is coming under assault, with the rise of some degree of medical consumer insurgency.

When the kin follow a sick relative into the hospital, unless this is at the beginning or very early in the trajectory, they are versed in the pragmatics of the case.

1. They are familiar with its history, including its complications and the various expedients that have heretofore proved to be successful or unsuccessful in its management.
2. They are familiar with the structure and dynamics of the family network: what resources it can command, who can be counted on to do what, and what kinds of problems family members can manage among themselves and which ones may require outside help.
3. They know the patient in his or her unique psychological and social dimensions and thus are in a good position to judge what conditions of life or disability he or she can be expected to accept and which may be beyond the limits of endurance.
4. They are aware of coterminous physiological problems whose implications may be overlooked by a hospital staff intently focused on the critical aspects of a single, if acute, phase of only one disease.

Although the kin have knowledge that can be of vital importance when hard and complex choices must be made among options for the next steps in treatment, they often have very little idea of the actual options. To participate intelligently in decision making, they must first seek out sources of reliable information—not always an easy quest.[4] Sometimes their attempts at information gathering are actively hindered by the staff but more often they are hampered inadvertently by hospital policies and customs that do not recognize that the kin have salient work to do and that its success may very well depend on the quantity and quality of the information available to them. The kin are at the bottom of an institutional hierarchy of information, whose code directs questions upward through the chain of medical command ending with the physician presumed to be in charge of the case, whose word is assumed to be final. This means that their questions, if they have any substance at all, will typically be met with the conventional, guarded advice: Ask the doctor! Asking the doctor, however, may be more easily recommended than realized. Between the telling and the doing lie knotty questions to be answered: Who is the doctor? Where is the doctor? How does one get him or her to talk?

Relevant to those questions are the following issues concerning the relationship of physician to patient. There is a prevalent American myth that patients are customarily in the care of a "primary care" physician who maintains close supervision over their health, including their psychosocial problems, and who is therefore equipped to advise them and orchestrate the various aspects of their medical treatment. However, once a chronic disease becomes a major problem for the patient, the picture changes. Patients with severe chronic illnesses are likely to be referred to the care of specialists, who become out of critical necessity the primary authorities in directing their cases. If there is more than one chronic illness, authority will be divided between two or more specialists. So, the position of the primary care physician can be largely anomalous. In the first place, contacts between patient and specialists will probably be more frequent and certainly more compelling than those between the patient and any physician of more general orientation. Second, generalists do not, by the very nature of their work, have the focused knowledge requisite for evaluating specific treatment options. Third, when the work of making critical decisions has to be done, patients and their family supporters may find themselves in a medical center far from where they live and where their family physicians, if they have one (or their local specialist) is located.

Therefore, the physician whom the kin seek to consult will more likely be the specialist in charge of the particular disease—or of a particular phase of a particular disease—than the primary care physician. Since, in the minds of many specialists, it is the primary care physician who should take responsibility for overseeing the broader physiological and psychosocial implications of the case, there can obviously be some slippage between kin and professional conceptions of what should be communicated by whom and to whom. This bears ultimately on the kin's ability to do the work entailed in making decisions important for their sick relatives as well as for themselves.

Further misunderstandings can arise when more than one specialist is simultaneously working on the case: "the" cardiologist, for instance, may in actuality be a *team* of cardiologists from whom it may be difficult to elicit a consistent opinion or body of information. In such an instance as this, the kin are often heirs to piecemeal, apparently contradictory testimony from individual team members, rather than the recipients of a well-thought-out, well-articulated, agreed-on, clearly communicated team position. The result can therefore be more distressing or disorienting than illuminating to the kin.

Even when the kin have ascertained which physician they need to consult in their search for information, they still face the problem of finding that physician—and finding her or him when she or he has enough time to permit full discussion of available options. For the family, the physical crisis of one of its members can be an emotionally challenging, timeless experience in which little else matters except the patient and the exigencies of his or her illness. Physicians, in contrast, not only have other patients competing for their time and attention, but also necessarily regulate their professional lives in accordance with their working hours. The ordered world of scheduled rounds and planned-in-advance, rigidly time-metered appointments is not readily adapted ot the inclusion of unpredictable, time-consuming encounters and conversations with the kin. In consequence, there often ensues an extended game of hide-and-seek in which the kin attempt to waylay and buttonhole physicians who, in turn, use various means at their disposal—including the protective intervention of nurses, receptionists, and answering services—to elude their grasp and avoid unplanned confrontation. The nature and outcome of the game vary with the nature and style of the participants: among the kin, for example, some will be diffident and easily discouraged in their quest for information and therefore are destined to fail in their efforts. Others will be bolder and more determined, less easily intimidated by the mystique of professionalism, and may as a result succeed in getting the information they need. However, they may also fail, especially if their determination is read by the staff as "pushy" or unreasonable behavior.

Much has been written about the problems of communication between physicians and their patients. The issue of bilingualism in medical practice is currently receiving a great deal of attention, particularly in regions of the United States such as California and Texas, whose populations include sizable concentrations of non-English speakers. All of the problems that hamper communication between physicians and their patients similarly impede the information-gathering work of the kin. Different perceptions, different lexicons, different standards of credulity and credibility—combined, varied, permuted—can make the exchange of even simple ideas a time-consuming and often mutually frustrating experience.

Additionally, there are problems that are especially exacerbated by the current state of the medical art. First, the more specialized the physicians are, the more difficult it is for them to explain the rationales for medical decisions, or indeed for the various options they recognize as feasible. Second, the increasingly experimental nature of treatment options, when a trajectory goes more and more awry, means that the physicians frequently do not themselves know what medical consequences can be reasonably anticipated to follow on a given course of action. Faced thus with a quandary, they may consider it better to conceal uncertainty, either to protect professional reputations or to spare the patient and kin from knowledge that might conceivably damage morale. Patients and kin, in their turn, may make the situation even more difficult by continuing to press insistently for conclusive answers even after they have been told that none can confidently be given. Ambiguity is not always easy to tolerate.

For all that, kin may be heavily involved in the decisions that will profoundly affect their sick relative's physiological and social fate. Of course, they may be called on by the medical and nursing staffs, quite literally, to join in or actually make such decisions, when either the staff cannot or wishes not to bear sole or full responsibility for the consequences of such decisions. This kind of work, then, becomes highly visible to everyone involved—more visible, in general, than the kin's involvement with other kinds of work in the hospital.

References

1. Massie, Robert, and Massie, Suzanne: Journey, New York, 1976, Warner Communications.
2. Strauss, Anselm, Fagerhaugh, Shizuko, Suczek, Barbara, and Wiener, Carolyn: Sentimental work in the technologized hospital, Sociology of Health and Illness **4:**254-278, 1982.
3. Strauss, Anselm, Fagerhaugh, Shizuko, Suczek, Barbara, and Wiener, Carolyn: The social organization of medical work, Chicago, 1984, University of Chicago Press.
4. Whipple, Lee: Whole again, Ottawa, Ill., 1980, Caroline House Publishing Co.

CHAPTER 13

COMFORT WORK IN THE HOSPITAL

Comfort work is familiar to us all, since so many illnesses are associated with aches, pains, nausea, and other discomforts. However, the hospital setting and the work done there together complicate the comfort work almost beyond belief, as compared with comfort work done during the pre-chronic illness era. The giving of tender loving care (the centerpiece of traditional nursing identity) has so many novel features that it warrants being awarded the status of genuinely new "news."

CHANGES AFFECTING COMFORT WORK

The overwhelming prevalence of patients bedded down with chronic illness in the hospital means there is a great deal of illness-related discomfort that requires handling by the staff and, inevitably, by the patients, too. Chronic diseases bring discomforts dramatically to the fore: each illness has its characteristic pattern of symptoms, and many of the symptoms represent some degree of episodic or persistent discomfort to the sick person.

Moreover, since many chronic illnesses bring about other systemic disturbances or impact on unrelated illnesses, the discomforts that afflict the sick person can be varied and feed into each other. Moreover, chronic illness is likely to be associated with long periods, even as long as life itself, of uncomfortable living. Not that discomfort is always at peak intensity, but the discomfort is apt to be intermittent, repetitive, sometimes persistent even if not so intense as to be completely immobilizing or debilitating.

SPECIALIZATION, TECHNOLOGY, AND COMFORT

Quite aside from the contingencies of disease itself, the contemporary explosion of medical specialization with its attendant therapeutic interventions contributes to the discomforts of ill persons and complicates their comfort care. In the hospital especially, during the acute phases of an illness, the interventions can be diverse and intrusive. Patients must be transported to and from machined sites, their bodies positioned in relation to the machines, their stomachs suctioned, and their arms punctured for intravenous connections or the drawing of blood. Numerous procedures also cause some degree of discomfort, both during and after the staff's procedural actions. Medications can also result in digestive disturbance, dizziness, headaches—any number of discomforts. The essential point here—one that is easily missed—is that medical interventions can and often do *inflict* discomfort.[2] That is so whether or not the personnel are competent and careful; when they are not, the chances of inflicting discomfort are of course greatly magnified.

For the management of many trajectories, the medications, procedures, or machine work deemed necessary are nearly continuous over the course of hospitalization (and often afterward), engendering discomforts that may feed into each other, raising the pitch of discomfort in geometric progression. This may sometimes stretch over many days or weeks of hospitalization.

HOSPITAL ORGANIZATION AND COMFORT

In addition to the changes in technology, medical interventions, and the chronic illness trajectories themselves, the characteristic organization of today's hospital also contributes to making comfort work a complex issue. The institution is organized principally around the giving of acute care, meaning an intense focus by the personnel around strictly medical aspects of diagnosis and therapy. This, combined with the general hustle and bustle of work life, and the great concern with clinical safety, means that comfort will take primacy only under such (not so frequent) conditions as touched on later in this chapter.

The various technicians who move in and out of patients' rooms are very much focused on their technical tasks and very little trained in the niceties or the physiological technicalities of comfort care. They have little knowledge of any given patient's current discomforts, unless told by the patient, and they may have little understanding of how to minimize their own unwitting or inevitable infliction of discomfort. Nurses are sometimes still educated at schools that emphasize comfort as well as more strictly physiological care, but the organization of ward work tends to pull them both toward the latter kind of care and toward the multitude of numerous mundane activities that help to keep the ward functioning as an organization. In general, also, the flow of information to nurses from physicians and from head nurses concerns work couched in medical and procedural terms that bears relatively little on patients' discomforts—except perhaps their relief by medications, when discomforts either are seen as affecting the disease course itself or are highly visible and perhaps have been complained about by the patients themselves.[1,4] Comfort tasks tend to be scheduled as routines, thus making the staff's total work easier: thus there is a time to bathe, to pass out fresh drinking water, to "look in on" patients. However, the intensity of the therapeutically oriented work schedule often competes even with the comfort routines. In short, all of these organizational features of the hospital tend to draw staff's attention away from engaging in the work of preventing, minimizing, or relieving discomfort, unless discomfort is perceived either as affecting the course of illness or as flowing directly from the illness (high temperature, dizziness) or the therapeutic maneuvers designed to manage it.

The work flow of departments other than the clinical wards also tends to complicate as well as to minimize greatly the amount and effectiveness of comfort work, which generally fares badly in the competition for staff's time and attention. For example, when doing an x-ray examination the highest priority is that of obtaining a clear picture, while patient comfort is entirely secondary if considered at all. On the patient's return to the ward, personnel there must cope with his or her normal reactions to such frustrating situations, as well as alleviate the discomforts thus engendered or magnified.

Inadequacies in goods and services required from supporting departments also enormously complicate the comfort work of ward personnel. A patient, for instance, may require frequent changes of bed linen because of excessive sweating or inability to control bowels, or may require a certain drug or comfort-abetting device. Yet there may be a shortage of necessary supplies on the ward or an exasperating delay in receiving them from elsewhere. It is not unusual for a nurse to be heard explaining that a drug or device or piece of equipment has been ordered, "but we have to wait until it comes." It is equally common to hear a patient say something like "What the hell does it take to get a pill for my headache?" or "Why don't you have that damn equipment right here, why do you have to send for it?"

DISCOMFORTS: IN THE HOSPITAL VERSUS AT HOME

Discomforts cover a wide range of physical conditions and sensations. Uncomfortable sensations include tingling, itching, soreness, pressure and fullness, coldness, hotness, stiffness, dirtiness, thirst. Uncomfortable physical states include weakness, dizziness, flatulence, constipation. These discomforts are of course a part of ordinary living, being associated with routine bodily functions (eating, sleeping, defecating, bathing), as well as with the daily activities of working, walking, sitting, interacting.

Outside the hospital, one's own body and its occasional or persistent discomforts tend to be private matters. People take care not to expose certain parts of their bodies in public, and personal body care is usually managed in private. Social conventions influence our talking about intimate "private parts" too openly, and such activities as passing gas or scratching oneself vigorously are frowned on when done in public. Nor does one dwell on body discomforts, burdening others with their details. In short, people usually maintain some semblance of healthy body normalcy, even when suffering much discomfort; even the sick tend to play down or literally hide their uncomfortable symptoms.

Everyday normalizing and managing of discomforts become drastically altered when someone is hospitalized. First of all, the medical orientation of personnel encourages viewing discomfort as symptomatic of disease. Symptom assessment is important for proper diagnosis, treatment, and periodically to locate the illness status, as well as to monitor physiological reactions to therapeutic measures. However, because discomforts tend to be ambiguous—stemming in part from their many possible sources that may or may not be directly related to disease or therapy—the patients themselves may experience difficulty in deciding which discomforts are important enough to tell the personnel about. Over time, as a result of questioning by staff and through their responses to expressions of discomfort, patients may learn which discomforts are significant to report, and for which ones they can successfully or at least reasonably request relief.

Second, in the hospital a patient's body becomes much more open to public scrutiny, shared territory for all kinds of personnel who lay claims to its examination and manipulation. When carrying out their various trajectory tasks, the nurses, physicians, technicians, and other health workers manipulate and expose the body, inserting instruments, needles, tubes into it. The status of the body is so openly discussed among the staff that even visitors and other patients may overhear the talk.

As for routine physical housekeeping tasks involving actual or potential discomfort for the patient, these are done under conditions strange for him or her and with unfamiliar equipment. Sometimes minimal information is given about how to go about these tasks: a basin of water is plunked down with the comment, "Okay, get started on your bath." Also some tasks are difficult, like cleansing oneself after using a bedpan; yet patients do not ordinarily request staff assistance, as this is a very private matter. Again, the ordinary upkeep routines are disrupted by the requirements of fitting into the various staff members' work routines, and patients do usually learn to do this if not always to accept it.

Third, hospitalized patients are required to cede management of their discomforts to others. Acutely ill persons generally readily relinquish this responsibility. However, chronically ill persons have had much experience and done much experimentation in managing their own discomforts. Often they have tried many different types of drugs, and they know which are more or less effective, how much to take, when, and what the potential side effects may be. They have learned which body positions "work best" and which to avoid "like poison." They know a great deal about pacing themselves and about which foods not to eat. So in many respects they are much more knowledgeable than any staff member can possibly be about managing their characteristic discomforts—however little they may know about managing other discomforts that result from medical interventions performed at the hospital. Additionally, since many suffer from two or more chronic illnesses, they are more likely than the staff, to be concerned with minimizing or alleviating discomforts associated with all except the primary illness, on which the health workers are focused almost exclusively.

Fourth, besides all the discomforts inflicted by the personnel while doing diagnostic and therapeutic tasks, patients' discomforts can be heightened by the hospital environment: it can be noisy, untidy, poorly ventilated, too hot, too cold, full of undesirable odors.

A fifth consideration is that the mundane quality of most discomforts tends to render invisible much of the comfort work engaged in by patients—or conversely, the necessity for staff members sometimes to do comfort work that goes unrecognized. For example, before a procedure begins, a sick person may prop a pillow because of "a touch of arthritis," or position his or her body in a specific way so as to "avoid having my back go out." If patients do not inform them, the personnel do not necessarily notice such actions; if they do notice, they may regard them as unrelated to comfort care. A counterpart of this blindness is that similar actions carried out by personnel, especially the nurses, may be invisible to or misinterpreted by patients. Comfort work often requires considerable knowledge about physiological functions, much skill, technique, and art; even the efficient accomplishing of body housekeeping tasks for or with a patient ("meeting hygienic needs") can be important in its therapeutic implications. Yet patients may regard this work or assistance as nontechnical, ordinary, or just being nice or helpful. Even close monitoring and assessing of discomfort-relieving procedures and medications can be quite invisible qua work (hence the often-heard criticism, "The only thing nurses do is pass out pills"—not knowing that monitoring and assessing may accompany this seemingly menial task).

In sum, management of discomfort at home and in the hospital must of necessity be enormously different. This is so even when patients rely to lesser or greater extent on their own tried and true or now desperately experimental methods. Everything in the hospital—organization, technology, work routines, staff orientations, the physical setting itself—compounds both the relative simplicity of comfort work done at home and the relative autonomy of sick persons (and kin) in doing their own comfort work. The contrast between home and hospital is epitomized by the remark of a longtime user of aspirin: "They even take away your aspirin, but don't pay attention when you ring the bell."

DIMENSIONS OF DISCOMFORT: RECOGNITION AND DISAGREEMENT

Adding further to the complexity of comfort work in hospitals is the recognition of, and agreement or disagreement over, various dimensions of discomfort. The dimensions include duration, graveness, specificity of cause, predictability, preventability, controllability, and rectifiability of any discomfort. Each dimension, of course, constitutes a continuum running from high to low, short to long, ambiguous to clear-cut, and so on.

In some illnesses, both the numbers and kinds of discomforts and their associated dimensions may not present particular problems insofar as they are easily recognized and easily agreed on, and measures for handling the discomforts are relatively effective. Standard surgery without undue complications thereafter is an instance of a trajectory characterized by those features. However, as noted earlier, problematic trajectories have markedly increased, hence the nonrecognition of and the disagreement over each and every dimension of a discomfort are a potential hazard to effective comfort work, as well as to harmonious relationships between staff and patient and among the staff members themselves.

In more specific terms, various participants in the trajectory dramas may misunderstand each others' readings of discomfort dimensions, not recognizing that others have placed different interpretations on or given different weights to whether a discomfort—if it is noticed at all—is important or unimportant, critically grave or not, ambiguous or unambiguous as to cause, will quickly pass or be persistent, is generally relievable or not, and so on. Even if each party recognizes how the other is reading the situation, misunderstanding being not really at issue, the disagreement still may result in impatience, irritability, frustration, anger, or downright fury. Consequently, rhetoric may flow easily, and action reminiscent of the battlefield is not uncommon.

DISCOMFORT TASKS: THREE VIGNETTES

The management of discomforts as engendered by the contingencies of the illness itself, the medical interventions, or the hospital environment, involves potentially eight different kinds of comfort work tasks: (1) preparing the patient for discomfort, (2) assessing discomfort, (3) preventing discomfort, (4) minimizing discomfort, (5) relieving discomfort, (6) legitimating discomfort, (7) enduring discomfort, and (8) expressing discomfort. The last three are the patient's potential jobs, although he or she may also engage in the others. Before scrutinizing what these tasks entail, we will present several vignettes taken from field notes to illustrate some of those jobs and sometimes failures to do them by the staff.

Mrs. Hofnagel's travail

Mrs. Hofnagel underwent surgery for an anal fissure; she was given a spinal block, sent to the recovery room for an hour, then back to her room. For the next day or two she had some anal discomfort but was readily given relieving medication, on request as well as at other times. However, one nurse the second day "struck me as really mean, implying 'you're a coward because you can't wait' " for the medication. "She said something also about how I was handling the packing when I was peeing, and I had to point out that I was trying to keep myself clean."

1. Discomfort and slight pain are anticipated following this operation by the physician, who writes orders for pain-*relieving* medication, including on patient's request.
2. However, one nurse has a different philosophy of pain *relief,* and perceives the patient as having a lack of proper *endurance.* She *assesses* the degree of discomfort differently than the patient, the latter having no effective means of *legitimating* the degree of her discomfort.
3. The patient is engaged in *preventing* potential discomfort from an unclean packing, an action that the nurse misinterprets.

Two days after the operation Mrs. Hofnagel had her first bowel movement. She had not been *prepared* by the staff for the potentially great pain that might attend this activity. There was an aide in attendance, called by the patient, who had been told that the first bowel movement might make her feel faint. The aide filled the bathtub with water while the patient began to defecate. "It was like passing splintered glass! I was shocked. You expect you'll be uncomfortable but—. And I had had no previous experience with this, so did not know what to expect." The aide helped her off the toilet and into the tub; after she had bathed, the aide helped her back to bed. A nurse then gave her clean packing and more medication.

1. The staff failed to *prepare* the patient for great discomfort.
2. Her discomfort was relieved by sitting in hot water.
3. Medication *prevented* or *minimized* more discomfort.

Mrs. Hofnagel's reaction to the episode on the toilet? "Horror! And scared about next time. When the physician came, I yelled at him: You didn't tell me! What if the aide hadn't been there?" The physician—whom she liked very much—only laughed. "He was pleased that I went, that I was functioning with no problems. He regarded all this like a minor cosmetic job—but up the anus."

1. The patient accuses her physician of negligence: *(a)* you did not *prepare me* for the discomfort; *(b)* there might have been nobody there to help *relieve* me.
2. The physician's focus is on the successful phase of the trajectory management, to the exclusion of any comfort work except his previous orders for medication on request. The physician sent her home—although she was frightened of future bowel episodes—with instructions to fill her bathtub in case of a repetition of the "splintered glass," and to sit in the hot water occasionally between bowel movements.
3. The physician was *minimizing or preventing* future discomfort.

Mr. Einshtein's enema

This patient managed a highly discomforting episode, which he later referred to as his "battle of the bowel." Two days before he entered the hospital with a severe cardiac attack, he had had a barium enema with an x-ray examination, to check a possible source of anemia. The first night in the hospital, a nurse gave him a milk of magnesia pill to prevent possible bowel blockage and attendant discomfort. The second night, however, although he had not yet moved his bowels, he was given no medication. The next morning, at about 7 AM he felt like defecating but was impacted; it really hurt, so he believed he needed an enema. He told the nurse about it two or three times, when she came to take blood pressure readings; finally he asked for the head nurse, repeating that he was in much discomfort. The personnel were very busy that morning, so they scarcely heard his relatively mild expressions of discomfort or his requests that they relieve it. The head nurse spoke of a bowel softener, but the patient insisted, the second time around but again to no avail, that he needed relief "right away!" An intern supported the head nurse's judgment about a bowel softener, although the patient repeated his own firm belief. By about 1 PM his discomfort was so extreme that he called for the head nurse and insisted flatly on an enema. The nurse acceded but said "in a while," because the necessary equipment had to be brought from a servicing department. In about an hour, the enema finally was administered. It yielded immediate relief: the discomfort vanished entirely.

1. The staff failed to *prevent* the discomfort, although it might have been anticipated.
2. The patient failed to *legitimate* the extent of discomfort and the need for its relatively immediate *relief,* for the staff *assessed* differently the extent and importance of the discomfort. They judged this in some part by either misreading or misinterpreting his *expression* of his discomfort.
3. The patient finally chose not to *endure* any longer, now *expressing* himself vividly and strongly; thus he managed to get *relief* for his discomfort.

Comfort work in the recovery room

The nurse changed the blood transfusion bag. She milked it down and took out an air bubble. Later she changed it again. Later still she managed to get the bottle part filled through mechanical motion. She drew blood and immediately put back new blood into the tube. She milked the urine tube once. She took a temperature. She put a drug injection into the nonautomated intravenous setup. During all this activity, however, she had in focus, though not necessarily glancing at it, the video screen that registered ECG and blood pressure readings. Once she punched the computer button to get the 15-minute readout on cardiac functioning. Once she milked the infection-purifying tube leading from the patient's belly. Periodically, she marked down both the readings and some of what she had done. Once the patient stirred as she was touching his arm: she said quite nicely then that she was about to give him an injection that would relax him. He indicated that he had heard. Another time she noticed him stirring and switched off the light above his head, saying, "that's better isn't it?"

1. Injections were given to *minimize* or *prevent* expected pain. To this should be added that the temperature of the bed was controlled by a machine, used to *minimize* potential discomfort and in the service of the trajectory itself.

2. In response to her *assessment* of the patient's *expression* of discomfort, the nurse switched off the light to *relieve* discomfort.
3. The patient is nonsentient so there is no need to *endure* or further *express* his discomfort—and certainly no need to *legitimate* because the discomfort is *expected* or "reasonable," given the phase of the trajectory.

To summarize this section as well as the whole thrust of this chapter on "comfort care," keeping patients maximally comfortable (and minimally uncomfortable!) can entail complex and subtle work. The patients' share of that work is considerable, for again they are very much a part of the hospital's division of labor. Although we have not especially emphasized the kin's participation in comfort work, of course that frequently is of much importance.

COMFORT TASKS: THE MANAGEMENT OF PAIN

Next, we discuss some complexities of comfort work in terms of pain management, focusing on the work of both staff and patients. What is true of pain management is simply a more evident instance of what transpires with nausea, dizziness, digestive discomfort, and other instances of discomfort. The material is taken from a book by two of the authors *(The Politics of Pain Management)*[2] and will consist of two segments: first, what happens when patients are hospitalized for routine surgery (mostly for their chronic illnesses), and then what often happens when pain is inflicted because of needed medical intervention.

Pain and routine surgical trajectories*

Routine surgical trajectories can be characterized as predictable, involving few risks, unambiguous, and of short duration. Barring complications, the recovery courses and their accompanying pains are predictable and nonproblematic. Both the hospitalization and the pain courses are anticipated to be short. The hospital stay is usually from a week to 10 days, and sometimes even shorter. Staff anticipates that pain will be relatively high for 24 to 72 hours postoperatively and will then quickly taper off.

There is a relatively high degree of specificity as to the causes of physiological (as opposed to psychological) pain and discomfort. So, patients generally need not legitimate the presence of pain, although there may be questions as to the degree of pain suffered by individual patients. Because of the physiological bases of pain, specific drugs and specific nursing and medical measures are used to relieve pains. Of equal importance to relief, however, are the prevention of complications and the returning of the patient to physiological equilibrium, both

---

*Material in this discussion is modified from Fagerhaugh, Shizuko, and Strauss, Anselm: The politics of pain management, Menlo Park, Calif., 1977, Addison-Wesley Publishing Co., pp. 61-67, 94-97.

of which may unavoidably require inflicted pains and discomforts.

Because of the familiar nature of the surgical trajectories, patients, too, are generally aware that they must endure some pains and discomforts from both the surgery and treatment. Usually they are aware that severe pain will last a few days, but that all pain will eventually end.

The staff's pain work. The pain tasks of the staff include assessment, prevention, minimization, and relief. The approaches to these pain tasks may be physiological, pharmacological, or psychological. The tasks are an integral part of the overall work done to accomplish a successful surgical outcome. Preoperatively, the staff attempts to minimize the degree of anticipated postsurgical pain by relieving the patient's apprehension about the impending surgery and pain. This is accomplished by talking with the patient about pain tolerance and anxieties concerning the surgery. The necessary preoperative procedures are explained, as are the surgical course, the accompanying pains, and the measures available for relief. The staff explains painful but necessary procedures that require patient cooperation and tolerance to avoid complications. In nursing vernacular this stream of information is called "preoperative patient teaching." Its purposes are not only to relieve patient apprehension and thereby reduce pain perception, but also to assure a cooperative patient for a successful surgery.

For the first 24 to 72 postoperative hours, staff are concerned with returning the patient to physiological equilibrium after the effects of anesthesia and surgical trauma. Staff members monitor vital signs, maintain fluid and electrolyte balance, prevent complications, and do other treatments specific to the surgery. Together, the treatments require a multitude of tasks, some involving no pain (taking blood pressure), others giving some discomfort (intravenous infusions, irrigations, or dressing changes). Circulatory, respiratory, and other complications associated with body immobilization must be minimized at the cost of "patient-induced pain" caused by deep breathing, moving around in bed, and early ambulation. Achieving patient cooperation is vital.

Incisional pain will probably be high for the first 24 to 72 hours postoperatively, but it depends on the type of surgery and an individual's pain tolerance. This pain is minimized by narcotics given at 3- to 4-hour intervals, as required. The nurses' tasks include assessing the pain and giving the drugs at appropriate intervals. When the dosage or frequency of administration of drugs does not "hold" the pain, then the surgeon or house staff are notified about changing the drug order. The pacing of drugs must be sufficient to control the worst pains, but it must not cause sleepiness or drowsiness when cooperation with treatment is necessary. Antinausea drugs are administered if needed. Appropriate drugs are also available for "gas pains." Other drugs, such as antispasmodics, are used with certain types of surgical courses.

There are many additional pain-minimizing tasks such as splinting the incision when the patient coughs, vomits, or changes body position. A variety of discomforts can be anticipated: dry mouth, headache, urinary and bowel retention, irritations from tubes placed in various body orifices, sore throat from an endotracheal tube used for the anesthetic. For each of these discomforts there are appropriate discomfort-minimizing measures. Reassuring and encouraging the patient are, of course, related pain-minimization tasks, as is relieving the family's apprehensions.

Usually by the third or fourth postoperative day, the patient is expected to be "over the hump" and is encouraged to be more physically active, take foods by mouth, and be more self-sufficient. As pain decreases, less potent drugs are used.

Patient pain tasks. When the patient accepts the decision to have surgery, an implicit contract is made with the staff. The patient must, first of all, trust the physician's judgment that surgery is necessary; the physician is responsible for as successful a surgery as possible and as comfortable a hospital stay as possible. The patient is to cooperate with the physician and other health personnel for this common goal. From the perspective of the staff, two of the patient's pain tasks are to apprise the personnel of existing pain and to give appropriate information (where, when, and the character of the pain) as requested. Using this information the staff assesses the pain and takes appropriate action. The patient also must keep pain expression within reasonable limits by avoiding prolonged loud crying and moaning, which might disturb other patients. One of the patient's major tasks is to cooperate with and endure painful but necessary procedures, such as insertion of needles. Noncooperation can unnerve the staff members and affect their technical performance.

Ward work and pain accountability. Considering, then, the properties of routine, low-risk surgical trajectories (predictable, unambiguous, short duration, and finite) and the specificity of approaches to pain prevention, minimization, and relief, we can assume that much of pain management is nonproblematic—as perceived by the staff. We can also assume that when the surgical trajectory is routine, there are well-developed, well-organized approaches for managing pain. There is a discrepancy, however, between what is possible and what is neglected in effective pain relief. This discrepancy can be understood only when viewed from the combined impact of (1) the work demands of the clinical setting, (2) the institutional accountability surrounding pain management, and (3) the complexity of patient-staff and staff-staff pain interactions.

Surgical units are usually very busy places, with innumerable and complex tasks requiring much skill, frequently involving a considerable use of machinery. Compared to medical units there is a constant flow of new patients, and the rate of patient turnover is quite rapid. There is a mixture of routine and complex problematic cases that require more or less of the staff's attention. When emergencies occur or when there is a shortage of staff or when there are several critically ill or problematic surgical cases, attention is naturally focused on the critical or problematic patients at the expense of the routine, low-risk surgical patients who are recovering on schedule.

The neglect of the latter results in part from competing tasks and time and staff shortages, but also from the lack of institutional accountability for some important aspects of pain work.

Relief versus minimization: reliance on drugs. Not only did we find a lack of psychosocial accountability in pain relief but also a lack of pain minimization through nursing comfort measures. Paradoxically, this dual neglect is partly caused by the very properties of routine, low-risk surgery. Because the causes of pain are unambiguous and of short duration, there is high reliance on manipulating either the frequency or the dosage of drugs in order to relieve pain. After all, the pain is anticipated, and specific drugs can be ordered for pain relief.

Thus when patients complain of pain, the nurse's immediate response is to check when last a shot was given and whether the drug can be administered again within the limits of prescribed frequency. The reliance on drugs for relief is also due to the fact that patients, like nurses, tend to see drugs as the only solution to pain relief. Consequently, patients tend to initiate pain interactions by saying, "I need a pain shot." This reinforces the nurse's stereotypical responses: "Let me check the last time you had a shot"; "It isn't time for your shot yet"; "You just had a shot an hour ago." These responses also reinforce a patient's perception of drugs as the major means of relief. When asked their reactions to the nurses' stock answers, patients replied: "It made me angry"; "I felt devastated"; "It made me feel stupid"; "I felt the nurses weren't very sympathetic"; "I knew I had to stand some pain, but not this much."

The anticipated short duration of the surgical pain also encourages reliance on drugs. Anxiety or no anxiety, when there is no danger of complications or problems of drug dependency, such as those that might arise with an extended trajectory, the severe pain will last only 2 to 4 days at the most. Adding a tranquilizer or increasing the dosage or frequency of medication will control the pain. Even if a given patient is overly expressive about pain, it lasts for a few days and does not ordinarily upset the ward's sentimental order.

Nurses have other measures available to minimize pain and give comfort, such as splinting an incision when the patient has coughed or turned, giving a back rub, positioning, or pacing the drug to minimize the pain in ambulation. But these are volunteered rather than mandated, as a result of the great emphasis on drugs as the relief measure.[5] The exceptions that we observed were in situations such as involved cardiac or respiratory surgery, when coughing was absolutely essential to avoid complications, and when the surgery itself caused much coughing with pain. Here the main minimization measures were "ordered."

Although the patients we queried were critical of both the staff's management of pain and care in general, they were not likely to express disgruntlement or to voice criticism directly to the staff. Several factors contributed to the lack of overt critical expression on the part of patients. Generally knowing that severe pain would be short-lived, the patients were concerned with getting past the acute phase of surgery and back on their feet to resume their former social roles and were therefore willing to endure the pain. They were also concerned about staff reprisal should they voice their criticism. Enduring pain and discomfort was also related to their comparisons of themselves with others who were more critically or seriously ill; they considered themselves more fortunate. The relative absence of overt fussing and complaining by patients tended to encourage the staff's assumption that their management of pain was adequate.

Variable pain philosophies: problematic aspects. What may be routine and nonproblematic to the staff because a patient does not complain may be very problematic for the patient. Patients know they must cooperate in the recovery process, but *how* they are to behave is not made explicit by the staff. This is partly a result of the routine nature of certain surgeries, which fosters a taken-for-granted attitude, so that the who, what, when, and how of patient-staff informational exchange and interaction are not considered essential. This results in each staff member interacting with the patient in terms of his or her own philosophies about pain. These philosophies may vary widely on issues like threshold assessment, pain legitimation, giving of information, kind of control administered to the patient, pain trajectory, and limits of endurance.

The staff usually assumes that drugs can control surgical pain, yet the effectiveness of drug control calls for a complex set of staff-staff and patient-staff interactions. The patient must know the appropriate times and ways to request pain relief, the amount of pain he or she is expected to endure, the rules governing drug administration, and so on. Unless the patient has had previous experience in hospitals or has been given explicit cues by the staff, drug transactions can become quite problematic.

The varied philosophies of pain greatly influence transactions involving drugs. Wide variations were noted in the decisional prerogatives of doctors and nurses regarding drug-related tasks. Some nurses thought that giving information to patients about pain medication was solely the responsibility of the surgeon; others thought it was a shared responsibility. Variations were noted concerning how much information should be shared with the patient about anticipated pain and about pain drugs, and who should give this information. When a patient asked about pain drugs, some nurses would respond, "You'll have to ask the doctor." Others freely gave information about the drug, its dosage, and frequency of prescription.

A nurse who believes that patients should be told about anticipated pain may have difficulties with a physician who believes that informing only increases the patient's "anticipatory pain." Variations were noted on the degree to which nurses adhered to the prescribed frequency of dispensing drugs. Variations were also noted on how much pain the patient had to endure before a nurse would consult a physician for changes of a drug order. In addition, physicians varied in the discretionary latitude they allowed nurses in dispensing drugs. For example, a drug order might be specific ("50 mg of Demerol every 3 hours") or allow more latitude ("50-75 mg of Demerol every 3-4 hours"). Given this latitude, however, some nurses consistently gave the lower dosage while others gave the higher dosage. Some lowered the dosage earlier than did others. The degree of discretion allowed by the physicians, and the acceptance of responsibility by the nurses, were related partly to their degree of consciousness of legal consequences and restrictions.

The consequences of varied philosophies such as these can strain patient-staff and staff-staff interactions. For example, a nurse tells a patient to wait for a pain shot. Immediately afterward, the surgeon visits the patient who complains of pain. The surgeon asks the nurse when the patient last had a shot. The surgeon then decides the patient can have a shot and orders the nurse to give it immediately. The physician thinks the nurse has shown poor judgment. The nurse feels betrayed; her reasons have not been taken into account. After all, she sees the patient for 8 hours a day while the surgeon is in only a couple of minutes a day. The patient begins to think the nurse is neither trustworthy nor sympathetic.

There are also staff variations on the amount of control patients are allowed to have, the willingness to act on patients' suggestions, and the degree of adherence to bureaucratic rules. In one instance, a patient was confounded by a nurse who rigidly adhered to the rules and could not tolerate any suggestions. The patient explained that the ordered drug was too strong and was causing sleepiness, which interfered with the coughing up of mucus—something the doctor had said was important. The patient requested that the dosage be decreased. The nurse insisted the dosage could not be altered. Since the doctor was not available, the patient, knowing about possible respiratory complications accompanying surgery, balanced the options and decided not to take the dosage at all, but rather to endure the pain resulting from coughing up the mucus.

The staff may assume that a patient has been given adequate information about his or her responsibilities in the drug transaction, but in fact the information may be far from adequate. Take, for example, a surgeon's assurance to the patient that pain shots will be available for controlling postsurgical pain. The patient is then faced with the problem of whether to ask for pain relief or to wait for the nurse to exercise judgment. The surgeon may have said the drug would be available every 3 hours. If 3 hours have passed, should the patient ask for the next shot or wait for the nurse to act?

Among the consequences of the many unshared, individual pain philosophies is a tendency for patients to become very confused and generally dissatisfied with their care, or to develop distrust of professionals. Here are some common statements made by patients:

> I don't get it. One nurse says don't hold off asking for pain shots. Another says hold off.

> Some nurses offer pain shots. Others give the shot only when I ask for it.

> Some nurses are regular time nuts, giving the shots to the minute. Others are not so exacting.

> When I complain of pain some nurses try to find out more about the pains. Others say, let me check the last time you had a shot.

> Some nurses plan the drug so it won't be so painful to get up and walk around. Others just come in and command: "It's time for you to walk now."

In addition to variations among nurses, there are group variations among work shifts on the same ward. The latter depend on the pain management philosophies and the degree of accountability demanded by the charge nurse for the given shift, on the numbers of staff assigned to the shift, and on the kinds of competing work demands. In one situation we found problems of pain management stemming largely from two charge nurses who had opposing pain philosophies. The day shift charge nurse was psychosocially oriented, allowing the patients more control over their pain management than the evening charge nurse. The patients were caught in a conflict of opposing philosophies.

It is noteworthy that when patients complained to the researchers about the ways their pains were mismanaged, they attributed many of the problems to personality defects in the ward personnel, calling them unsympathetic, unkind, mean, and so on. The patients were totally unaware that the personnel were acting on the basis of their individual pain philosophies. Nurses criticized each other on the same basis. We should add that the patients often had *their* own pain philosophies, which they might or might not openly express.

Inflicted pain: accusations of incompetence or negligence

It is easy to see that the implicit (sometimes explicit) contract that allows the accomplishment of the primary medical task can be violated, either in actuality or in the opinion of one of the contractual agents. There is considerable fragility that characterizes the basic contract. Since the obligations of the contract are reciprocal, a patient of course can be reprimanded for breaking his or her side of the bargain. The stage is set, on both sides, for accusations of bad faith or bad conduct. The blaming, as in any political arena, will often be mutual.

From the staff's viewpoint, the patient can be blamed for failing to endure the pain; after all, it is only a by-product of a task done for the patient's own good. He can also be blamed for failing to control extreme expressions of displeasure and slowing up accomplishment of the primary tasks.

A number of conditions underlie the possibility that the patient will also make accusations. The most general set of conditions is that the patient, like the staff, makes a distinction between necessary and unnecessary pain. The latter, of course, pertains to pain that is an unanticipated by-product of the primary task, pain that the patient either has not been told about or has been told would not occur. However, unnecessary pain pertains also to necessary pain when the pain is more intense or of longer duration than expected. The inflicter is usually held responsible for all types of unnecessary pain: unanticipated, overly intense, and long-lasting.

As the patient sees it, the unnecessary pain can be caused either by *incompetence* (lack of skill) or *negligence* (carelessness, indifference). The patient may erroneously accuse pain inflicters, believing they have been careless when in fact they are inexperienced or they have made errors involving skill. Alternately, the patient may think the staff less than competent when in fact there has been some actual negligence displayed. Experienced patients, such as those on extended physiotherapy regimens, are more likely to spot the difference between incompetence and negligence.

Before discussing the conditions and consequences of experience in assigning blame, it will be useful to note some common organizational reasons for a staff member's actual negligence or incompetence. Concerning incompetence, the main fault usually lies with personnel who are insufficiently skilled either at their techniques or at "working on" particular kinds of patients. That deficiency of skill can stem from insufficient basic training, from lack of enough in-service training to keep up with advances in technologies—at the very least, from inadequate information about types of patients new to the personnel (a newness often caused by such factors as staff rotation).

The organizational conditions fostering negligence are perhaps more complex. To prevent or minimize pain engendered in cardiac patients by postoperative breathing regimens, patients must receive their drugs before doing the breathing, and receive them at exactly the right time. Unfortunately this involves a more complex intermeshing of staff work than is usually accomplished. Hence this kind of pain infliction through organizational negligence seems fairly frequent on CCUs. Other contributory organizational factors include a staff on a tight schedule, or one with a heavy load of medically difficult patients. A staff focused on technical aspects of care to the almost total exclusion of the humanistic aspects is also likely to be negligent in its infliction of pain during the pursuit of its main tasks.

Hospitals and clinics also seem often to proliferate a tendency to discount the patient's opinions on medical and even procedural matters, so that when a staff member and patient do not really know each other, a discounting of the patient's cues or utterances is likely. Patients are even more likely to be disregarded if they have earned a negative reputation on the ward or clinic—a frequent phenomenon, alas, in our health facilities.[3] Quite aside from an actual reputation, however, certain people get additional short shrift, or at least less concern is shown for them, because they are of "low social value": for example, some of the drunks, suicide attempters, victims of knife slashings, "accident cases," and various of the lower socioeconomic or "undesirable" ethnic and racial groups who appear regularly at the emergency rooms of our hospitals.

Now let us return to the differences a patient's experience might make in accusations of incompetency or negligence. Even without experience with specific procedures, treatments, or regimens, lay persons can sometimes recognize lack of skill in the manner, approach, style, or actual words of the pain inflicter. Experience leaves the patient less at the mercy of such negligence. A patient who time and again goes through the same regimens or procedures can quickly learn to judge the skill of personnel. Essentially, each new potential pain inflicter is on trial. Patients also become better at distinguishing between individual reasons (unpleasant person, does not like me) and organizational reasons (overworked, not enough staff) for negligence. Such comparisons go hand in hand with the repeated infliction situation. Also, if a number of patients know they are undergoing the same treatments, as with physical therapy, they will share their evaluative comparisons, so that certain staff members, like certain patients, receive reputations. Naturally, if a staff member is viewed as *both* competent and negligent, then patients would rather not have their fate, or at least their comfort, in such hands.

Patients differ in the manner in which they express themselves to staff when they believe they have suffered from some degree of incompetence or negligence. Sometimes they can be very direct; at other times they choose to remain silent. Conditions eliciting direct comments are fairly obvious: the patient is surprised into angry exclamation or fears that the same inflicter will return unless somehow reprimanded. Patients may even be quite fearful of potential damage, as well as of the pain itself, and command, as one did to a physical therapist: "Don't touch me again! You obviously don't know what you're doing." Among the reasons for keeping silent are the pain is insufficient to complain about, or the procedure is only done once, or the person is shy, does not like to complain, or is simply overawed by the staff's authority. Silence can also be a response when the patient fears, sometimes accurately, that there may be reprisals for complaining or blaming. An experienced person may recognize the dangers of being defined as a "bad" patient.

Those accusations that patients do level at a staff member are often met by two kinds of counterstatements. The first is based, whether justified or not, on the strategy that the strongest defense is an offense: "You moved!" or "What do you expect with all that racket you've been making?" In other words, the staff member accuses the patient of failing to keep his or her part of the implicit contract.

The second type of defense is to retort that someone has misread the situation: the task is very difficult and a certain amount of pain is inevitable, or what looks like undue and unseemly haste or careless procedure is really nothing of the sort. In short, signs are at best ambiguous, and only the truly experienced (that is, the professional) can read them correctly. Both types of counterstatement can be delivered with a variety of gestural and tonal expression, signifying a range of disapproval running from reluctant countercomplaint through annoyance, anger, fury, disgust, desperation. After all, the main job simply must be done, with or without the patient's cooperation. Understandably, such sets of tactics and countertactics may end in an increasingly vicious spiral of bad feeling, bad temper, and bad health care.

References

1. Byers, V.: Nursing observations, Dubuque, Iowa, 1975, Wm. C. Brown Publishing Co.
2. Fagerhaugh, Shizuko, and Strauss, Anselm: The politics of pain management, Menlo Park, Calif., 1977, Addison-Wesley Publishing Co., pp. 61-67, 94-97.
3. Glaser, Barney, and Strauss, Anselm: Social loss of dying patients, American Journal of Nursing **64:**119-121, 1964.
4. McBryde, C., and Blacklow, R.: Signs and symptoms, Philadelphia, 1970, J.B. Lippincott Publishing Co.
5. Schatzman, Leonard: Volunteerism and professional practice in the health professions. In Folta, Jean, and Deck, Edith, editors: Sociological framework for patient care, New York, 1966, John Wiley & Sons, Inc., pp. 45-155.

CHAPTER 14

HOSPITALIZED PATIENTS AND THEIR CLINICAL SAFETY WORK

Because the raison d'être of hospitals is the giving of medical and nursing care to patients, a substantial proportion of their personnel inevitably are involved with issues of clinical safety. We shall use this term, "clinical safety work," to indicate an important distinction, that between the safety work for patients and considerations for the safety of the personnel or the environment in which they work. At the ward level the immediate aim is to manage hazardous courses of illness, so that the ill are saved or made safer from the contingencies of their illnesses. On each ward, varying kinds of degrees of potential hazard are antici-pated and resources organized to cope with them.

This blocking, slowing up, or reversing of hazard that derives from patients' illnesses is, after all, the core of the staff's work. However, attached to that phys-iologically derived core are risks engendered by medical interventions (surgical, procedural, pharmacological, mechanical) that can threaten the safety of patients, whether their illnesses are similarly threatening or not. Many of the illnesses for which people are hospitalized today do not immediately threaten their lives; nev-ertheless, some of these lives are threatened immediately, or soon, unless there is skilled intervention. Ironically, that very intervention can be exceedingly hazard-ous either to life itself or at least to body functions. In the pages to follow, we will for purposes of clarity refer to the hazards of medical intervention as "risk," reserv-

---

This chapter is a portion of a forthcoming monograph[1] on the research project that provided materials for the three preceding chapters.

ing the term "danger" for those arising from the illness itself and from various contingencies arising to threaten the clinical safety of the patients. We will focus on the patient's safety work in conjunction with, as well as in parallel with, the personnnel's work.

PATIENTS' MONITORING, ASSESSING, AND RECTIFYING OF CLINICAL HAZARDS

Just as health workers are busily engaged in monitoring, assessing, and occasionally rectifying clinical danger and risk, so are the patients themselves (and often their families.) The patients' monitoring and assessing are quite intense, since it is their bodies and selves that are endangered. Their watchful eyes are not simply on potential dangers and risks as such, but also on the possible negative consequences of either staff's or their own mismonitoring and misassessing. They make their appraisals about themselves and others in highly charged situations. Their judgments may be very different from the personnel's. What may appear to be a major risk or danger to the patient may be trivial to the staff. Structurally, too, the context within which the patients must indicate their fears, anxieties, judgments, and even discoveries (they do indeed discover dangerous errors) makes expression of those additionally difficult. First, patients may be part of the hospital's division of labor (see below), but not formally so, and often only implicitly or in scarcely recognized ways. Second, when indicating to staff judgments of actual or potential hazard, they not infrequently operate from weakness in any accomplishing, persuading, or negotiating that they deem necessary.

Division of labor: implicit and explicit

In the actual division of labor during the monitoring and assessing, varying degrees and types of cooperation may be required of a patient. For the staff to make accurate assessments, a patient may have to engage in important collaborative actions, for instance, by accurately supplying information requested about physical and emotional reactions to the illness and to various medical interventions, or by "complying" in the carrying out of various diagnostic tests and therapies. When patients cannot collaborate because of the severity of their illnesses, or are unable to talk, are confused, hard of hearing, and so forth, then families and other appropriate resources may be substituted. Thus in pediatric units parents are important agents for assessing and monitoring. Patients also aid the staff in their monitoring and assessing by apprising them of something being "not quite right," or "going wrong"—new or altered physical signs and discomforts, altered machine sounds, or a disconnected tube. Supplementary action can be essesntial for instituting measures to prevent or reverse a potential risk. How well a patient performs these actions depends on whether the patient and kin understand both the degree of danger or risk, and the degree to which participation in the work is deemed necessary by the staff. Also important is the degree of patients' medical sophistication and other capabilities.

However, because mutual participation and responsibility remain largely implicitly understood rather than explicitly stated, much of the monitoring and assessing is done independently. It is also often invisible to each and is not shared. Also these invisible and unshared actions guide each person's managing of danger and risk, so that when the judgments differ—either in items or their dimensions, or in priorities—the management actions may be at cross-purposes and are apt to be mutually misconstrued. Thus they become the basis for inter- actional difficulties that arise between the respective parties. Making explicit the monitoring and assessing that the staff judge as appropriate for a given patient is not without its problems for the staff. Patients vary widely in their experiences with illness and in personal experiences, medical sophistication, and willingness to accept responsibilities. Judgments must be made about a patient's competence to take on the requisite tasks.

There is also the question of timing. This may call for varying degrees of interactional skill by the personnel, so that potential hazards can be made explicit to patients and families without their being unduly upset by the information. Then, of course, many illnesses and medical interventions can be so uncertain in out- come that the attendent risks cannot be specifically predicted to the patients. A great deal of information about biographical, illness, and medical experience is required from the patient before the staff can reasonably make his or her respon- sibilities clear. This task is becoming especially important with the increase in chronic illnesses, since patients now are having long and complicated illnesses and associated experiences. This calls for much interactional skill on the part of the staff members and also much time spent with the ill—time often not available on a busy ward. Thus a considerable amount of patients' monitoring and assessing goes unnoticed by the personnel unless directly brought to their attention or called for explicitly by the need to have patients "cooperate" in therapeutic and diagnos- tic actions.

Mutual assessment of risk potential

Since both patient and staff can be a source of danger and risk, both play a silent game of assessing each other's potential for those hazards—whether the other is competent, alert, reliable, and trustworthy. The cues and signs used by each may be accurate but also sometimes can be quite off the mark. For instance, a patient who has a reputation as a "crock" or a "whiner" will experience extreme difficulty in getting the personnel to accept the reliability of his or her assessments concerning the seriousness of, say, a physical reaction. A tricky silent game is played wherein both parties size each other up, as well as present themselves in such a manner that they are accepted as reliable, competent, and believable. Patients' conversations with each other and with kin replete with judgments of staff competence: "Boy, nurse so-and-so sure knows her stuff." "You got to watch Miss Jones." "I feel worse today because I don't think he knows how to do the treatment." Patients and families are constantly engaging in consulting about and comparing observations concerning the competences of various personnel.

More often than not, patients are at a disadvantage, because they have neither the experience nor medical knowledge (and they often recognize that) to make accurate judgments about hazard. However, some become quite expert. For instance, kidney dialysis patients, because of their treatment sessions each week, become expert not only in assessing staff competence but also in monitoring both the treatment and their bodies while on dialysis.

A patient's focus on assessment as well as on monitoring is often based on very personal experiences with illness, health personnel, and hospitals, often unknown to the staff. These experiences color the patient's priorities, making some hazardous items quite important, whereas others may actually be of equal or greater importance "medically." As an example, one patient had gotten an infection at the intravenous puncture site during his previous hospitalization, so he assessed and closely monitored the personnel who were now doing that procedure—whether they washed their hands, and so on. He even refused to have anyone whom he judged to be clumsy or physically untidy to carry out the procedure. The staff, in turn, thought of this patient as "being a bit fussy," and "a little on the paranoid side."

Patient-staff differences in criteria

A central problem in getting a better matching of patients' and staffs' assessment of hazard is that generally they apply different criteria. Health professionals tend to rely on technical medical measures, whereas patients rely on body reactions and sensations, mainly pains and other discomforts. As noted in the last chapter, pain and discomfort are highly subjective matters, many discomforts are highly ambiguous, and this poses particular problems of assessment for both the patient and the staff. Understandably this differential assessing of discomforts may be extremely relevant to the more crucial assessing of clinical safety.

It is important to understand that patients use their physical reactions to assess their trajectory locations, whether out of danger or not. When the felt body reaction and discomforts do not match the medical criteria used by the staff, interactional conflict may arise and endanger the future trajectory. Staff may discount the patients' expressions of discomfort, or the patients may discount the staff's assessments. These differences in assessment have consequences for how patients cooperate in the treatment process. Thus patients may engage in risky activities because they "feel better," or refuse to engage in activities because "I'm not over the danger." (This is a particular problem when patients engage in self-assessment and monitoring while at home. Drugs and treatments may be discontinued, or monitoring of bodies may be discontinued because they feel better.) By the same token, staff's discontinuing of the physical indicators as reported by patients may have serious consequences. Horror stories abound about serious dangers being neglected because of staff's heavy reliance on objective measurable medical approaches.

Also, as we have seen, in the highly technologized hospital, many of the pains and discomforts are technologically or staff inflicted. Sometimes the suffering that patients must withstand may be well beyond their tolerance for discomfort, not to mention their abilities to retain their composure. In other words, a patient assesses pain and discomfort not only in terms of their relevance to the illness trajectory but also in terms of very personalized composure. When a necessary pain or discomfort exceeds the composure limit, a patient may pull out a tube or refuse further painful treatments. Of course, other balancing factors may enter into the decision to cooperate in the treatment, such as tolerating terrible discomfort and pain just to live a bit longer. Patients' communications to staff about their pains and discomforts may constitute assessments of perceived dangers, but they also may amount to a request for relief. Thus those communications can be fraught with ambiguity or carry double messages. All of that adds to interactional difficulties between patients and personnel, which in turn can negatively affect the safety work of both.

INFORMATION WORK AND SAFETY

Patient-staff interactions concerning hazards and risk, exchange of information, and disclosure by the staff are extremely difficult. They call for considerable interactional skills and the giving of much biographical information both by patients and their families. Moreover, disclosure may be complicated by the ambiguity surrounding many illnesses and their associated technological interventions. In fact, debates among health professionals about safe options and when and how they are to be applied are not uncommon occurrences. In addition, when there are multiple illnesses, as is often the case, multiple specialists and experts are involved—so that the primary physician may well be reduced to a lay person vis-à-vis another specialist, perhaps deferring to that expert more blindly than is warranted.

The ambiguity of risks and dangers can become the basis of misunderstanding between the patient and health professionals. For example, the physician may hesitate to disclose information because the situation is ambiguous or requires further data; the patient, however, may construe the physician's silence as deliberate evasion. In another situation, when the ambiguity is disclosed because the patient is directly involved in the danger, the latter may press for nonambiguous answers that the professional cannot deliver. Aggressive patients pressing for nonambiguous answers can pose difficult patient-staff interactional problems.

An instructive account can be found in *A Coronary Event* by Dr. Michael Haberstram who treated the patient, Stephan Lesher, who had his first myocardial infarction while in his 30s.[3] The two authors write of their mutual experiences: how they experienced and perceived the many events, each other, and other hospital personnel. The patient was an investigative reporter (then much involved in the Watergate investigation), skilled in information gathering, aggressively seeking information, using such tactics as checking out the validity and reliability of information by asking the same question framed differently to the same or different physicians and confronting them with inconsistent information. Information was compared by him from reading medical literature and talking to other cardiac patients, then confronting the staff with treatment variations and with inconsistencies of medical information. Misunderstandings and misconstruing of information by him were frequent. Information given by professionals in the early phases of hospitalization, when the danger prognosis was still unclear, was doggedly pursued by him after conditions had changed in the latter phases. Information and responses from the attending physician meant to relieve the patient's anxiety were interpreted as being evasive or patronizing. Seemingly innocuous information from residents and interns was used against the attending physician or blown out of proportion. All of that earned the patient a unit-wide unfavorable reputation, resulting in staff meting out subtle and not-so-subtle punishment for his "uncooperativeness." Eventually the two sides were able to achieve mutual trust, but not without considerable interactional tension between them. The tactics used by this patient-author to obtain information and to establish its reliability and validity are not dissimilar to those used by other patients, only perhaps differing in degree of sophistication and interactional style (not as aggressive or as brash).

The case of the coronary event ended happily, but a contrasting case is Robert and Peggy Stinson's account in "On the Death of a Baby."[5] They were the parents of a premature infant who, at the extreme margin of human viability, was placed on a respirator against parental wishes and consent, and cared for in a neonatal intensive care unit. The infant died after months of heroic efforts to save him. These efforts had resulted in a long list of iatrogenic afflictions, and ultimately the parents expressed great bitterness and anger against the medical staff. Their tragic account describes the tremendous difficulties they faced in obtaining information from the medical staff, forcing them finally to find information on their own at the medical school library. Attempts to seek information from the medical staff and to participate in treatment decisions were rebuffed. In addition, the parents' efforts were harshly judged as "not wanting the child," "hostile," "emotionally fragile," and so forth.

The contrast between the two cases (the investigator-patient's coronary event and the dying infant) concerning the gaining of information about hazard and risks can be explained away entirely as due to the differences in sensitivity and humanity of the respective medical staffs. The physician in the coronary event had considerable sensitivity toward the patient; in contrast, there was insensitivity by the neonatal critical care medical staff. However, the two cases can also be analyzed from the perspective of the conditions bearing on the two trajectories relative to dangers and risks and their relevance to disclosure. In general, it is safe to say that the ease and dis-ease of disclosure for the staff, and obtaining information for patients and families, are related in part to the degree to which the dimensions of the dangers from the various sources in the trajectory phases can be accurately assessed, anticipated, and controlled. The more problematic the danger and risk, their dimensions, their sources, and the illness phases, the greater is the variability in assessment and of danger and risk being balanced between patient and the staff, and among the staff members. Moreover, anxiety and stress for both the patient and staff are high. All of that fosters the misunderstanding and misconstruing of information, and the misjudging of the appropriateness (what, how, and when) of information disclosure.

In comparing the two trajectories, first of all they are vastly different in terms of the medical-historical time frame, or the medical-technological biography. The application of high technology in coronary care had been in use for some time (partly as a result of extensive federal financial support for research and development in coronary care technology during the 1960s). In spite of the many ambiguities in the coronary event, the hazards and risks in coronary care could be more accurately assessed and controlled than in the neonatal intensive care situation. The application of high technology in neonatal care and the development of neonatal intensive care units have been later developments, so that in 1976 (when the event occurred) much of the technology was then fraught with many unknowns and uncertainties. Then, too, as is characteristic of pioneering medical situations, the desire to find answers and solutions to a technical medical problem on the part of the medical staff tends to foster an experimental stance in dealing with the patient at the expense of pain and suffering for the patient.

Second, the two illness trajectories were very different. The coronary trajectory was limited to a single illness; information exchange and disclosure could be handled by one person—the cardiologist. The infant's case involved multiple body systems, which called for multiple specialists; also there were new interns and residents rotating through the intensive care unit. The ability to extend lives today brings with it, then, a high probability for trajectories becoming what we term a "cumulative mess," with multiple health professionals who may each have quite different approaches to assessing hazards and risk and to balancing risks, and who may also hold different moral and ethical philosophies regarding disclosure and regard life and death quite differently.[2] Coordination of care and of information within the health team tends to break down, resulting in great problems for the patient and family and for the staff as well.

In spite of the professional effort to share information, the Aesculapian authority (power based on physicians' expertise and on patients' faith in them and their almost mystical powers) continues often to be so strong that equitable patient-professional interactional approaches are very difficult to attain. To go against this traditional authority is very difficult even for medically sophisticated persons. This difficulty is described by Beatrice Kalisch, a prominent nurse, in an account describing her decision to have surgery. The title of her paper tells the story: "On Half Gods and Mortals: Aesculapian Authority."[4]

Establishing the validity and reliability of information received is also a frequent problem for patients. Patients, of course, as do health professionals themselves, rely on the usual formal hierarchy of expertise (nurse, intern, resident, attending physician, specialist, chief of staff, and so on) to determine the degree of reliability. Having inadequate criteria to make reliability judgments, they closely watch how professionals present the information, along with their accompanying facial expressions and body languages. For example, a patient comments, "I know I'm over the hump because today the doctor smiled when he said, 'You're coming along fine.' Two days ago he said the same thing, but his face was grimmer." Another patient will say, "I am wondering if indeed the risks are not so serious, he seemed so circumspect." Patients search for approachable health personnel to give them answers, quite often also seeking out acquaintances and relatives (hopefully someone with some medical knowledge). Indeed, during the course of our research, patients would question whether we were familiar with a given technology or procedure, or with the reputation of a physician. In the search for validity and reliability, nurses frequently are sought out, in part because of their availability. Not infrequently, a nurse may hesitate because she or he, too, may accept the Aesculapian authority, answering, "You'll have to ask your doctor," or fear the consequences of a certain physician's anger because he or she does not believe in open disclosure. Kalisch points out that physicians' exercising of authority is the villain most frequently singled out, but nurses are also involved and must be guarded against.

Currently, much hazard and risk disclosure in nursing takes the form of "patient teaching." Quite often the teaching is formalized and follows protocol.

More often than not, the protocols are formulated quite late in the technological development of equipment, after much trial and error and after the "bugs" are worked out. Certainly, patient teaching has improved the exchange and disclosure of information, but the limitations of the teacher-learner model used in the teaching, as noted earlier, tend both to encourage a hierarchical relationship and to discourage a more equitable sharing of information.

References

1. Fagerhaugh, Shizuko, Strauss, Anselm, Suczek, Barbara, and Wiener, Carolyn: Clinical safety work in hospitals. (Forthcoming.)
2. Fagerhaugh, Shizuko, and Strauss, Anselm: The politics of pain management: staff-patient interaction, Menlo Park, Calif., 1977, Addison-Wesley Publishing Co.
3. Halberstram, Michael, and Lesher, Stephan:

A coronary event, New York, 1976, Popular Library.
4. Kalisch, Beatrice: On half gods and mortals: Aesculapian authority, Nursing Outlook **23**:22-28, 1975.
5. Stinson, Robert, and Stinson, Peggy: On the death of a baby, Atlantic Monthly **244**:64-72, 1979.

THE HEALTH CARE SYSTEM AND CHRONIC ILLNESS

CHAPTER 15

PROVIDING BETTER CARE

"Now," the reader may well comment, "Parts 1 and 2 of this book are quite illuminating: I have gotten both a general picture and many vivid illustrations of the problems of the chronically ill—but what about the practical side of all this? How can this information help a nurse (or social worker, or physical therapist, or whomever) like me to provide better care to the patient?"

That is a perfectly legitimate question, but one must approach its answer with considerable caution. What we have in mind is that when anyone uses a phrase like "provide better care to the patient," rather than "how can we help these people," then one has already begun in a subtle way to lay professional claim to a domain that perhaps belongs more properly to the sick people and their families.

In the preceding pages, we have seen these people attempting, with more or less success and courage, to manage their lives, often in the face of extreme adversity. Their management is *their* business. Even when they get good aid and counsel from health personnel, they themselves ultimately bear the responsibility for facing *their* problems, making *their* adjustive arrangements, handling *their* social relations, and sometimes even taking the decision of whether to continue living or to die right out of the hands of the medical authorities, who ordinarily tend to maintain life as long as possible. Given the realities of this situation, health personnel may well ask: What then is our responsibility, really? For how much should or can we be responsible, and about what? Responsibility only inside the health facilities, or somewhat inside "their" homes, too?

Currently, health personnel tend to require that patients delegate maximum responsibility to the staff whenever they enter a health facility, especially a hospital. The staff expects, and if necessary demands, that responsibility. The terrain is theirs and they have virtually complete autonomy over it. This is why some patients prefer to die at home, wishing to die as much as possible in their own ways rather than in a hospitalized style. "At home" they do not have to delegate or even share the responsibility for dying—or living while dying—with outsiders, no matter how medically skillful or well-meaning.

Health personnel observe this same dichotomy between home and health facility. In fact, it is notable that inside the facility they bear heavy burdens of responsibility for the well-being and care of a patient, at times fighting for that person's life. They may become "overinvolved" in their patients care and health. Rather frequently they appear, or actually become, brusque and unconcerned, pulling away from psychological investment in a patient, so as not to become drained of emotion and energy. Ironically, when the patient leaves for "the outside" all will quickly tend to forget him or her, except the physician (if the person has one, and many people do not). They forget that person, that is, until he or she again enters the hospital or visits the clinic. Home is the patient's domain. The corollary to that is, whatever happens to a person at home is essentially that person's own business, just as what happens to him or her at the health facility is believed to be the staff's business. That is a somewhat overdrawn picture of the home-facility dichotomy, but there is a great deal of truth to the picture.

That dichotomy made sense, perhaps, when disease was primarily of an infectious kind. The patient then was under medical care while in the hospital and sent home when pretty much out of danger. (In earlier periods, or with milder illnesses, patients were perhaps treated at home entirely by an attending physician.) With the advent of widespread chronic disease, however, any sharp division between home and health facility would seem to be far too simple a solution to the problems faced by the chronically ill.

In light of these problems, a more rational approach is to soften the line between the two realms. Probably this would involve two major kinds of changes.

1. Sick people, when at the health facilities, would have a generally greater participation in the decisions made both about their care and its implementation.
2. The health care "system" would be extended in systematic ways so that health personnel could play more of a role in aiding sick people and their families, to cope with problems attendant on chronicity.

Those changes involve at least a two-pronged attack. In the next chapter we will approach these issues on the level of broad "public policy" considerations. Before doing that, however, we will look at the issues from the standpoint of health personnel themselves. Since most are not now engaged in servicing patients at home but are working at various kinds of facilities, our discussion will pertain mainly to those facilities, and especially to those that we know best, namely hospitals and clinics.

●   ●   ●

Staff members certainly need to know more about the chronically ill who visit such facilities than they can have learned from reading this book. What they need additionally is rather *specific* information—either about individual patients or about types of patients who suffer from the particular diseases "seen" at the staff's work site. This information surely will not be only medical but will also include the kinds of social and psychological data discussed in the foregoing pages. While many staff members are quite capable of getting such information, certain features of health facilities militate against the personnel's obtaining this information, sharing it, and acting effectively in terms of it.

"DOING" TASKS VERSUS UNDERSTANDING THE PERSON

Staff members are first of all focused on "doing"—that is, on carrying out their primary jobs. These inevitably are quite medical and procedural. To do these tasks requires obtaining information. One needs to know the kinds of physiological, biochemical, pharmacological, and procedural information that typically finds its way into the patient's medical record. This information, of course, is gathered by a variety of different personnel and by a variety of methods. However, we would emphasize that very little of it is of a social or psychological nature.

When it is, then either it tends to be fragmentary and unsystematic by comparison with other types of recorded data, or it is gathered and reported because the patient is "difficult." If the latter, then the staff members may genuinely be attempting to discover why the patient is "difficult," or they may understandably be giving vent to their feelings by reporting what they believe is true about him or her. Some personnel (especially nurses and social workers trained in schools that emphasize "interpersonal" aspects of care) may pay considerable attention to the psychological and social difficulties of patients. Often, however, they find themselves not getting much support from other personnel in this particular side of their work. Likewise, some personnel, such as the nursing aides in hospitals and clinics, may come to learn quite a bit about the personal lives of the patients, but they are not often called on by their "superiors" or supervisors to report what they have learned. This kind of information is simply not much valued.

ACCOUNTABILITY AND NONACCOUNTABILITY

The chief reason for this general neglect of the experiential aspects of the chronically ill is that those aspects are regarded as quite peripheral to the responsibilities of the health personnel. By responsibilities, we mean not merely the staff's perceived task-oriented responsibilities, but its actual organizational and even legal ones. The staff is only genuinely *accountable* for getting and reporting certain types of information and for doing certain kinds of tasks.[3] The corollary is that it is *not* accountable, not organizationally responsible, for other kinds of information and other kinds of interaction with patients (and their kin).

One can see this very clearly, for instance, with patients who have come to the hospital or clinic with pain related to a chronic disease. Even cursory inspection of medical-nursing records, or listening to reports from personnel to their superiors, makes it quickly evident that staff members are responsible only for communicating about certain actions and not about a great many others. Among the former actions, of course, are the giving and carrying out of orders about medication. There is also staff communication, although it is not necessarily required, concerning the problems of assessing a patient's pain, about his or her "complaints" of pain, about certain other "problems" with the patient, and so on. The larger array of detail, however, pertaining to interaction with the patient, or what was learned about her or his biography or experiential history with disease and pain, is reported only fortuitously. Everyone has done more, observed more, knows more, than he or she reports or talks about to colleagues and superiors. Certainly, they know much more than is put into the official records. What is true of patients in pain is equally true of patients who are dying from their chronic illnesses.

In connection with accountability and the flow of information among staff members, it is worth examining what happens when they encounter an especially difficult or troublesome patient. Then the personnel are likely to talk over ways of "working with" him or her. Into the deliberations may enter much shrewdness and experience with similar patients. When this happens, what was essentially invisible action—actions by patients or personnel not reported back or observed by other personnel—becomes part of the staff's organized effort. This kind of temporary organization and accountability of effort can be termed ad hoc, because it arises around specific patients rather than being a permanent feature of the facility's organization.

In fact, so little does this ad hoc organization usually carry over to permanent organization that a rather peculiar situation develops at most health facilities. Each time that another difficult patient appears, the personnel will draw, either personally or collectively, on their experiences with similar patients encountered in the past. ("She's just like Mrs. Frisbee. Remember the problems we had with her? And how we managed her?") In that sense, there is a carryover of staff learning and experience. (It is often bitter experience and rather biased or ineffective "learning.") However, a neutral observer might note that there develops a rather amazing pattern of repeated interactional difficulties around particular kinds of patients—and wonder why the staff does not effectively work out sensible, permanent ways of either preventing or coping better with these recurrent difficulties.

The reason is that they are organizationally responsible for quite another order of events, namely the carrying out of medical and medically supportive tasks. Behavior and interaction are important to personnel only insofar as they permit or hinder the carrying out of primary tasks. Hence each person develops his or her own style of working with patients. That individualized style may be relatively unnoticed by other personnel (as with night nurses or staff who draw blood or position patients for x-ray examinations). In contrast, someone's style of working with patients may influence others, either because it seems effective or because the person has supervisory power. Nevertheless, such modes of handling patients are only infrequently raised to the level of self-conscious organizational approaches, based on a careful consideration of biographies and experiences of the types of patients most frequently seen by the staff. As for the patients' families, they are even less likely to be thought about in those considered terms.

The exceptions to this usual nonaccountability of the psychological and social aspects of medical or health care are most conspicuously found at special, and usually rather innovatively oriented, facilities whose staffs must deal with such matters as the problems of families of children dying of leukemia or of patients who have special kinds of diseases (such as kidney transplants). At such locales, the organizational effort is not necessarily effective, but at least it *is* organized. It is a genuine attempt to deal with repeated patterns of difficulty rather than merely to cope with the patterns on an ad hoc basis.

It is probable that until health personnel are genuinely responsible for the social and psychological aspects of giving care (as they are for the more purely medical and procedural aspects), there will be limited improvement in those aspects of care, except that which is effected fortuitously or temporarily because of an unusually skilled or compassionate or sensible staff member. Genuine accountability about the neglected aspects of care can be built into facilities only if their major authorities understand the crucial importance, for chronic care, of those aspects. Then they will convert that understanding into a commitment that will result in necessary changes in written and verbal communication systems. This kind of understanding and commitment is likely to come about only after considerable nationwide discussion, such as is now taking place about terminal care. That kind of discussion about chronic care seems only in its initial phases, although it is certainly beginning. Inevitably it must evolve, if only because of mounting concern among the citizens of most industrialized countries with the quality of life rather than with only standards of living or, as in less fortunate nations, with sheer individual physical survival.

Having read all that, our readers may feel discouraged by visions of the insignificance of their individual efforts. If one must wait for genuine organizational accountability, then what can be done all by oneself! The answer is, quite a bit.

THE PATIENT'S MULTIPLE BIOGRAPHIES

Undoubtedly, the place to begin is to recognize that health personnel, especially those who do not visit sick people at home, see them from a very peculiar angle of vision. They are apt to see only that portion of a patient's biography that pertains to their own work or that they learn during the course of doing their work with or around him or her. Distortion aside, and assuming they do learn true things about the patient, they are likely to grasp only a *small slice* of the total relevant biography—relevant, that is, to giving good health care.

One way of comprehending what is meant by a small slice of biography is simply to think back to the foregoing pages of this book wherein we considered the complexities of the chronic experience, even for people sick from comparatively mild or uncomplicated diseases. There is another way of comprehending the same point. Sick people have at least three different types of biographies. First, they have had sequential (or chronological) experiences with their disease. Second, they have had biographical experiences with medical and health care—that is, with physicians and other health personnel ("legitimately medical" or not) and with various kinds of facilities. Third, they have had what may be termed a social biography, that is, a personal history of encounters with kin, friends, acquaintances, work colleagues, and strangers.

The important question is, then, for any given patient or type of patient: which of these biographies does the caring staff tend to overlook, and how much of it? Surely it would not be contentious to claim that rather little of the second biography and sometimes very little of the third biography are regarded as directly relevant by the personnel in the course of their various duties. Sometimes even the disease biography is little comprehended in its experiential aspect; that is, the staff comprehends very little of what the patient has lived through in terms of symptoms and regimens or even medical crises.

Yet each of the three biographies can present major interactional problems—even affect the providing of good care—when the sick person visits a health facility. As a minor, but frequent, instance, consider the psychological and physiological difficulties of a man who has been accustomed to taking pain medications of a certain kind, a certain strength, and at certain intervals of time. He comes to the hospital, where the staff takes over the work of giving him relief from his pain and, without consulting him, changes one or more of those variables. Patients sometimes warn nurses and attending physicians about specific drugs that they know from experience will be ineffective as pain killers or trigger allergic reactions, only to have warnings ignored, at cost to themselves. In general, nursing and medical personnel get to know little or nothing about their patients' past experience with pain—including their own methods of dealing with it, other than the present or current evolving pain.[2] That is, they understand little of their patients' experiential or management biography with regard to this kind of symptom.

Patients with severe chronic back pain, for instance, often come into hospitals for operations, hopeful that "this one" may accomplish what one or more other operations did not, but, at the same time, highly mistrustful of health personnel who previously have misdiagnosed, misoperated, mismanaged, or just plain scoffed at their "complaints." So they often prove to be difficult patients.[4] As for those with considerable experiences in hospitals, they can cause plenty of bad feeling when they make nasty comparisons between the handling of the medications here and there, or comment pointedly about what they think is the incompetent production of unnecessary pain, as when certain procedures or tests are done on them. To continue with examples from pain, back pain patients are frequently regarded by kin and friends as, at least, somewhat hypochondriacal, as not having "that much" pain. By not grasping the sick person's own understanding of pain and of his or her experiences with others' definitions of it, health personnel are failing to give themselves the basis for providing more adequate care. Indeed, they are likely, by dubbing a patient neurotic or "a complainer," simply to be adding to his or her unfortunate social and medical care biographies.

So the very first place to begin improving the care of the chronically ill is to develop effective methods for discovering their actual biographies. That is true for each patient. It is also true for patients who suffer from the most typical diseases encountered at given locales. Surely, the next step is to utilize this information. Although its fullest utilization cannot take place until there is an organized accountability for its collection and use, is there any question that considerable improvement of care can occur even without systematic accountability?

INTERVIEWING FOR BIOGRAPHICAL DATA

How, then, does one obtain this biographical information? Clearly, the first requisite is an attitude: "this information can be useful." If one believes otherwise, the effort to obtain the information will not be long extended—and it will be all too easy to slip back into disregarding or misconstruing whatever information has been discovered. Given a belief in the crucial importance of biographical data, however, it is still necessary to learn or develop effective methods of getting those data.

A social scientist would tend to say that the methods already exist. They need only be adjusted to the specific situations obtaining at any given health locale. What he or she would mean is that personnel could learn or be taught to use interviewing and observational techniques where they do not now really use them, or to use them more skillfully than they do now. A brief list of possibly useful books and articles about such techniques is given in the bibliography. Short of exhorting readers to peruse them—and to urge supervisors to institute in-service courses on interviewing and observation—what specific instruction can be given here?

INTERVIEWING WHILE WORKING: "ACTION INTERVIEWS"

Let us look at interviewing, which is the chief instrumentality for getting biographical data. Seemingly, interviewing takes a great deal of time, and time often or usually is a scarce commodity for personnel. By contrast, social science researchers are paid or have proper incentives to spend all the time required to get good interview information, but health personnel are not paid for that kind of work! A researcher may be able to spend 1, 2, 3, or more hours with "an interviewee," thus getting the requisite information. What health worker can work at that leisurely, talkative pace?

Wasted time or time given to other priorities aside, the issue of time is very germane. Yet, there are certain advantages that can accrue to a health worker that even a researcher does not always, or indeed usually, have. The basic fact about the patient–health worker relationship is that it is a service relationship. So the personnel are repeatedly doing something for, or at least around, the sick person. Thus most interviews—that is, conversations designed to get information—will be "action interviews." The conversations will take place while the staff member is in action—working. Of course, sometimes the patient (or relative) and staff member can just be chatting or spending relatively free time together, but most often they meet only when something is to be done to or for the patient.

Interviewing while working has its disadvantages, of course, but it can also have great advantages. To begin with, often the talk can go on while the work is proceeding. The staff member may initiate the talk or the particular topics, but so may the sick person. It is easier for some people (both patient and staff) to talk, in fact, about certain topics under such work conditions. One does not have to look directly into the other's face. One can take cues about what to say or ask from the very action itself. One can choose this time and place to say something, precisely because he or she does not expect the conversation to go on—or deeper. One can tentatively introduce a topic—as patients do—to see whether the staff member will pick up the conversational invitation, or turn away, or "turn the conversation off." (A skillful or determined staff member can do that with patients, too.)

Moreover, these action interviews usually need not be confined to a single session. A staff member is very likely to work with, or around, a patient repeatedly (although the intervals between sessions are shorter in hospitals than in clinics). Consequently, not all the information-getting need be jammed into a single encounter. Indeed, the very nature of "repeated sessions" means that the conversations are likely to be relatively short. However, the next conversations can continue where preceding ones broke. That is, the total conversation is a continuing one, even though it may not be carried on whenever the two people meet. Repeated meetings also mean that each can more easily choose when and when not to talk. Thus a patient who seems not inclined to talk today, or this morning, need not be pushed to talk. One waits for a more appropriate mood.

Furthermore, continuing conversations yield at least two other potential advantages. As the interviewer learns more and more, he or she will find that this cumulative knowledge will allow the asking of better questions. (By questions, we do not necessarily mean direct questions posed to the patient, but kinds of information about which the staff member will seek information.) Thus the information obtained not only is quantitatively cumulative but has a tendency to become qualitatively better. Besides that, continuing interviews tend to go "deeper," because both parties feel increasingly free to express themselves. This is especially true of many patients in health settings. The reasons are several but include previous bad experiences with health workers or mistrust of health personnel in general. Some patients do not feel free to talk about themselves in a setting so different from their own home. Some just take time to reveal themselves. Besides, most people of course, need to test out listeners before going deeper into what matters to their private selves. Will the listener really listen? Understand? Pass a bad judgment? Be sympathetic? Naturally, the more a staff member reveals of himself or herself—if only that he or she is sympathetic, empathic, compassionate, or has had similar personal experiences—the deeper this continuing conversation can go.

INTERVIEWS ARE CONVERSATIONS

That is all very well, the reader of this book may say, but how can a person who is not specially trained in interviews do this kind of interviewing? A partial answer to that query is that, perhaps, too much of a mystique has been built around the idea of the skilled interviewer. We would not for a moment assert that training is unnecessary or that some people can be taught to be skillful at interviewing while others are pretty hopeless. However, in our opinion, it makes eminent sense to think of interviews quite as if they were conversations. An interview is different only insofar as its special purpose is to get information from the talk that flows between the conversationalists. If the conversation does not yield good information, then it may be good talk but a poor interview. Talk and conversation it is, however, and not much more.

Now, the fact that every interview is supposed to yield information has important implications for health personnel. Possibly foremost is that they need not be especially frightened of, or anxious about, the *idea* of interviewing. All of us attempt to get information from certain of the conversations in which we engage our friends, relatives, strangers, officials. Some of us are better at getting that information than are others, but all of us can get some information—especially if it matters!

Another implication of the idea of interview-as-conversation is that all of us are better at some conversations than at others. Some people can talk more freely with intimates than with strangers, and some just the reverse. (For instance, some persons can talk easily with strangers in the park; others find it nearly impossible to strike up or even engage in such conversations.) Some can talk better on the run, or while doing something, than when self-consciously face to face with some-one. Some people are marvelously good listeners, so by their very presence and posture they invite others to confide private detail to them; others are very good at getting people to express themselves by dint of aggressive questioning or lively verbal interplay.

In consequence, everybody (including every research interviewer) is better at some kinds of conversations than at others. No one can be equally good at all of them or hope to learn to be very competent at every variety. The most that can be hoped is that one can discover and be aware of one's genuine limitations. It is precisely at the margins of conversational competence that people need special training. They need to learn what they think, or feel, they cannot do—or cannot do very well. Then they need to stretch themselves to discover whether, in fact, that is really where their limits are; perhaps instead they need to "push themselves" or perhaps get special encouragement or a few specific techniques in order to get over some temperamental or experiential barrier.

It seems safe to say that it is far more important that interviewers learn the limits of their natural repertoire, and learn how to extend those limits, than that they learn very specific techniques. Certainly techniques are useful; the problem, however, is that they apply only to certain kinds of conversations (interviews) and not necessarily to others. Advice not to interrupt the other's flow of talk is certainly useful for success at certain kinds of interviews but scarcely applies to interviews that involve putting the informant under great pressure, as with captured spies or suspected criminals. Similarly, the techniques used especially by psychiatrists, or derived from their teachings, are not necessarily going to work effectively with patients who are asking explicitly for information—and thus yielding information about themselves to an astute interviewer, who needs to be answering to inter-viewees as they are requesting rather than in terms of his or her conception that they need therapeutic handling.

These last examples allow us to raise another useful issue about interview-ing. Information obtained from conversations is valid only to the extent that one can make good judgments about what the conversation was really all about. To take an obvious example; if the interviewee is deliberately faking, putting one off the scent, then her or his falsified story simply ought not to be believed. However, one cannot make that judgment unless one knows, or suspects, that falsification actually transpired. From the very nature of the conversation what really transpired is not necessarily an easy thing to determine, though obviously we can be far more certain about some conversations than others. At any rate, the injunction to the interviewer is to discover with as much probability as possible what kind of identity the other person assigned both to "himself" and to "me" during the conversation. Who was I to him, as he saw it, and what was he explicitly or implicitly trying to be to me? (This matter of estimating the situational identities of interviewee and interviewer is so important that one must wonder about even social science research, based on interviews or questionnaires, if the research does not make clear what those juxtaposed identities were.) What will help the health worker in making those kinds of estimates is precisely that the interviews, characteristically, are repeated, continuous, and based generally on a service relationship. For all that, health personnel will need to develop to the utmost their sensitivities about the identity aspects of their interview-conversations.

MULTIPLE INTERVIEWS

Finally, a word is in order about another advantage that personnel may enjoy in their interviewing. Chronic illness, as we have repeatedly said, usually involves the relatives as well as the sick person. Consequently, when relatives show up at the facility, some ought to be interviewed also. Naturally there will be discrepancies among their views and between each of them and the patient. That difficulty should not persuade any staff member from the duty of having, somehow, the responsibility of putting together as accurate a story as is possible. In fact, the very existence of discrepancies sometimes is not so much a deterrent to discovering the truth as an aid in discovering how the different people in the family see what has happened both to the sick person and to the family relationships. That is immensely important information for the health personnel to have if—in accordance with the viewpoint of this book—they are to give better care to the patient.

Moreover, health personnel have the special advantage of often being in the position of talking not merely with each family member separately but with two or more (including the patient) together. Naturally, there are also disadvantages to these multiple-people interviews. This type of interview situation can also yield very useful information. People will say certain things—and in certain ways—in this context that they might not when alone with an interviewer.

PATIENTS WILL TALK!

Before leaving the topic of interviewing for biographical data, we should make *the* most important point: the chronically ill (and their families) usually are more than willing to give those data. Many sick persons, as we have noted earlier, are not able to tell other people about their difficulties, or they refrain from doing so for a variety of reasons, and some suffer from genuine social isolation. The researchers who have interviewed sick persons have discovered how eager most of them are to talk about themselves and their disease-related problems. (To quote from an apt speech by Mr. Doolittle in G. B. Shaw's *Pygmalion:* "I'm willing to tell you, I'm *wanting* to tell you. . . .") Health personnel who are genuinely interested in the chronically ill should have not less success in engaging them in informational conversations. Although the researchers had more time, and perhaps greater interviewing skill, health personnel have the great advantage of direct access and a service relationship to the sick persons.

USES OF BIOGRAPHICAL INFORMATION

The next question is, after the biographical information is obtained, what does one do with it? The answer is, use it! Any innovative person can surely figure out how to do so. In general, however, there are three ways to use the information. The first, and most obvious, is that any individual staff member will shape his or her own responses to sick persons in accordance with what is known about each one of them so that, presumably, more individualized care can be given. It may even be possible to persuade other staff members that one's information helps to give a fuller picture of a patient's current state. If so, more than one staff member will act on that information. Staff discussion, even when debate then ensues, should lead to more considered action toward the patient than if no interview had been reported.

More important than improving care for specific patients, however, is what interviews can do for the care of patients in general. What we have in mind is that every facility and every subpart of the facility draws patients who have certain kinds of illness. Whether that means this particular clinic gets arthritic clients while another gets asthmatic ones, or whether the latter clinic draws both elderly and adolescent asthmatic patients—in either case, the disease-related experiences of their respective clients will vary. The implication is that interviewing should be focused not merely on individual patients but also on patterns of patients. Once a staff begins to obtain this more extensive—and deeper—knowledge of the biographies of "our types" of patients, then interviews with specific patients and families will be easier to carry out and be far more revealing. If staff members do not feel confident to do this kind of interviewing, then it may be sensible to attempt to persuade the administration to hire a researcher who can help get that information. However, many staffs could get the data once they believed in their usefulness or, as we would claim, in their necessity. In any event, the road to genuine accountability, to organizational responsibility, lies in the direction of discovering these more general biographical patterns and then in a concerted effort to respond to them.

SHARED RESPONSIBILITY

Getting and interpreting biographical data brings us squarely up against the next important and indeed crucial question. How much responsibility for their care should be left to patients when they are at the health facility? As noted earlier, the sick person has almost total responsibility when at home, but what about "here"? In general, the answer to the question is that once staff members really begin to respect their patients' biographies (medical, medical care, and social), then they will listen more closely to what patients think good care must include for themselves. We need not always take their views "straight," but most of the time they should be taken into account. Again, innovative personnel should be able to determine the limits of a given patient's responsibility for aspects of care when at the facility. They will thereby not only save themselves much trouble with so-called difficult patients but greatly contribute to the betterment of care. Most important, perhaps, they will give the patient that much additional support for dealing with symptoms, regimens, disease, and people in the outside world. Also, they may even elect to organize the facility's work in somewhat different or at least additional ways.

References

1. Schatzman, Leonard, and Strauss, Anselm: Field research: strategies for a natural sociology, Englewood Cliffs, N.J., 1973, Prentice-Hall, Inc.
2. Strauss, Anselm, Fagerhaugh, Shizuko, and Glaser, Barney: Pain: an organizational-work-interactional perspective, Nursing Outlook **22:**560-566, 1974.
3. Strauss, Anselm, Glaser, Barney, and Quint, Jeanne: The non-accountability of terminal care, Hospitals **38:**73-87, 1964.
4. Wiener, Carolyn: Pain assessment, pain legitimation and the conflict of staff-patient perspectives, Nursing Outlook **23:**508-516, 1975.

CHAPTER 16

PUBLIC POLICY AND CHRONIC ILLNESS

Beyond the responsibility and, indeed, the power of individuals who work as health personnel is the task of changing the present societal status of the chronically ill. Nevertheless, there surely is a place in this book for at least a brief discussion of general policy considerations. Some health workers could play a role, and others now are certainly doing so, in getting policy changes effected.

The larger public is aware, of course, of the special difficulties of being sick when old or poor, and a few well-publicized diseases have their interested and involved publics. Yet the chronically ill, as such, are not defined, at least in the United States, as what sociologists call "a social problem" (poverty or pollution or the American racial problem). Perhaps chronic illness should not be defined as a social problem. Nevertheless, a more general awareness should be fostered of how society is arranged, physically, socially, and financially, for normal people and of what this means for sick people. Doubtless, the efforts of specific interest groups would be rendered more effective if such an across-the-board awareness were to develop. Currently the approaches tend to be categorically oriented, that is, focused on specific diseases or types of disease (heart, cancer). If the chronically ill are to be aided in their own efforts to live more effectively and happily, the categorical approaches simply will not get them very far. That is, after all, one of the chief messages of this book.

NEGLECTING THE MOBILITY NEEDS OF ILL PERSONS

A telling way of underlining how disregarded, or at least unnoticed, are the needs of the chronically ill is to consider briefly how American streets and public buildings are ordinarily organized, then to raise questions about that in terms of sick people who have persistent mobility problems because of lack of energy or physical disablement. On the downtown streets of most towns and cities are there many (or any) benches—including at the bus stops? Are the curbstones set low enough to make them manageable or are they troublesome and difficult? Are the entrances to public buildings (including the hospitals and clinics) provided with ramps or steps? Are they with or without railings? Are the entry doors easy to manage or do they require great expenditure of energy to open? Is seating at theaters—and churches—arranged for normal people, or are some seats, at least, arranged for people with mobility difficulties? That list of questions could easily be extended, and to each there is usually a negative answer.

That the standard terrain can be so difficult is realized by normal people only when they are temporarily incapacitated in limb or energy. Ordinarily, they are no more aware of such a list of obstacles than of how a similar terrain might look to a cat or a giraffe. To prove this point to themselves, health personnel might have a look at the entries and entrance doors to their own facilities, also at the floors of their lobbies and corridors (polished and shining or carefully carpeted?).

The mobility difficulties of the chronically ill when in public places provides a clear exemplification of a crucially important issue. Not only is chronicity much more than a medical problem; it is also a problem in which the public, whether with recognition or not, is deeply implicated. Of course, one cannot fault public authorities, or private builders either, for aggravating the physical difficulties of the ill, since they do not realize their own contributions in that matter. Indeed, there exist specialized books and articles written by disabled persons for disabled persons that give information about how to get in and around in specific public places and buildings. While these writings are of help to their readers, they ordinarily do not reach public officials or carry an accusatory argument to the general public. By the same token, however, only a public awareness and an arousal of conscience about these issues will ease the mobility difficulties of sick people when in public places.

TREND TOWARD HEIGHTENED AWARENESS?

The basic problem is that neither the general public nor the health professionals are yet aware of the implications of chronic illness prevalence, even if many of them recognize it as a new phenomenon. So there is a continued dominance of the older conception of illness as requiring "acute care"—which in turn means, as noted often in this book, a continuance of health institutions organized primarily in terms of acute care concepts, however adapted they are to the realities of the changed diseases* of their clients. It is safe to say, for example, that the health care emphases in most industrialized countries are still on acute medical

---

*This section is modified from Strauss, Anselm: Editorial Comment, Soc. Sci. Med. **140:**351-352, 1980.

care (at medical facilities) rather than on an integrated system of home–medical facility care, and that far greater prestige, power, and resources go to the highly technologized medical specialties than into research and care on illnesses like multiple sclerosis or to those most widespread of afflictions, arthritis and "back pain". Even where, as in kidney dialysis treatment, hospital or clinic staffs are keenly aware of details of patients' lives, and where systematic linkages are made between home and medical facility—even there, the approach is primarily in terms of acute medicine, despite the growing consciousness of "quality-of-life" considerations. There are also attendant questions that are as much or more social than medical—for example, initially, the selection of patients for dialysis (in the United States at least), and more lately (as in a British hospital that we visited in 1977), the quasi-institutional fate of older patients who can survive only by virtue of returning to the hospital each night, not to mention the family strains engendered by dialysis machine-tending and patient-attending by the kin.

In fact many health-related movements and tendencies can be viewed as related to the prevalence of chronic illness, although people who are involved in those movements and tendencies probably do not see that larger chronic illness picture. Here are some examples.

The death and dying movement

Since the middle 1960s the concern with "proper and more humanistic" dying has mounted steadily—principally, perhaps, among the nonphysician health workers and religious personnel—along with the growth of hospices, death counseling, grief counseling, and the like. This movement and its associated phenomena began among hospital staffs who bear a heavy burden of caring for people who are dying lingering deaths from their chronic illnesses. Often there is great strain not only for patients and kin, but for the staff themselves. The changed condition of dying from diseases like pneumonia to illnesses like the cancers, lies behind this dramatically arresting social movement.

Bioethics

The evolution of "bioethics" arises from professional and lay concern alike over moral issues that accompany today's medical care. There has been an explosion of bioethics literature, the development of the bioethics specialist, and attempts to get bioethic perspectives into the curricula of the professional schools. Again, this movement can scarcely be divorced from the problems attendant on giving care to patients on dialysis, or whose care poses moral dilemmas for hospital staffs as the ill lie dying or are trying to decide among various possibly fateful, options. Yet the bioethics specialists, like the participants in the death and dying movement, do not grasp the larger implications of their own relationship to a host of chronic illness issues.

Self-help groups

We have seen the rapid proliferation of self-help groups, whose members may or may not work in close collaboration with "the medical system." All those groups are composed of chronic illness sufferers, who are dealing with the issues of daily living with their illnesses and with the regimens prescribed by physicians. We can expect the further increase of those groups everywhere, and with many more of the chronic illnesses, as well as their participants' growing sophistication about health care. They are likely, too, to become increasingly politicized, as some groups seek to put pressure on the requisite authorities.

Alternative care

In the United States at least, increasing numbers of citizens are vocal about supplementing or even supplanting "established medicine" with alternative modes of medicine. In turn, avant-garde health practitioners are trying to incorporate some of those alternative modes into the hospitals and clinics. The alternative care enthusiasts sometimes are totally distrustful of medical technology, medical facilities, and medical personnel; sometimes people are simply searching, often desperately, for effective relief from their chronic symptoms, when standard medical procedures have failed them.

Intractable pain centers

Another trend is the development of pain centers. Their practitioners are invested in various supporting ideologies about pain and its relief, utilizing a plethora of diverse methods believed—or hoped—to relieve previously intractable pain, that is, pain not relieved and even enhanced by previous modes of medical treatment. Chief among visitors to those centers are those who suffer from back pain or arthritic pain, precisely those who believe they have (and often they are correct) received ineffective, and sometimes brutalizing, "management" for their pain in standard medical facilities.

Dehumanization

A host of articles and books have been published around the theme of how dehumanized modern medical care has become. There are an appropriate number of diverse explanations for this state of affairs. Whatever else dehumanization may represent, it reflects the conditions under which care increasingly is given to people in facilities profoundly affected by complex medical technology designed for diagnosis, treatment, and life support of the chronically ill. The changed nature of this technology (below) and the organization of facilities around it, produce both the accusation of dehumanization, and a counter-reaction: attempts to lessen dehumanization, including getting the "social aspects" of illness and medicine into the bloodstream of health care.

Costs

Here again, there are a multitude of prescriptions for attacking the rising costs of medical care, these prescriptions resting on the villains perceived as responsible for the rising costs: physicians' cupidity, ineffective hospital management, overuse of expensive tests, and so on. One current prescription for reducing cost rests unquestionably and obviously on early twentieth-century thinking about acute disease: the plea that people take more responsibility for preventing their sicknesses (they should be more self-reliant, live more properly, not be so self-indulgent about running to the health services for every ailment).

As the medical institutions move in piecemeal fashion toward adapting to the vastly changed and changing chronic illness conditions, what else can be observed? Here are a few other important instances that can be seen, at least in the United States, where the public debate is largely over rising costs and the pros and cons of federal health insurance:

1. Patients are going home with complicated drug and machine technology that they and their kin must manage. So, inevitably there are the beginnings of increased attention to "teaching" patients and kin in the hospitals and clinics, as well as some sort of continuing support services, especially for patients on such equipment as pacemakers and dialysis machines. Likewise, increased attention is being placed on the need for "professional training for home care," although the institutional accompaniments are still, in the United States at least, quite meager except in the immediate weeks or months after hospital.

2. Physicians are more and more dependent on a host of other personnel, although they are still legally responsible for the care of patients; however, their judgments increasingly rest on the judgments of others (such as clinical laboratory technicians, consultants) or indeed are really taken over by other personnel at various points during very problematic courses of their patients' illnesses. All that is linked both with the rise of medical technology and with the difficulty of predicting accurately for specific patients their courses of chronic disease.

3. Following closely behind the recent pharmacological revolution is another, involving the introduction of various types of machinery into the hospital. The evolution and diffusion of specialized intensive care units, dense with machinery and attendant technicians, is evidence of this. These units are becoming differentiated into intensive, intermediate, and ambulatory care spaces. Machine technology has resulted in architecturally outmoded hospitals, which are constantly under reconstruction and with many poorly designed spaces. Patients and machines shuttle back and forth to each other, crowding the halls and the elevators. A host of safety regulations cover these new technologies, tying the hospitals in complex ways to various levels of government. Technol-

ogy and associated medical knowledge are accompanied by an explosion of technicians, and a proliferation both of specialized function and of special occupational interest groups. Problems of coordinating the tasks of these many specialists abound—and hospital administrators in the larger medical centers call on social engineers, experts in organizational theory, to advise how to handle those coordination problems. Nurses on the more specialized services (like ICU, CCU) tend to be young, vigorous, and challenged by their work—but also to be subject to intense stress because of the pace and variety of physical tasks and the difficulties or working with dying, and often psychologically demanding, patients and kin: the popular word for this state is "burnout."

4. All this is also linked with the new and problematic courses of chronic illness that are being seen and treated—new and problematic because technology and knowledge are keepig alive patients who would previously have died but who are now back at the hospital in "acute condition," presenting unpredictable reactions to current treatment modes. (Many have multiple chronic illnesses, which only further complicate this unpredictability.) Physicians have an increasing number of treatment options, hence often require other specialists to help with their choices. However, if a patient fails to progress, or worsens, in response to disease or the regimen, then people other than the chief physician make on-the-spot decisions (nurses, staff physicians, respiratory therapists, consultants). Courses of illness often go (at least) temporarily awry, are managed for a while, only to go awry again repeatedly. (As researchers we have seen courses of illness and treatment go so awry that the end product can be termed a "cumulative mess," not only in the medical sense but insofar as the various actors and the entire organization become profoundly and negatively affected.)

That listing of changes in the health scene, public and professional, suggests that it will not be much longer before chronic illness will be recognized—to coin a phrase—as a chronic, here-to-stay, "acute health and social problem." Furthermore, the rising costs of medicine, which we will discuss later, are perhaps going to force more attention on less expensive modes of care. "Less expensive" in this instance quite possibly could mean less care and inferior care, but alternatively the term might point to an awareness of the need for alternative and supplemental modes of care, as opposed to those now provided in hospitals, clinics, and physicians' offices. The professionals themselves, so slow to recognize chronic illness as the source of many institutional, economic, and care problems, are moving—albeit with seemingly glacial slowness—to some awareness of the implications of the phenomenon. Books with "chronic illness" in their titles (written mainly by and for nurses) are appearing with increasing frequency, although at this writing their emphasis is still overwhelmingly "medical"; indeed a recent (1982) issue of *Hospitals* is devoted to chronic illness. Although not overly optimistic ourselves about quick progress in heightened professional and law awareness about all of this, we are inclined to think wistfully of Shelley's unforgettable lines, to the effect: if winter's here "can Spring be far behind?"

HEALTH COSTS AND CHRONIC ILLNESS

As an instance of how the crucial significance of chronic illness can go unrecognized, with accompanying untold cost of dollars and suffering, let us look at *the* major debate concerning health care today: the rising and frightening costs of health care. The debate is worth examining closely, in terms of our own thinking about what might be done for the chronically ill—how money might best be spent to ease their travail. From the perspective of the authors of this book, the participants in the cost debate are circling around the chronic illness issue but not directly grappling with it: so their phrasing of the cost problem and their suggested solutions miss the essential target.

We will begin with noting four points apropos of health costs*:

- Costs are even greater than most estimates and are going to increase, despite the various assumptions—and policies based on them—about the source of increased cost.
- The impact of specialization is also greater than the most extravagant criticism of it, and this process is bound not only to continue but to proliferate.
- The diffusion of medical technology will continue, and blaming specialization for this diffusion is a distortion of the issue.
- The notion that consensus can be reached regarding the efficacy and use of medical technology is an unreachable objective.

Concerning the first point: in *Technology in Hospitals: Medical Advances and Their Diffusion,* Louise B. Russell examined available statistics for four industrialized countries—the United States, Sweden, Great Britain, and France—and found they have all assumed, until recently, that technology is beneficial for patients (in some fashion) and therefore worth having. She concludes this may reflect the fact that the problems to be addressed—the rapid growth of costs in general, and the arrival of a number of expensive new technologies in particular—are relatively recent. However, the more pressing problem is still not faced by her head-on: the needs of increasing numbers of chronically ill people. There is now, and will continue to be for some time, competition among the various chronic illnesses for priority. The technologies for these illnesses are at varying stages of their development—for example, hemodialysis well established although still

---

*Modified from Wiener, Carolyn, Fagerhaugh, Shizuko, Suczek, Barbara, and Strauss, Anselm: Published by permission of Transaction, Inc., from Society **19**(2):22-30, Copyright © 1982 by Transaction, Inc.

being refined, the artificial pancreas as yet in the development stage. "Overuse" of technology makes a convenient target, but it is much more realistic to acknowledge that costs are bound to increase because of this intertwining of new technologies with new and more problematic illness trajectories.

While it is generally assumed (even by critics of applying cost-benefit analysis to the health arena) that costs are easier to measure than benefits, the costs are even greater than the most dire estimates. A host of organizational costs are omitted from discussion:

- Interdepartmental coordination (time spent working out strategies for coordinating and troubleshooting; since the more options, the more possibilities of coordination breakdown, unexpected contingencies, disrupted schedules, and so forth)
- New personnel to handle these contingencies, such as unit managers, ward clerks, material management experts
- Body to machine transportation, and vice versa, within the hospital
- Machine purchase, maintenance, repair, monitoring; bioengineers to handle this in large hospitals, outside contracts in smaller hospitals
- Drug purchase, storage, and handling
- Auxiliary supplies (throwaway tubes, catheters, connections, needles) and their purchase, storage, and distribution
- Staff to understand, monitor, and enforce regulatory compliance
- Safety monitoring, including building and maintaining whole departments of safety engineers
- Time, effort, and space required for backstopping of machines and drugs
- Resource building of skills; in-service in every department, time spent working and reworking protocols as technology undergoes rapid change
- Record keeping and reporting
- Building and rebuilding space to accommodate continually changing needs of departments and wards
- Nonroutine trajectory decisions: meetings and debates over options, more monitoring; then the next round per phase, and the coordination of these phased decisions
- Time spent working out the idiosyncrasies of a particular machine, or assessing it for feedback to the manufacturer
- Continuing care at home—clinic costs, technology and supplies at home, posthospital home visits, and new personnel to handle this (for example, discharge nurses and liaison nurses)
- Phone networks from hospital to outlying areas in less populous states

Discussion of indirect costs due to chronic illness rarely goes beyond suggesting loss of work time and restriction of activity. There are, however, other costs, equally hard to measure (and many borne principally by patients and their families):

• Help in the home for patients who are incapacitated, as, for instance, stroke patients
• Transportation to and from clinics, hospitals, and physicians' offices
• Increased burden on middle-aged, middle-class working taxpayers (for Medicare, Medicaid, and increased insurance premiums)
• Counseling to cope with disease-induced stress
• Tutoring for children with chronic illness
• Technical services (in the use and maintenance of home equipment, such as dialysis machines and respiratory equipment)
• Inflationary cost of products as employers respond to increased benefit packages offered employees

Concerning the impact of specialization: it is also greater than the most extravagant criticism of it. An example is the development of electronic prosthetic devices (an implantable electronic inner ear, electronic vision) brought about by the increased miniaturization of electronic circuitry and the combined work of engineers, chemists, and biologists. Consider the artificial pancreas, a still nascent development dependent on all kinds of basic science: mathematical models constructed through experimentation in a metabolic research unit, enzymatic methods for measuring blood sugar, improvement of chemical films that allow immobilization of enzymes despite the risk of infection, computer analysis to measure insulin levels, production of refined biomaterials, creation of a machine that measures a patient's blood sugar over a 24-hour period. This machine finally confirmed what the researchers had long suspected: that the diabetic taking insulin every day is never fully under control; that no diabetic is being treated very well.

Obviously, the expanded medical knowledge and the technology that evolves through the combined efforts of specialization are then mirrored at the level of application. Thus we have witnessed the emergence not only of cardiologists, nephrologists, and neurosurgeons, but also that of pediatric cardiologists and hematologists with a subspecialty in leukemia—sharpening the mastery ever more finely by limiting the focus. What is more, medical knowledge is developing at such a rapid pace that many medical options are experimental, involving increasingly higher risk, which further increases the requirements of the limited focus.

Although medical specialization is usually singled out in this regard about cost, the nursing profession is also specializing at an ever-increasing pace—again in response to the clinical expertise demanded by specialized equipment and more problematic trajectories. There are now numerous special-interest nursing groups for nephrology, neurosurgery, oncology, rehabilitation, and critical care, to name a few. Combined nursing specialties are mushrooming, again in response to perceived need.

As for the problem just listed, the third point to be made is that the diffusion of medical technology will continue to increase, and to target specialization as a scapegoat for medical-technology diffusion is a misrepresentation. For instance, critics assert that a technology is more likely to be adopted, or is adopted sooner, by hospitals with residency programs.

The California State Health Plan remarks pointedly that a specialty promotes use of its own technologies and the development of new ones, thereby starting the cycle over again of forming additional specialties. Omitted from the cycle by these critics are the needs (and demands) of the chronically ill. At a recent meeting in a metropolitan hospital, a physician reflected this as he struggled for clues in the referral process: "People are already going to the high-volume hospitals. So if we could find out why referrals are happening, we could perfect the system." People go, or are referred, to oncologists because they are better at treating cancer; they go to pediatric cardiologists because they are more skilled at treating heart disease in children. The incidence of open-heart surgery is higher in large medical centers with medical school affiliation, because both patients and their referring physicians know that is where the most skilled cardiologists, the best equipment and supporting staff are to be found. True, graduates of these large research and training centers then seek opportunities to practice their skills. True also that competition among hospitals forces equipment requirements on them. However, the assumption that supply is affecting demand ignores the evidence that there is a chronically ill population "out there" on whom these skills are being practiced. Blaming specialization itself for the diffusion of medical technology is like blaming the cure for the disease.

Let us turn now to the fourth point outlined above: the vision of consensus regarding the efficacy and use of medical technologies is an unattainable goal. Some people, in fact, call the decisions about what medical services we need and can afford "social decisions," requiring "political consensus" about technological assessment. The debate takes notice of the formidable obstacle of professional stakes biasing the outcome of evaluation studies, but the discussion tends to soft-pedal the genuine diversity in assessment. The political aspects aside, it has been very difficult to get consensus about most technological innovations.

Yes, but

The debate about cost as it pertains to medical technology misses the mark by not focusing on the very real and central problem of an increased number of people with chronic illnesses.[3] However, since many of the proposals in this debate appear reasonable, it is important to emphasize just where our quarrel with them lies, by offering a series of "yes . . . but" qualifications.

Yes, inequities have evolved in the reimbursement system, suggesting that panels might be able to adjust rates of payment to provide more incentive for nontechnical services. Although this will arouse opposition from some quarters, presumably a committee representative of the medical and insurance worlds could surmount the obstacles. *But,* it should not be assumed that this will meet the problem of "overspecialization" and diffusion of medical technologies. Nor will legislative interventions designed to create a better balance of primary care physicians and specialists and a better geographic distribution of physicians alleviate this situation. Such measures have in the past "either failed to demonstrate the desired impact or have created secondary, almost intolerable, side effects," according to Charles Lewis, Rashi Fein, and David Mechanic in *A Right to Health.* Furthermore, the geographical distribution of physicians is not the prime condition explaining the use of medical technology.

Yes, offering alternative health plans is desirable in that competition might force more comprehensive coverage. *But,* it should not be assumed that this will deal with either equality or quality of care. Although data released to the public from the Health Maintenance Organization (HMO) experience is sparse, indications are that the principal cost-control mechanism is not decreased hospital stay, but decreased number of hospital admissions—the supposition being that these people are being treated on an ambulatory basis. Yet is is common knowledge that those who get quality care in an HMO are those who know how to manipulate the system (such as how to find a trustworthy doctor and ensure assignment to him or her, and how to circumvent the administrative barriers to ambulatory care). Furthermore, that the consumer can make an enlightened choice among health plan options is a questionable assumption; buying a health plan, unlike buying a television set, does not lend itself to consumer cost-benefit analysis.

Yes, assessing "appropriate use" of medical technology and achieving consensus on that assessment sounds like a reasonable expectation. *But,* given all the barriers to evaluation (the inconclusiveness of evidence, the lack of uniform values in medical practice, the constant modification that characterizes new technologies, the variation of use from setting to setting, the long period needed for assessment, the fiscal disincentives for those doing the evaluation, and the ambiguity in the relationship between processes of care and outcomes), assessment in the aggregate is an impossible goal.

Yes, building in early prevention (one of the major arguments in this arena), may reduce eventual costs. *But,* it will be a long time before the results of prevention programs become evident. In the meantime, HMOs as presently constituted, for example, sell themselves on the basis of prevention but are still based on an acute care model; patients learn that the best way to get prompt attention is on an acute or emergency basis.

Yes, the cost of medical technology can be reduced through rationing devices such as prospective reimbursement, administrative barriers to treatment, explicit criteria for allocation of new techniques. *But,* such proposals fly in the face of equality of care, for it is the poor who will suffer most from rationing. Medical servicing of the lower income groups still exhibits considerable deficiencies. Yet it is people with lower incomes who have the highest incidence of chronic illness, who need the support and preventive work, who are cheated out of the best technology. Rationing will only mean, as it has in England, that the elite get better care; they are able to go around the system because they want and can afford the state-of-the-art. Discussion of distribution of medical technology as it pertains to cost is based on the assumption that if you decrease the supply you decrease the demand. In contrast, we are saying that the distribution should be *more* extensive—that most poor diabetics cannot afford a correct diet, often do not have the family structure to help them maintain a regimen, and delay diagnosis and treatment because of their focus on "the deadly earnest present." Far from cost containment, what are needed are additional services that *may* in the end reduce total costs—but at least they should markedly improve health care.

A 1979 *Social Policy* editorial called for an expansion of new forms of services—forms that add the health consumer to the existing means for the production of health care: "With some 50 percent of health care directed to chronic illness and about 70 percent of doctors' visits for the maintenance of chronics, support function can be readily, and best, served by self-help/self-care systems." The editorial added that self-care and mutual support as a national program must be developed in concert with the professional services that complement them, and with the financial support and planning of government. Borrowing from groups like Alcoholics Anonymous and Weight Watchers, health self-help groups are expanding: I Can Cope for cancer patients, Mended Hearts for heart patients, Parent to Parent for parents of intensive care nursery graduates. Aside from the valuable contribution these groups make in terms of mutual support and exchange of information, they are performing a reverse service: teaching health professionals what it means to "live with" chronic disease—knowledge the professionals can impart to future patients. Insofar as there could be a greatly supplemented guidance of patient work in the home, and greater support of self-help groups, the health consumer would be provided with enhanced ability to read signs that portend a crisis of his or her disease, improved skill in responding to the crisis of the moment, and greater motivation to establish and maintain a regimen. Certainly the health sciences schools and professional associations (medical, nursing, and so on) could accord greater weight to the potential of self-care in chronic disease management, and the training of students and practitioners to teach patients to use self-care. Such proposals in the end could reduce total cost by freeing the physicians from work that other health professionals can do, by slowing up the rate of return to hospitals, by reducing the severity of disease in the population.

Not insignificantly, such a course might break the vicious cycle that characterizes health care for lower income patients—patients who delay too long in seeking treatment for themselves and their children, do not follow regimens, come back in worse condition, and are then further alienated by professionals who have not been trained with the special skills necessary to deliver quality care to these people.

Perhaps the most fruitful aspect of the consumer movement in the health field is its potential for demonstrating the force that the concept of patient work can be in increasing productivity of service.[5] Alan Gartner and Frank Riessman make the point, in *The Service Society and the Consumer Vanguard,* that consumers are workers: they already contribute heavily to the human services through the less obvious ways in which they assist practitioners in getting "their" work done. The tie-in of health services to other service industries has been underscored by Victor Fuchs in *The Service Economy:* "Productivity in many service industries is dependent in part on the knowledge, experience and motivation of the customer."

Modern medical care is far too complicated to allow *equal* partnership between patients and physicians in the decision making over treatment options. Both health professionals and patients could benefit, however, from a realization on the part of consumers that good medical care is not, as Norman Cousins has commented wryly, just a matter of shoving one's body onto the doctor's table.

The value of a consumer movement notwithstanding, there is always the danger of any movement being used to counter the good intentions of its designers. Berenice Fisher has warned of the danger in "The Work of Helping Others":[1]

> Since this movement itself takes place in a context in which resources are still limited and directed by those in power, it runs the risk of being coopted by them, of doing the society's dirty work by getting the poorest and most disadvantaged people to serve themselves—to fulfill the old bourgeois admonition that they ought to be taking care of themselves anyway.

A cruel distortion of the consumer movement would be to use it as a wedge in the argument for decreasing health dollar outlay. For in the forseeable future, despite consumer mobilization, self-help, and prevention through health screening, there will remain a need for expert professional help and massive technological resources. Americans are thus faced with the following options: we can let more people die faster, or let many people be very sick. As in most industrialized countries, we do not choose to do either of those things, for our health priorities are fairly high. There is yet another option: we can give health care even high priority—we can make people less sick for a longer time (perhaps by building fewer bombers or nuclear submarines).

A GENERAL STRATEGY

All this suggests a general strategy for attacking the question of the division of labor among those who might be responsible for better management of the problems attendant on chronic illness. In the first place, the sick person *and* his or her agents are much concerned with handling those problems. For health personnel, or anyone else, to attempt to usurp their responsibilities would be ultimately ineffective, and also quite possibly immoral in implications. Nevertheless, it is in the public interest, and perhaps eventually will impinge on the public's conscience, that normal arrangements should take into account at least some of the problems of the chronically ill. Questions of cost are involved, of course, but as the mobility illustration implies, cost may be far less consequential than simple lack of awareness.

NEED FOR A WIDER RANGE OF SERVICES

Beyond those considerations, what else might be said specifically about the health personnel themselves, along with the occupations, professions, and institutions they represent? What overall role should they play? The answer, perhaps, is twofold. On occasion, they can act as members of interested publics with respect to specific issues. Generally, however, they should be concerned with extending the so-called health care system (such as it is in the United States), extending it, that is, so as to aid the sick and their families much more than at present.

Since that is only the most sweeping of positions, what about more specific policy suggestions? Here, the very pertinent suggestions of Laura Reif[2] can be quoted. They were written in 1974 and appeared in the first edition of this book. Although there have been some improvements in the services available to the chronically ill since then, most of her suggestions in all categories listed below are, alas, still very pertinent, while services in some categories are still virtually negligible. (With current cutbacks, as of 1982 in federal and state funding, and possibly more to come, even current services will be curtailed.)

Here are Laura Reif's suggestions:

> A wider range of services [for the chronically ill] is imperative. . . . The numbers and types which could be utilized . . . are legion. . . . The following broad categories of help are relevant:
>
> *Broad-spectrum counseling and education* addressed to the sick person *and* his associates: counseling on both the medical and social-psychological aspects of managing a chronic illness (i.e., help in tailoring regimes so they entail fewer costs and obtain greater benefits for overall functioning; assistance in developing social skills in dealing with visible disability, stigma, social isolation; managing the impact of illness on others; renegotiating responsibilities with family and employers, taking account of the constraints of illness; help managing the social, personal, and medical aspects of terminal disease; legal

counsel regarding the ramifications of diagnosis and treatment—as help dealing with employer discrimination, termination of insurance coverage, and loss of license due to illness).

Assistance in *revamping the physical environment,* taking into account the limitations resulting from illness and disability (i.e., designing or modifying living accommodations, work areas, transportation facilities in order to improve the physical settings in which the chronically ill live and work).

Assistance with *funding* and *money-management:* providing financial resources, budget-planning, and other economic-management help to the sick person and those affected by the economic ramifications of his chronic illness (this involves extension of economic assistance to cover not only the medically related but the social and personal "costs" of chronic illness—i.e., the expense of revamping work areas, the cost of equipment to facilitate functioning, reimbursing lost pay, etc.).

Redesigning social arrangements: organization of individual and group effort in the interest of providing the necessary man-power for dealing with the ramifications of chronic illness (i.e., working with the sick person and his associated others, or with groups of chronically ill in the interest of providing emergency back-up systems, task exchange networks, or social support arrangements—for the purpose of sustaining persons who must regularly deal with the ramifications of chronic illness).

Supplying technical aid and equipment: designing and providing new equipment and techniques to facilitate daily activities for those who have disabilities, and for those who care for the chronically ill (i.e., such equipment might be designed to facilitate regime procedures, household tasks, mobility, etc.).

Medical intervention: provision of broad-spectrum medical services, including use of paramedical resources such as dietary counseling, rehabilitation services, speech therapy, services of voluntary groups—these efforts directed toward improving the overall functioning of the individual, *taking into account* the potential existence of multiple diseases, co-existing disabilities, and the resulting personal and social ramifications of illness.

Daily-maintenance services: supplying assistance with various aspects of daily living—household tasks, personal care, chauffeur and other travel services, and so forth.

Public education and *informational services:* These would be the counterpart of counseling of the sick person—they involve educating those persons who are likely to encounter or care for the chronically ill; they also involve attempts to increase understanding, lessen misconceptions, and limit prejudicial behavior on the part of those who are likely to affect the lives and opportunities of the chronically ill and disabled.

Managerial assistance: making available to clients an agent (whether brokers, contractors-of-services, ombudsmen, or advocates) who could ensure access to, and effective provision of, services to the sick person and his involved associates. Such client-representatives could provide assistance in the following sorts of areas: (1) obtaining information and services; (2) assisting clients in decision-making re use of services; (3) coordinating specialized services; (4) ensuring quality care; and/or (5) facilitating feedback from consumers, with respect to existing and needed services.

Mrs. Reif goes on to say that these:

> potentially effective resources are much broader in scope than those presently utilized. Because current services tend to revolve around medically pertinent interventions, the resources most frequently utilized tend to be medical and paramedical. There is no reason to believe that many—if not the majority—of services . . . need to be supplied by medically trained personnel, or provided through specifically medical institutions.

The providers of such services could include unions, commercial and industrial organizations, lay self-help groups, the mass media, and agencies both private and governmental.

Since the actual or potential unemployment of the chronically ill is an important problem for them and their families, a substantial public effort needs to be directed at protecting their rights to work. This means getting the appropriate legislation passed and enforced by governmental agencies or the courts. Mrs. Reif also suggest employer education regarding the work potential of various groups of the chronically ill, tax incentives for employers who retain or hire the chronically ill worker, and union support against companies for members who are unjustifiably denied employment. Thus in the matter of employment, as in other areas, there probably will be need for informational campaigns, private (and consumer) action, and also a certain amount of governmental action, in order to protect what hopefully will be defined as the rights of chronically ill citizens.

NEEDED: A MORE RESPONSIVE HEALTH INDUSTRY
Redesigning current health facilities

Finally, what about the host of personnel who are involved in what is sometimes called the health care industry? Basically, the two main issues here are as follows: first of all, as emphasized previously, within health facilities personnel should work toward establishing accountability for the behavioral and interactional aspects of chronic care, along with giving sick persons more "say" in their care when within the facility. In addition, the organization of the facilities needs to be redesigned so that the chronically ill can better use their services.

As many observers have noted, clinics and medical centers are often awkwardly located and their services are inconveniently scheduled for many of their potential clients. Chronically ill people, low in energy, with mobility problems and difficult regimen schedules and the like, are often hard put to get to certain facilities and at the institutionally scheduled times. Moreover, the sources of information that they or any other sick person—but especially they—need about available services are far from adequate. Generally the facilities

> have not considered the larger problem of making their services known. . . . Little has been done to locate those who want or need help in dealing with chronic disease and its ramifications.[2]

Those who do get to the facility often fail to gain entry: they cannot handle the admission procedures, cannot adequately verbalize or justify their need for aid, leave treatment programs because they lack time or energy or sufficient help in finding their way around the health system, and so on. "What [they] need most is help in routing themselves through the organizational network [of facilities] and into the kinds of services they can most effectively utilize."[2] Moreover, although the selection of clients by facilities understandably functions to get the desired match between services and clients, the selection procedures do leave many sick persons with no ready access to health services.

Extending the facilities

The second direction in which the health care system must go is toward proferring far more and additional kinds of counsel and aid to the chronically ill and their families. This would require building a more general recognition of the range of management problems attendant on suffering from various chronic conditions. It means the training and education of health personnel in these matters. Presumably, new categories of personnel (health or health-related) would also be needed including health consumer advocates, social-psychological counselors, and coordinators of various health and health-related services. Again, we turn to the adjective "innovative" to suggest that brains combined with practical experience would allow health personnel to invent new modes of offering services (and to fill gaps between current servicing agencies). The kind of extended and comprehensive medical-health program needed for many chronically sick persons is exactly what they rarely get today. If they are so unfortunate as to suffer from two or more disease, those deficiencies of service are even more pronounced.

A last few words

Beyond that, it is necessary to emphasize again that helping sick people to live more satisfying lives is not only, or even principally, the responsibility of health personnel. If the many kinds of services listed earlier are to be offered to the ill and their families, then many other interested participants must enter into what now looks like the "health" arena. Among the participants in this era of consumer movements will surely be ill persons themselves as well as their legislative and legal agents—also additional types of agents who will voluntarily or on a paid basis take up their cause. Health personnel should be only too pleased, or perhaps relieved, not to have to shoulder the entire burden of work. Part of the aim of this book has been to suggest how they can *offer* better service to the chronically ill. Remember, it is the *chronically* ill who constitute the bulk of the sick population in "advanced" nations.

References

1. Fisher, Berenice M.: The work of helping others, Unpublished manuscript, New York, 1980, New York University, School of Education.
2. Reif, Laura: A policy perspective and its implications, unpublished manuscript, San Francisco, 1974, University of California, Department of Social and Behavioral Science, School of Nursing.
3. Schroeder, Steven, Stowstack, Jonathan, and Roberts, E.: Frequency and clinical description of high-cost patients in 17 acute care hospitals, New England Journal of Medicine **320:**1305-1309, 1979.
4. Strauss, Anselm: Editorial comment, Social Science and Medicine **140:**351-352, 1980.
5. Wiener, Carolyn, Fagerhaugh, Shizuko, Suczek, Barbara, and Strauss, Anselm: Patient power. complex issues need complex answers, Social Policy **11:**30-38, 1980.
6. Wiener, Carolyn, Fagerhaugh, Shizuko, Suczek, Barbara, and Strauss, Anselm: What price chronic illness? Society **19:**22-30, 1982.

EPILOGUE

Just as the first edition of this book was nearing completion, we happened to read Joshua Horn's *Away with all Pests*,[1] a moving account of what Horn, a British physician, saw in China from 1954 to 1969 while working as a surgeon, teacher, and medical field worker. Once incident that he recounts, although not about chronic disease as such, is so relevant to our own inquiry that we cannot refrain from commenting on it.

Horn begins the description by saying that his concept of full responsibility had taken on a deeper meaning after coming to China. "Although in the past I always thought of myself as being responsible, it is becoming clear that to be fully responsible requires more than good intentions." Horn then tells about a middle-aged peasant on whom he had operated. Terribly burned in a home accident, the man was rushed to the hospital where emergency treatment temporarily saved him. "At this point we paused to consider the problem as a whole"—"we" being the surgeons. "Some of the doctors thought it was impossible to save his life and doubted whether we should fruitlessly prolong his agony." But the two villagers who had rushed the unfortunate man to the hospital urged attempts to save him. "They explained that he was chairman of the Association of Former Poor Peasants in his Commune, that everybody respected him for his unselfish service and would look after him very well."

So the physicians resolved to do everything possible. However, two opposing views of how to proceed then developed: should amputation of his legs be delayed until his condition had improved sufficiently to get him through the formidable operation, or was a delay even more dangerous? "Gradually, through argument, it became clear that these opposing viewpoints did not result from different estimations of the medical aspects of the case but, in essence, reflected two different attitudes toward responsibility and taking risks." No surgeon, Horn says, wants the risk of a patient's death on the operating table; it is distressing and "harmful to his reputation." So, "concern for one's reputation and peace of mind may, even though unconsciously, influence a surgeon's decisions." However, they began to realize the nonmedical bases of their potential decision, and "determined to be guided by Mao's insistence on a full sense of responsibility" (that is, communal responsibility), they finally reached agreement on doing the kind of operation—and doing it immediately—that perhaps might be successful. (It was.)

What lessons can one draw from this story? After all, China is a communist society and not an "advanced" industrialized, urbanized nation like the United States. We do not have communes or even the kinds of village communities that take total and personal responsibility for caring for a permanently incapacitated man; nor do surgeons so respect the head of state as to follow his perspective on responsibility in guiding their professional ethics and procedures. Nevertheless, Horn's narrative does underscore what might be striven for and possibly attained in countries like ours—but of course in our own political and social styles.

We have in mind that the implications of Horn's incident include the following:

1. There can be a much more explicit and better balanced division of labor between health personnel and the rest of the population. The latter should have much more responsibility for decision making and more explicit functions in caring for the sick.

2. Yet health personnel should be appreciated (provided they earn the appreciation) for their skills, judgment, and trained wisdom.

3. Health personnel should also be regarded, and regard themselves, as acting in the service of their clients—not dominate them, especially in the health facilities, or make decisions for them (indeed often decisions unknown to them).

4. They should listen closely to the sick persons and their representatives and not impose their own viewpoints—which at best will be unheeded (away from the health facilities) and at worst can be disastrous.

5. In short, for the best care, there need to be *intelligent transactions* carried out among sick persons, their representatives, and health personnel.

Horn's village peasant was not a "patient," a "case," or "client"—he was a fellow citizen. He was brought to the hospital for traumatic emergency care. Chronic disease necessitates even more urgent attention to what Horn refers to as a deeper sense of responsibility. The challenge, presumably, is whether this can be achieved in noncommunist countries as well as the Chinese seem to have met the challenge. Whether communist China has been able to institute this kind of civic responsibility as well as Horn claims is not the point; rather, can this be achieved in other countries, including the United States, each in its own style? Yes? No? Maybe?

Reference

1. Horn, Joshua: Away with all pests, New York, 1969, Monthly Review Press.

BIBLIOGRAPHY

Anderson, J.: The social construction of illness experience: families with a chronically-ill child, Journal of Advanced Nursing **6**:427-434, 1981.

Benoliel, Jeanne Quint: Becoming diabetic, doctoral thesis, San Francisco, 1969, University of California, School of Nursing.

Benoliel, Jeanne Quint: the developing diabetic identity. In Batey, M.: Communicating nursing research, Boulder, Colo. 1970, Wiche.

Bury, Michael: Chronic illness as biographic disruption, Sociology of Health and Illness **4**(2):167-182, 1982.

Calkins, Kathy: Shouldering a burden, Omega **3**:23-36, 1972.

Charmaz, Kathy C.: Time and identity: the shaping of selves of the chronically ill, doctoral thesis, San Francisco, 1973, University of California.

Christ, Adolph E., and Flomenhaft, Kalman: Psychosocial family interventions in chronic pediatric illness, New York, 1982, Plenum Press.

Christ, Grace: Dis-synchrony of coping among patient, family, and staff. In Social Work Oncology Group: Social work in cancer care. Proceedings of second national conference, July 2-3, 1981, Berkshires, Mass., Boston, 1981, Sidney Farber Cancer Institute, pp. 37-48.

Chu, George: The kidney patient: a socio-medical study, doctoral thesis, Berkely, 1975, University of California, School of Public Health.

Cogswell, B., and Weir, W.: A role in process: development of medical professionals' role in long-term care of chronically diseased patients, Journal of Health and Human Behavior **5**:95-106, 1973.

Crewe, N., and Zola, I.: Independent living in America, San Francisco, 1983 Jossey-Bass, Inc., Publishers.

Dana, Bess: The integration of medicine with other community services. In Catastrophic illness: impact on families, challenge to the professions, New York, 1966, Cancer Care, Inc., National Cancer Foundation.

Danowski, T., editor: Diabetes mellitus, New York, 1964, American Diabetic Association.

Davis, Fred: Deviance disavowal: the management of strained interaction by the visibly handicapped, Social Problems **9**:120-132, 1961. Also reprinted in Davis, Fred: Illness, interaction and the self, Belmont, Calif., 1972, Wadsworth Publishing Co.

Davis, Fred: Passage through crisis: polio victims and their families, Indianapolis, 1963, The Bobbs-Merrill Co., Inc.

Davis, Marcella: Living with multiple sclerosis, Springfield, Ill., 1973, Charles C Thomas, Publisher.

Davis, Marcella Z.: Rehabilitation care in the skilled nursing facilities: the mismatch of organizational structure and patient need, Journal of Nursing Administration **7**:22-27, 1977.

Dubuskey, M., editor: The chronically ill child and his family, Springfield, Ill., 1970, Charles C Thomas, Publisher.

Dudley, D.L., Wermuth, C., and Hague, W.: Psychosocial aspects of care in the chronic obstructive pulmonary disease patient, Heart and Lung **2**(3):389-399, 1973.

Fagerhaugh, Shizuko: Mismatched properties: problems in managing mentally ill TB patients, doctoral thesis, San Francisco, 1972, University of California, School of Nursing.

Fagerhaugh, Shizuko, and Frankel H.: Behind the scenes, the skid row hotel manager who sees that Ernie takes his TB drugs, The Bulletin, National TB Respiratory Disease Association, **56,** 1970.

Futterman, E., and Hoffman, I: Crisis and adaptation in the families of fatally ill children. In Anthony, E., and Koupernik, C., editors: The child in his family: the impact of disease and death, New York, 1973, John Wiley & Sons, Inc., pp. 127-143.

Futterman, E., Hoffman, I., and Sabshin, M.: Parental anticipatory mourning. In Kutscher, A., editor: Psychosocial aspects of terminal care, New York, 1972, Columbia University Press, pp. 243-272.

Glaser, Barney, and Strauss, Anselm: Awareness of dying, Chicago, 1965, Aldine Press.

Glaser, Barney, and Strauss, Anselm: Time for dying, Chicago, 1968, Aldine Press.

Goffman, Erving: Stigma: notes on the management of spoiled identity, Englewood Cliffs, N.J., 1963, Prentice-Hall, Inc.

Goldstein, V., Regnery, G., and Wellin, E.: Caretaker role fatigue, Nursing Outlook **29**(1):24-30, 1981.

Griffith, C.: Sexuality and the cardiac patient, Heart and Lung **2:**70-73, 1973.

Gussow, Z.: Behavioral research in chronic disease: a study of leprosy, Journal of Chronic Disease **17:**179-189, 1964.

Gussow, Z., Knight, E., and Miller, M.: A theory of leprosy stigma and professionalization of the patient role, unpublished manuscript, New Orleans, 1965, Louisiana State University Medical Center, Department of Psychiatry.

Gussow, Z., and Tracy, G.: Strategies in the management of stigma: concealing and revealing by leprosy patients in the U.S., unpublished manuscript, New Orleans, La., 1965, Louisiana State University Medical Center, Department of Psychiatry.

Hoffman, Joan: Nothing can be done: social dimensions of the treatment of stroke patients in a general hospital, Urban Life and Culture **3:**50-70, 1974.

Isaacs, J., and McElroy, M.: Psychosocial aspects of chronic illness in children, The Journal of School Health **50:**318-328, 1980.

Jennings, Bonnie M., and Muhlenkamp, Ann F.: Systematic misperception: oncology patients' self-reportive affective states and their caregivers' perceptions, Cancer Nursing **4:**485-489, Dec. 1981.

Kassenbaum, G., and Baumann, B.: Dimensions of the sick role in chronic illness, Journal of Health and Human Behavior **6:**16-27, 1965.

Katz, Alfred, and Bender, Eugene: Self help groups in Western society: history and prospects, American Journal of Applied Behavioral Sciences **12:**265-282, 1976.

Koocher, G.P.: Adjustment and coping strategies among the caretakers of cancer patients, Social Work in Health Care **5:**145-150, 1979.

Koocher, Gerald, and O'Malley, John: The Damocles syndrome: psychosocial consequences of surviving childhood cancer, New York, 1981, McGraw-Hill Book Co.

Krulik, T.: Successful "normalizing" tactics of parents of chronically-ill children, Journal of Advanced Nursing **5:**573-578, 1980.

Lamb, H.R.: Staff burnout in work with long-term patients, Hospital and Community Psychiatry **30:**396-398, 1979.

Lawrence, S., and Lawrence, R.: A model of adaptation to the stress of chronic illness, Nursing Forum **18**(1):34-43, 1979.

Lefton, E., and Lefton, M.: Health care and treatment for the chronically ill: toward a conceptual framework, Journal of Chronic Disease **23:**339-344, 1979.

Leiberman, Morton, and Borman, Leonard, editors: Self help groups for coping with crisis, San Francisco, 1979, Jossey-Bass, Inc., Publishers.

Lenneberg, E., and Rowbotham, J.: The ileostomy patient, Springfield, Ill., 1970, Charles C Thomas, Publisher.

Lewis, Charles, Fein, Rashi, and Mechanic, David: A right to health, New York, 1976, John Wiley & Sons, Inc.

Lifchez, Raymond, and Winslow, Barbara: Design for independent living: the environment and physically disabled people, Berkeley, 1979, University of California Press.

Litman, Theodor: The family as a basic unit in health and medical care: a social-medical overview, Social Sciences and Medicine **8:**495-519, 1974.

Louie, Theresa: The pragmatic context: a Chinese-American example of defining and managing illness, doctoral thesis, San Francisco, 1975, University of California, School of Nursing.

MacVicar, M., and Archbold, P.: A framework for family assessment in chronic illness, Nursing Forum **15**(2):180-194, 1976.

McKeever, P.: Fathering the chronically ill child, American Journal of Maternal-Child Nursing **6:**124-128, 1981.

Mattsson, Ake: Long term physical illness in children: a challenge to psychosocial adaptation, Pediatrics **50:**801-811, 1972.

Norbeck, J.S.: Social support: a model for clinical research and application, Advances in Nursing Science **3**(4):43-59, 1981.

Peedling, Edward: Heart attack: the family response at home and in the hospital, London, 1982, Tavistock.

Quint, Jeanne: The impact of mastectomy, American Journal of Nursing **63:**88-92, 1963.

Reif, Laura: A policy perspective and its implications, unpublished manuscript, San Francisco, 1974, University of California, Department of Social and Behavioral Science, School of Nursing.

Roth, Julius: Timetables: structuring the passage of time in hospital treatment and other careers, Indianapolis, 1963, The Bobbs-Merrill Co., Inc.

Russell, Louise B.: Technology in hospitals: medical advances and their diffusions, Washington, D.C., 1979, The Brookings Institute.

Schneider, J.W., and Conrad, P.: In the closet with illness: epilepsy, stigma potential and information control, Social Problems **28**(1):42, 1980.

Schwartz, Charlotte: Strategies and tactics of mothers of mentally retarded children for dealing with the medical care system. In Bernstein, Norman, editor: Problems and care of the mentally retarded, Boston, 1970, Little, Brown & Co.

Strauss, Anselm, Fagerhaugh, Shizuko, Suczek, Barbara, and Wiener, Carolyn: The social organization of medical work, Chicago, 1984, University of Chicago Press.

Strauss, Anselm, and Glaser, Barney: Anguish: case history of a dying woman, San Francisco, 1970, The Sociology Press.

Tracy, George, and Gussow, Zachary: Self help groups: a grass roots response to a need for services, Journal of Applied Behavioral Sciences **12:**381-396, 1976.

Turk, J.: Impact of cystic fibrosis on family functioning, Pediatrics **34:**67, 1964.

Westbrook, M., and Viney, L.: Psychological reactions to the onset of chronic illness, Social Science and Medicine **16:**899-905, 1982.

Wiener, Carolyn: Pain assessment, pain legitimation and the conflict of staff-patient perspectives, Nursing Outlook **23**(8):508-516, Aug. 1975.

Zola, Irving: To find the missing piece: about having a handicap in a healthist society, Philadelphia, 1982, Temple University Press.

INDEX

217